THE APPLE OF HIS EYE

Jews, Christians, and Muslims from the Ancient to the Modern World

EDITED BY MICHAEL COOK, WILLIAM CHESTER JORDAN, AND PETER SCHÄFER

A list of titles in this series appears at the back of the book.

The Apple of His Eye

CONVERTS FROM ISLAM IN THE REIGN OF LOUIS IX

William Chester Jordan

PRINCETON UNIVERSITY PRESS

PRINCETON & OXFORD

Published by Princeton University Press
41 William Street, Princeton, New Jersey 08540
6 Oxford Street, Woodstock, Oxfordshire OX20 1TR

press.princeton.edu

Library of Congress Control Number 2018949930
First paperback printing, 2020
Paperback ISBN 978-0-691-21041-4
Cloth ISBN 978-0-691-19011-2

British Library Cataloging-in-Publication Data is available

Editorial: Brigitta van Rheinberg and Amanda Peery
Production Editorial: Jill Harris
Cover Design: Layla Mac Rory
Cover Credit: Muslims expressing a (false) desire to convert in the crusader camp
before Tunis, August 1270. From Angers: Archives départementales, Maine-et-
Loire, MS 3 F 6 / 5, Jean de Vignay, *Histoire de s. Louis et de Philippe
le Hardi* (fragment from chap. 32–34), fol. 2 v.
Production: Erin Suydam
Publicity: Jodi Price and Julia Hall
Copyeditor: Katherine Harper

This book has been composed in Miller

Printed in the United States of America

To

Leila Grace Gorman (aged 4) and
Oliver Parker Gorman (2)

and

Ruth (Mays) Apilado (110)

CONTENTS

ILLUSTRATIONS

Figures

Maps

ACKNOWLEDGMENTS

I AM PLEASED to thank a number of people who listened to my thoughts about the matters addressed in this book and reacted with suggestions and criticisms or helped or offered to help in other ways. These conversations and email exchanges were sometimes brief but always enormously enlightening. My interlocutors, in alphabetical order, included Peter Brown, Zoë Buonaiuto, Andrew Collings, Angela Creager, Merle Eisenberg, Eileen Gardiner, Dov Grohsgal, John Haldon, Anne Hedeman, Christine Jordan, Lorna Jordan, Victoria Jordan, Robert Leonard, Erika Milam, Ron Musto, Laurie Nussdorfer, Randall Pippenger, Jennifer Rampling, and Troy Tice. Unbeknownst to him, Menachem Butler also had a role to play. The attachments to his emails often brought valuable relevant studies to my attention, studies which I would otherwise never have known about.

I had opportunities to present the argument and some of the evidence to two audiences. The first was at the American Academy in Rome, where I was the Lester K. Little Distinguished Visiting Scholar in Residence in October and September 2017. Those who heard the talk I gave included a few classicists, medievalists, and scholars of more recent periods but mostly artists, composers, musicians, architects, and writers. Their positive feedback convinced me that the topic had a certain general appeal. I wish to thank the Academy, its former director, Kim Bowes, who arranged my appointment, and the current director, John Ochsendorf, who was my host while I was there.

I had promised to do a second presentation as a plenary lecture at the International Congress on Medieval Studies at Western Michigan University (Kalamazoo) in May 2018. Before that could take place, I finished a more or less complete draft of the book and submitted the manuscript to Princeton University

Press. My editor, Brigitta van Rheinberg, and her assistant, Associate Editor Amanda Peery, were enthusiastic (my thanks to them both) and quickly sent the manuscript out to referees. These anonymous referees provided me with a number of suggestions, which turned out to be very valuable and for which I am grateful. Moreover, their reports persuaded the Press's Editorial Board to authorize publication of the book. By the time the International Congress came around, less than a month after this approval, I was able to summarize before a large group of specialists what I thought was a finished manuscript. Public discussion does not follow plenary lectures at the International Congress, but the feedback I received in the long aftermath of my presentation also turned out to be a great motivator for a final rereading and revision before publication.

IN THIS BOOK, I have followed the usual scholarly conventions: (1) I typically provide the original forms of personal names in Medieval Latin or Old French in the translations of direct quotations from those languages, but elsewhere I have translated them into English, where such equivalents exist, or into Modern French. Where no equivalent exists in English or Modern French, I have retained the original in italics. (2) Citations of primary sources ordinarily precede those of secondary sources. (3) I refer to French currency and monies of account in Medieval Latin *libre, solidi,* and *denarii,* or in Old French *livres, sous* or *sols,* and *deniers,* and use the abbreviations l., s., and d. Money of Tours, *tournois* (t.), and of Paris, *parisis* (p.) correlated at the time at a rate of five to four: 5 l. t. = 4 l. p.

THE APPLE OF HIS EYE

Converting the World

SINCE THE ANTIQUARIANS of the sixteenth and seventeenth
centuries established the scholarly rules and conventions that
govern the professional study of the past, historians have put an
enormous amount of effort into investigating the Crusades.[1]
Many aspects of the Crusade experience, however, remain un-
derexplored. Despite a few valuable studies, conversion is one of
the more neglected topics. Interested, as I have long been, in the
Crusades of the French king Louis IX, who reigned from 1226 to
1270, I have returned frequently to the relevant sources in order
to see what more can be learned about his two exceedingly well-
planned and yet, from the point of view of his Christian contemporaries, disappointing expeditions of 1248–1254 and 1270. The
specific aspect scrutinized in this book is the king's program
for the conversion of Muslims, which incorporated, because of

1. Florida State College at Jacksonville professor Andrew Holt's blog assem-
bles the views of a large number of leading historians of the Crusades, whom he
invited to identify the most important books on the subject. Taken together, this
has turned out to be one of the more comprehensive and by far the most engross-
ing review of crusade literature presently available: https://apholt.com/2017/07
/27/historians-rank-the-most-important-books-on-the-crusades/. See also Jonathan Phillips, Thomas F. Madden, Marcus Bull, and Andrew Jotischky, eds., *The
Cambridge History of the Crusades* (Cambridge, UK: Cambridge University
Press, forthcoming).

circumstances, a small number of pagan refugees as well. This was part of a complex of conversionary impulses long associated with Louis IX. There are notable differences among his various efforts, but there are also remarkable parallels and similarities. I shall first be summarizing for the reader these other, better-investigated endeavors, as well as some related developments in the thirteenth century, in order to set the scene for the king's attempts to bring Muslims and pagans to the Catholic faith.

Before doing so, I want to acknowledge that in order to fill in gaps in the story of the king's project, I have sometimes had to press the evidence hard. However, I do acknowledge explicitly which assertions are only possibilities or plausibilities, and I have tried to avoid introducing statements as potentially true and then presuming them to be true thereafter. Rather, I have hypothesized in the manner, "if this is the case, then such-and-such should follow." Often enough, hypotheses without direct proof have generated conclusions for which I believe the evidence is compelling. In any case, I hope this explanation of my approach encourages an open-minded reading of the reconstruction of events presented in this book.

In general, the policies and programs that Louis IX instituted to encourage conversions—in particular those targeting dissenting Christians, notorious sinners (prostitutes and manifest usurers being two such groups according to medieval moral thought), and Jews—had a very hard edge to them. In order for them to reconcile with him, the king demanded the converts' full renunciation of the beliefs and practices that defined their fallen state. The transformation of Christian dissidents into faithful Catholics was primarily a task for the ecclesiastical authorities. The effort had come to have an urgency about it in the late twelfth and thirteenth centuries, in large part because clerical elites claimed that heresy had long been spreading and would continue to do so unless rigorous means were employed to arrest its extension and, indeed, to extirpate it as a whole. These perceptions and their consequences constitute an almost classic theme in the scholarship; historians such as Robert Moore and Malcolm Lambert have treated them with great sensitivity.[2]

Some scholars do not think the nature and extent of the threat to Catholic orthodoxy was as serious as contemporary churchmen believed.[3] Yet, however misguided the clerics may have been, they made it their mission to find and expose heresy. They did so eventually (in the mid-1230s) by the implementation of inquisitions of heretical depravity. These became the principal mode of ferreting out religious difference among baptized Christians. The crown, in the reign of Louis IX, fully embraced the mission "with all thankful support."[4] The goal of these inquisitions was conversion, securing the return of contrite dissidents to the Catholic fold. Yet sometimes the inquisitors failed to achieve their goal. Contumacious heretics not only put their own salvation at risk, the orthodox observed, but could also lead other Christians astray and jeopardize their chance to enter into Paradise.[5] In cases of contumacy, clergy turned to secular authorities for assistance. Clerics could not impose capital punishment in such instances because the church abhorred blood ("ecclesia

2. Robert Moore, *The Origins of European Dissent* (New York: Blackwell, 1985); Malcolm Lambert, *Medieval Heresy: Popular Movements from the Gregorian Reform to the Reformation*, 3rd ed. (Oxford: Blackwell, 2002). See also Christine Ames, *Medieval Heresies: Christianity, Judaism, and Islam* (New York: Cambridge University Press, 2015). On Moore's views, see the respectful but nonetheless critical assessment in John Arnold, "Persecution and Power in Medieval Europe: *The Formation of a Persecuting Society*, by R. I. Moore," *American Historical Review* 123 (2018): 165–74.

3. Mark Pegg, *The Corruption of Angels: The Great Inquisition of 1245–1246* (Princeton, NJ: Princeton University Press, 2001).

4. William of Chartres, "On the Life and Deeds of Louis, King of the Franks of Famous Memory, and on the Miracles That Declare His Sanctity," in *The Sanctity of Louis IX: Early Lives of Saint Louis by Geoffrey of Beaulieu and William of Chartres*, ed. M. Cecilia Gaposchkin and Sean Field (Ithaca, NY: Cornell University Press, 2014), 142, paragraph 19.

5. Jacques Le Goff, *Saint Louis* (Paris: Gallimard, 1996), 58–59, 785–88; William Chester Jordan, *Louis IX and the Challenge of the Crusade: A Study in Rulership* (Princeton, NJ: Princeton University Press, 1979), 157–58.

abhorret a sanguine"). Instead, they "relaxed" (delivered) contumacious heretics into the hands of secular rulers for execution, typically by burning.[6]

As to prostitutes, Louis IX articulated policies of social segregation piecemeal before 1254 and more comprehensively thereafter, expelling them to the peripheries of towns and away from main roads and holy places, threatening the loss of their goods if they violated these directives, and criminalizing the actions of people who leased them dwellings too near the prohibited spaces. He expected these measures to motivate them to abandon their profession.[7] With the king's support, the bishop of Paris, William of Auvergne (d. 1249), provided group housing in the city and financial support for those who promised to reform themselves and live quasi-monastic lives. This meant also furnishing religious instruction and the necessary endowments to sustain the women over the years.[8] The temporary relief from financial vulnerability, often a key factor in taking up sex work,[9] offered some repentant prostitutes the opportunity to reenter society and to marry.[10] For others, it allowed for the possibility of later professing at a genuine monastic house, taking their conversion to a higher stage.[11] The king's and similar other programs subjected the women temporarily or permanently to the stringent disci-

6. Edward Peters, *Inquisition* (Berkeley: University of California Press, 1988), 50–51 and 68–72.

7. Keiko Nowacka, "Persecution, Marginalization, or Tolerance: Prostitutes in Thirteenth-Century Parisian Society," in *Difference and Identity in Francia and Medieval France*, ed. Meredith Cohen and Justine Firnhaber-Baker (Farnham, UK: Ashgate, 2010), 185–86 and 190–91.

8. William Chester Jordan, *Men at the Center: Redemptive Governance under Louis IX* (Budapest: Central European University Press, 2012), 90; Jordan, *Challenge of the Crusade*, 188–89; Le Goff, *Saint Louis*, 218–19, 292, 400.

9. Nowacka, "Persecution, Marginalization, or Tolerance," 181–82.

10. Nowacka, "Persecution, Marginalization, or Tolerance," 190–91.

11. Nowacka, "Persecution, Marginalization, or Tolerance," 190; Joëlle Rollo-Koster, "From Prostitutes to Brides of Christ: The Avignonese *Repenties* in the Late Middle Ages," *Journal of Medieval and Early Modern Studies* 32 (2002): 115.

pline of the church and secular authorities in the communal housing furnished to them. This may not have been to their liking, but authorities had not forced the women (by contemporary understandings of force) to take up residence. Over time, though, some of them may have chafed under the discipline and come to rue their choice.

Usurers, as remarked, also attracted the king's attention. He and his mother, Blanche of Castile, as regent, prohibited lending at interest in a series of pronouncements, the centerpiece of which was the Ordinance of Melun of 1230.[12] Moreover, Louis IX took extraordinary measures to follow up on the prohibition and eradicate usurious practices.[13] The goal, expressed in language drawn from Ephesians 4:28, was for the usurers to give up traditional moneylending and "live by the honest work of their own hands," not, as the criticism went, by mulcting poor people in distress by means of high-interest consumption loans.[14] Jews were the principal focus of the anti-usury campaign because of their prominence as moneylenders in the lower reaches of the consumer credit market.[15] In time, despite manifest subterfuges and clandestine practices, the campaign drastically reduced usurers' profits, causing widespread pauperization.[16] It is not clear that any immediate occupational shift improved the financial situation for Jews, however, since other than moneylending, they were restricted to producing goods for the small market of their coreligionists.[17]

As dissenters from the Christian faith, the Jews also stimulated the king's interest in other aspects of moral reform and, of

12. William Chester Jordan, *The French Monarchy and the Jews from Philip Augustus to the Last Capetians* (Philadelphia: University of Pennsylvania Press, 1989), 131–32.

13. Jordan, *French Monarchy and the Jews*, 132.

14. Jordan, *Challenge of the Crusade*, 154–55 n. 15.

15. Jordan, *French Monarchy and the Jews*, 26–29.

16. Jordan, *French Monarchy and the Jews*, 154–76.

17. Jordan, *French Monarchy and the Jews*, 148–49.

course, in *religious* conversion.[18] To turn this interest into reality, he imposed a whole range of crippling disabilities on them. For example, at his command his officials consigned hundreds of copies of the Talmud to destruction by burning, the justification being that it contained passages that appeared to insult Jesus and the Virgin Mary and taught doctrines that deviated from those of the written Torah or Old Testament.[19] A series of orders preserved for Normandy for 1235 show that Louis IX also forbade Jews to go to brothels or to prostitutes who were working independently. He limited their access to taverns in an evident effort to cut down on drunkenness and contact with Christians, though he mitigated this last prohibition slightly; travelers who needed to rest overnight in a tavern that doubled as an inn might do so. Nevertheless, the suspicion of "negative outcomes," if there were too many occasions for proximity between Jews and Christians, was unrelieved, as the Norman evidence also reveals. The king particularly charged Jews to dismiss Christian servants in their employ who had been excommunicated and who thus might have their animus for the church reinforced by Jewish expressions of hatred for Christianity.[20]

There is no doubt that the restrictions detailed above extended beyond Normandy. Moreover, in the culmination of its program in the 1250s and 1260s, the government obliged individual Jews everywhere in the kingdom to wear distinguishing signs on their clothing and to endure sermons preached in their synagogues and in Christian spaces—the Dominican convent in Paris, even the royal palace in the capital—urging them to aban-

18. Juliette Sibon, *Les juifs au temps de saint Louis* (Paris: Albin Michel, 2017), 22–64.

19. Jordan, *French Monarchy and the Jews*, 137–41; William Chester Jordan, "Marian Devotion and the Talmud Trial of 1240," in *Religionsgespräche im Mittelalter*, ed. Bernard Lewis and Friedrich Niewöhner (Wiesbaden: Harrassowitz, 1992), 61–76.

20. For a discussion of the Norman directives, see Jordan, *French Monarchy and the Jews*, 135.

don Judaism for Christianity.[21] None of these measures, illiberal as they may now appear, constituted force in the dominant contemporary moral calculus governing permissible incentives to convert.[22] Yet, there were also less-disciplinary inducements. These included the patronage that came with royal and aristocratic sponsorship at baptism and yearly pensions for the new Christians.[23]

The groups mentioned above do not exhaust the objects of Louis IX's or his contemporaries' concerns. The impulse in the thirteenth century was to convert—"to christianize and evangelize," in Geraldine Heng's words—the whole world.[24] It was to convert every part of it to a purity of devotion and, indeed, of moral living, as contemporary Catholics understood it. The hopes and strategies that emerged out of this impulse have stimulated a good deal of sophisticated scholarship. Some episodes are particularly vivid indicators of this totalizing vision. Although there are undoubtedly more that are worth addressing than those discussed here, I will concentrate on a small handful that are most directly relevant to the current study. These include the rise of the friars and the *béguines*, the eschatological and apocalyptical movements and discussions common in the period, the reform program of the Fourth Lateran Council and later church councils, the striking efflorescence of relic devotion, and the crusading enterprise itself. I do not attempt to offer comprehensive reviews of these issues in the pages of this introduction or to

21. Jordan, *French Monarchy and the Jews*, 149–50, 160, and 163. To the sources cited there, add "Notes sur quelques manuscrits du Musée britannique," ed. Léopold Delisle, *Mémoires de la Société de l'histoire de Paris et de l'Île de France* 4 (1877): 189.

22. Sibon, *Juifs au temps de saint Louis*, 32–33.

23. Jordan, *French Monarchy and the Jews*, 128–50.

24. Geraldine Heng, *The Invention of Race in the European Middle Ages* (Cambridge, UK: Cambridge University Press, 2018), 304 (see also 50–51 nn. 31–32).

pretend that they are not themselves interrelated, but I hope to provide sufficient background to situate readers and deepen the story told in the chapters that follow.

Even if churchmen exaggerated the threat of religious dissent, the array of ecclesiastical and political reactions to the reputed danger had a transformative effect on Christian society. In the first instance, it appeared to justify a resort to violence for its suppression in the Albigensian Crusade (1209–1229), a precedent of immense importance and long-lasting impact.[25] In addition, as we have already seen, the threat churchmen imagined gave rise to the inquisitions of heretical depravity in the aftermath of the war. Another reaction, the one I shall be stressing, was the growth of preaching by men of evangelical disposition, whose aim was the spread of true doctrine and enforcement of the proper performance of the Christian life in a way that would challenge and ultimately nullify popular and potentially heretical criticisms of the basic practices of the church.[26]

Not all of the groups that one associates with this antiheretical outpouring escaped the suspicion of heterodoxy themselves. The Humiliati, for example, endeavored to live what they took to

25. Mark Pegg, *A Most Holy War: The Albigensian Crusade and the Battle for Christendom* (New York: Oxford University Press, 2008); Christine Ames, *Righteous Persecution: Inquisition, Dominicans, and Christianity in the Middle Ages* (Philadelphia: University of Pennsylvania Press, 2009); James Given, *Inquisition and Medieval Society: Power, Discipline, and Resistance in Languedoc* (Ithaca, NY: Cornell University Press, 1997); Lucy Sackville, *Heresy and Heretics in the Thirteenth Century: The Textual Representations* (York: York Medieval Press, 2011); Peter Diehl, "Overcoming Reluctance to Prosecute Heresy in Thirteenth-Century Italy," in *Christendom and Its Discontents: Exclusion, Persecution, and Rebellion, 1000–1500*, ed. Scott Waugh and Peter Diehl, 47–66 (Cambridge, UK: Cambridge University Press, 1996); James Given, "Social Stress, Social Strain, and the Inquisitors of Medieval Languedoc," in Waugh and Diehl, *Christendom and Its Discontents*, 67–85.

26. Jeannine Horowitz, "Popular Preaching in the Thirteenth Century: Rhetoric in the Fight against Heresy," *Medieval Sermon Studies*, 60 (2016): 62–76; Sackville, *Heresy and Heretics*, 41–87.

be the simple gospel life implicit in the name they bore.[27] Their endowed fraternal communities were patterned on the coenobitic life, accepted a hierarchy of internal discipline, and gave a nod to episcopal oversight. However, their insistence on preaching, though many were laypeople, got them into trouble with bishops. They responded to criticisms by means of strategic compromises in ways that ultimately allowed them to survive and to carry out their missionary tasks, but not everyone was convinced. Nevertheless, their communities satisfied many of the critics, including the popes. Louis IX of France, on the contrary, while clearly sharing many of their values, was suspicious of the Humiliati and refused to endow houses for them in France or even to let them expand there from Italy.[28]

The king's reason may relate to another group, called loosely Waldensians. Although the scholarship on this group/movement has been characterized by skepticism, as Peter Biller has nicely mapped,[29] a few matters seem certain, at least to me. The Waldensians shared the missionary zeal of the Humiliati and other contemporary or near-contemporary groups, but were divided about making strategic concessions to the demands of the institutional church, such as promising to preach only with episcopal licenses. Their name possibly stems from a merchant, Valdès or Waldo of Lyon, who renounced his wealth and assumed the garb and behavior of a poor holy man. Inspired by his example, the Waldensians preached a gospel of renunciation of worldly possessions. Many also appear to have begun to challenge the priesthood's authority and, following from this, to attack the sacramental system. Those Waldensians who were willing to submit

27. Frances Andrews, *The Early Humiliati* (Cambridge, UK: Cambridge University Press, 1999).

28. William Chester Jordan, "Louis IX: Preaching to Franciscan and Dominican Brothers and Nuns," in *Defenders and Critics of Franciscan Life: Essays in Honor of John V. Fleming*, ed. Michael Cusato and Guy Geltner (Leiden: Brill, 2009), 224–25.

29. Peter Biller, "Goodbye to Waldensianism?," *Past & Present* 192 (2006): 3–33.

to ecclesiastical censure—or pretend to—were, like the Humiliati, reconciled and did effective (exemplary) work in the communities in which they resided and preached under license. Others who refused to reconcile fell victim to prosecution as heretics or fled to the mountains to practice their faith as they wished, in anticipation that a final end-time reckoning was near at hand. God would come to rescue the truly good and faithful men and women who burned with the fervor of their love for Him.

A Spaniard named Dominic and an Italian named Francis, as most readers know, were critical personalities in the further expansion of these evangelical movements.[30] Dominic of Calaruega (1170–1221), in some ways a more opaque personality, was motivated to convert heretics in southern France (conventionally referred to as Cathars, whether the terminology is appropriate or not) and ultimately the losers in the bitter war of annihilation referred to above, the Albigensian Crusade.[31] Francis of Assisi (1182–1226), who first focused on the towns of northern Italy, took his message to Christians who were orthodox in name but failed to live up to the values they otherwise accepted. These people included, as one might expect, usurers and prostitutes, but extended to merchants, bankers, shopkeepers, and the middle and lower orders in general. Francis in particular had an irrepressible zeal in his missionary activity and an explicit belief that he was God's holy agent. Neither he nor Dominic rejected the authority of the institutional church, and both found their patrons in a succession of popes.

The men and, soon, women[32] who flocked to the new orders—the Dominicans (Order of Preachers) and Franciscans

30. On Dominic, see Ralph Bennett, *The Early Dominicans: Studies in Thirteenth-Century Dominican History* (Cambridge, UK: Cambridge University Press, 1937), 18–30. On Francis, see Jacques Le Goff, *Saint Francis of Assisi* (London: Routledge, 2004) and Augustine Thompson, *Francis of Assisi: A New Biography* (London: Cornell University Press, 2012).

31. Pegg, *Most Holy War*.

32. Marie-Humbert Vicaire, "La naissance de Sainte-Marie de Prouille," in Pierre Mandonnet, *Saint Dominique: l'idée, l'homme et l'oeuvre*, vol. 1, 99–114

(Order of Friars Minor)—set about to transform the world. The Dominicans dedicated themselves to propagating right doctrine through learning, and they were early on attracted to the higher schools, including the University of Paris. As their name implies, they were also dedicated to persuasion by preaching. When all else failed, however, they resorted to repression. It was a short step to Dominican involvement, preponderant involvement, in the inquisitions of heretical depravity. In its early years, the Franciscan order's attraction to the schools was peripheral. They were rather more like animate symbols of the faith, wandering mendicants living off alms. Their male adherents (not the women[33]) traveled about like holy men of old, and they preached and exhorted their listeners to amend their lives in preparation for the Lord's return.

While Dominicans and Franciscans came to dominate the scene in terms of evangelical piety, the impulse to prepare the world for the Second Coming of Christ had many other partisans. There were the Brothers or Friars of the Sack, the Pied Friars, and the like, all licensed to preach and exemplify the simple life for the Christian faithful.[34] As the Dominicans and Franciscans found a powerful patron in the French royal family, including Louis IX, so too did these friars. Eager as they were to pledge obedience to the pope, they did not evoke reservations such as the king had about the Humiliati.[35] One ought to note, however, that in the reckoning of some critics, all of these groups were defective in that their devotion did not culminate in the highest

(Paris: Desclée De Brouwer, 1937); Miles Pattenden, "Canonisation of Clare of Assisi and Early Franciscan History," *Journal of Ecclesiastical History* 59 (2008): 208–26.

33. Catherine Mooney, *Clare of Assisi and the Thirteenth-Century Church: Religious Women, Rules and Resistance* (Philadelphia: University of Pennsylvania Press, 2016), 47–48.

34. Frances Andrews, *The Other Friars: The Carmelite, Augustinian, Sack and Pied Friars* (Woodbridge, UK: Boydell, 2006).

35. Andrews, *The Other Friars*, 25, 105–6, 183, and 199; Jordan, *Challenge of the Crusade*, 185 and 190.

form of conversion, namely the taking of *monastic* vows, signaling the move from the lay to the religious life. Very troubling to conservatives was many friars' refusal to live in enclosed and scrupulously regulated and disciplined communities.

If wandering friars failed to meet some of the traditional mid-thirteenth-century criteria of the perfected life, so too did another group of people who shared the moral fervor of the day. Discussing them reveals some additional fault lines in the reform movement. *Béguines* were typically widows or never-married laywomen who dressed plainly but did not take vows and often lived independently rather than in groups. They represented themselves as practicing renunciation of worldly life, but it was up to them as to whether to persist in the practice. Unlike nuns, they were not de jure obliged to do so. Thirteenth-century Paris was replete with such women. Their "halfway" conversion, from the critics' point of view, seemed dangerously incomplete, even though the king was an ardent supporter.[36] To take another example, the king's sister Isabelle (d. February 1270) was no béguine, but she embraced virginity, rejected marriage, lived a rigorously ascetic life in many other ways, and founded a convent of nuns on the then-existing Franciscan model, whose rule she helped to write.[37] Yet she herself refused to take the veil, even though she kept an apartment at the convent. Ultimately this provoked clerical displeasure, as Sean Field has shown.[38] In other words, conversion was itself a contested category in the thirteenth century. How much did one have to change for observers to reckon one a genuine convert and thus a person contributing to that improvement of Christian society that would bring a final reconciliation with God?

36. Tanya Miller, *The Beguines of Medieval Paris: Gender, Patronage, and Spiritual Authority* (Philadelphia: University of Pennsylvania Press, 2014), 25–34.

37. Sean Field, *Isabelle of France: Capetian Sanctity and Franciscan Identity in the Thirteenth Century* (Notre Dame, IN: University of Notre Dame Press, 2006).

38. Sean Field, *Courting Sanctity: Holy Women and the Capetians* (Ithaca, NY: Cornell University Press, in press).

It comes as no surprise, perhaps, that the eschatological and apocalyptical were expressed both in tandem with the growth of the mendicant, béguine, and similar movements (such as the Italian "Order of the Apostles"[39]) and in opposition to their spread. So the teachings of the Calabrian mystic Joachim of Fiore (d. 1202) prophesying a new status or phase in salvation history came to be associated—though, as David Burr has demonstrated, not always uncritically—with the mission and person of Francis, canonized in 1228 less than two years after his death.[40] To be sure, conservative thinkers disliked this association, another theme in Burr's book. Saint Francis was wildly popular, and as stories spread about his life and miracles, men and women accepted that God had specially chosen him to support His church. This did not mean that the saint's life had opened up a new dispensation that in the extreme imaginings of Francis's admirers might even be the critical act in a new age of the Holy Spirit.

Other conservatives and cynics respected Francis without believing that his followers lived up to his model or that the model was worthy of imitation by, say, kings such as Louis IX. The author of the harshest academic critique of mendicant spirituality was a professor at the University of Paris, William of Saint-Amour. He referred to his treatise *De periculis novissimorum temporum* as a commentary on the end-times.[41] In this rendering, the friars' coming was the bad omen, an aspect of the Antichrist's plan, a conclusion echoed by the prolific northern French poet Rutebeuf, one of the professor's zealous supporters.[42] William's work

39. See, for example, Jerry Pierce, *Poverty, Heresy, and the Apocalypse: The Order of the Apostles in Medieval Italy, 1260–1307* (New York: Continuum, 2012).

40. David Burr, *The Spiritual Franciscans: From Protest to Persecution in the Century after Saint Francis* (University Park: Pennsylvania State University Press, 2001).

41. Editorial introduction to William of Saint-Amour, *De periculis novissimorum temporum*, ed. Guy Geltner (Paris: Peeters, 2008), 1.

42. For the reference to the Antichrist, see *Oeuvres complètes de Rutebeuf*, ed. Edmond Faral and Julia Bastin (Paris: A. and J. Picard, 1977), vol. 1, 254–55, ll. 93–117. For other works and passages in Rutebeuf's works in support of William of Saint-Amour, see vol. 1, 243–48, 258–66, 273 ll. 92–105, and 311 ll. 193–215. As

occasioned papal censure and exile from France at the behest of the French king.[43]

The point is that the coming of the apocalypse was the framing narrative for multiple discussions of reform and crisis in the thirteenth century, a fact established meticulously in the work of Nicholas Vincent.[44] The Fourth Lateran Council of 1215 was "a show with a meaning," in Brenda Bolton's memorable words.[45] Drawing directly and indirectly on the writings of the ancient fathers of the church, especially Pope Gregory the Great, and on the magisterial teachings of the late twelfth-century Parisian scholar Peter the Chanter and his circle, its canons envisioned a thoroughgoing purification of the Catholic religion from the top down.[46] One may infer from the canons that this would reach the lowest levels by a new stress or reemphasis on pastoral care carried out by a metaphorical army of energetic prelates.

The fathers of the Council, especially Pope Innocent III, himself an avid supporter of the Dominican and Franciscan orders, envisioned a long, ongoing program that would require incredible effort:

> Indeed, *it is time*, as the blessed apostle said, *for judgment to begin at the house of the Lord* [1 Pet. 4:17]. For all corruption in the people comes first from the clergy, because *if the priest, who is anointed, sins, he makes the people guilty* [Lev. 4:3].

----

a guide to understanding Rutebeuf's medieval French, Michel Zink's translation into Modern French (Rutebeuf, *Oeuvres complètes* [Paris: Bordas, 1989–1990]) has been extremely helpful.

43. Editorial introduction to William of Saint-Amour, *De periculis*, 1–22.

44. Nicholas Vincent," 'Corruent Nobiles!': Prophecy and Parody in Burton Abbey's Flying Circus." In press.

45. Brenda Bolton, "A Show with a Meaning: Innocent III's Approach to the Fourth Lateran Council, 1215," in *Innocent III: Studies on Papal Authority and Pastoral Care*, 53–67 (Aldershot, UK: Variorum, 1995).

46. In general, see John Baldwin, *Masters, Princes and Merchants: The Social Views of Peter the Chanter and His Circle* (Princeton, NJ: Princeton University Press, 1970); and specifically on the appeal to Gregory the Great's authority, vol. 1, 24, 53, 57, 90–91, 95, 115, 196, and 339.

It is certain that when the laity see [the clergy] sinning shamelessly and outrageously they also will fall into sins and ungodliness because of the [clergy's] example. And when they are reproved by anyone, they immediately make excuses for themselves saying, *The Son can do only what he has seen the Father doing* [John 5:19] and *It is enough for the disciple if he is like his master* [Matt. 10:25].

So this prophecy is fulfilled, *The people will be just like the priest* [Hosea 4:9]. Indeed now the sea says, *blush with shame, O Sidon* [Isa. 23:4] for this is where evils have come into the Christian people: faith decays, religion grows deformed, liberty is thwarted, justice is trampled underfoot, heretics emerge, schismatics grow haughty, the faithless rage, the Agarenes conquer.[47]

In such manner the pope addressed the prelates of the Council in 1215 in anticipation of the deadly struggle between Muslims (Agarenes) and Christians to turn back the former's conquests as an element or even the culmination of universal reform.

Innocent III threw himself into the reform effort immediately, only to die a premature death in 1216 at the age of 56.[48] The First Council of Lyon in 1245, despite Norman Tanner's assertion that concerns for reform had begun to wane, "promot[ed] and confirm[ed]," as he himself recognized, "the general canonical legislation for religious life"—in other words, continued Innocent III's program.[49] In 1274, and with greater emphasis, the fathers at the Second Council of Lyon kept up the pressure to reform the world.[50] Moreover, both the Fourth Lateran Council, as we

47. Translation in Aden Kumler, *Translating Truth: Ambitious Images and Religious Knowledge in Late Medieval France and England* (New Haven, CT: Yale University Press, 2011), 21.

48. John Moore, *Pope Innocent III (1160/61–1216): To Root Up and to Plant* (Leiden: Brill, 2003), 254–55.

49. *Decrees of the Ecumenical Councils*, ed. Norman Tanner (London: Sheed and Ward, 1990), vol. 1, 274.

50. *Decrees of the Ecumenical Councils*, 305–6; *Crusade and Christendom:*

have seen, and the Second Council of Lyon emphatically yoked the crusade to this process, like oxen to the plow.[51] The mid-thirteenth-century archbishop of Rouen, Eudes Rigaud, who will make an appearance later in this book, was a Franciscan, a crusader, and a close friend of King Louis IX. He would come to embody all these impulses.[52]

Yet, long before the Fourth Lateran Council, Pope Innocent III had already linked his vision of the reform of the world to the crusade by authorizing the expeditions that now go under the collective name of the Fourth Crusade (1204) and strategizing about similar wars. To the pope, "it was essential," in the words of Danielle Park, *"to eradicate sin from Christian society* in order to bolster the crusade efforts" (my emphasis).[53] The planners of the Fourth Crusade targeted Muslim power in Egypt and the Holy Land.[54] A small expedition, separate from the main body of forces, did adhere to this goal, but the brunt of the military effort, for reasons it is not necessary to go into here, was diverted to an attack on the Byzantine Empire and led to the Frankish conquest of Constantinople and, in its wake, the establishment of the Latin Empire.[55] When Pope Innocent III first heard the news, he vented his dismay at a crusade gone wrong, but on re-

Annotated Documents in Translation from Innocent III to the Fall of Acre, 1187–1291, ed. Jessalynn Bird, Edward Peters, and James Powell (Philadelphia: University of Pennsylvania Press, 2013), 449–73. For a full treatment of the Council, see Burkhard Roberg, *Das zweite Konzil von Lyon [1274]* (Paderborn: Ferdinand Schöningh, 1990).

51. *Decrees of the Ecumenical Councils*, vol. 1, 267–71 (canon 71 of Lateran IV), 297–301 (canon ii.5 of Lyon I), 309–14 (constitution i of Lyon II).

52. Adam Davis, *The Holy Bureaucrat: Eudes Rigaud and Religious Reform in Thirteenth-Century Normandy* (Ithaca, NY: Cornell University Press, 2006), 65–129.

53. Danielle E. A. Park, *Papal Protection and the Crusader: Flanders, Champagne, and the Kingdom of France, 1095–1222* (Woodbridge, UK: Boydell, 2018), 99.

54. David Nicolle, *The Fourth Crusade 1202–04: The Betrayal of Byzantium* (Oxford: Osprey, 2011), 2; *Crusade and Christendom*, 56.

55. Jonathan Phillips, *The Fourth Crusade and the Sack of Constantinople* (New York: Viking, 2004); Nicolle, *Fourth Crusade*.

flection, and probably influenced by the dominant providential, even millenarian, narratives of the victorious First Crusade, he managed to interpret the conquest as another powerful sign of God's plan and a further step in the coming transformation of the world. Only now this would include the (impending) conversion of the schismatic Greeks.[56] As he expressed it later in the decrees of the Fourth Lateran Council, even while excoriating practices in the Eastern Church that were deemed deviant, "we would wish to cherish and honour the Greeks who in our days are returning to the obedience of the apostolic see."[57]

The conquest of Constantinople did more. The victors took the spoils back to the West. Its sanctuaries and palaces received wave after wave of relics that returning crusaders had taken from the caches of holy objects in church treasuries and private collections in Constantinople; of course, there was an existing market in Holy Land relics returning with pilgrims.[58] By implication, the West was supercharged with holiness by the transfer of these relics.[59] Not all of the spoils from Constantinople came to the West immediately after 1204. Many of the victors who

56. Marco Meschini, "The 'Four Crusades' of 1204," in *The Fourth Crusade: Event, Aftermath, and Perceptions*, ed. Thomas Madden, 27–42 (Aldershot, UK: Ashgate, 2008), 30–32. On millenarian expectations in the First Crusade, see Jay Rubenstein, *Armies of Heaven: The First Crusade and the Quest for Apocalypse* (New York: Basic, 2011), and Jay Rubenstein, "Lambert of Saint-Omer and the Apocalyptic First Crusade," in *Remembering the Crusades: Myth, Image, and Identity*, ed. Nicholas Paul and Suzanne Yeager, 69–95 (Baltimore: Johns Hopkins University Press, 2012). See also the rather more intricate picture painted in Philippe Buc, "Crusade and Eschatology: Holy War Fostered and Inhibited," *Mitteilungen des Instituts für Österreichische Geschichtsforschung* 125 (2018): 304–39.

57. *Decrees of the Ecumenical Councils*, vol. 1, 235, canon 4.

58. Michael Angold, *The Fourth Crusade* (Abingdon, UK: Routledge, 2014), 227–35. See also Nicholas Paul, *To Follow in Their Footsteps: The Crusades and Family Memory in the High Middle Ages* (Ithaca, NY: Cornell University Press, 2013), 102–4.

59. Alexis Charansonnet and Franco Morenzoni, "Prêcher sur les reliques de la Passion à l'époque de saint Louis," in *La Sainte-Chapelle de Paris: Royaume de France ou Jérusalem céleste?*, ed. Christine Hediger (Turnhout: Brepols, 2001), 61–99; Anne Lester, "What Remains: Women, Relics and Remembrance in the

established residence in the Empire retained the most precious relics for themselves, but regularly fiscal pressures obliged them to sell some of these to westerners or to allow westerners to redeem them from Italian moneylenders who held them as pledges for loans. This is how in the late 1230s King Louis IX obtained the Crown of Thorns and other relics of the Passion, for which he erected over the next few years a new chapel reliquary, the Sainte-Chapelle, in Paris.[60] As Sophie de Sède pointed out long ago and more recent historians have confirmed, there are many themes in the glass of the magnificent royal chapel, one worthy of note being the salvation history that looks forward to the conversion of the world under David's messianic successor (as evoked, for example, in the Tree of Jesse).[61]

Louis IX of France, like many Christians in Europe, was actively concerned, even as the construction team brought this monument to the triumph of Christianity to fruition, about just how this transformation would come about. What kind of endtime events would signal it? One interpretation predicted a titanic clash between the forces of good and evil. The contemporaneous invasion of Central and Eastern Europe by Central Asian warriors, the Mongols, appeared to support this.[62] Although images of the Mongols were not fixed, Westerners frequently

Aftermath of the Fourth Crusade," *Journal of Medieval History* 40 (2014): 311–28.

60. See the collection of articles in *La Sainte-Chapelle de Paris*.

61. Sophie de Sède, *La Sainte-Chapelle et la politique de la fin des temps* (Paris: Julliard, 1972). See also Alyce Jordan, "Seeing Stories in the Windows of the Sainte-Chapelle: The *Ars Poetriae* and the Politics of Visual Narrative," *Mediaevalia* 23 (2002): 39–60; Elizabeth Reynolds, "The Development of Stained Glass in Gothic Cathedrals," *JCCC Honors Journal* 4 (2012): 1–11 (4); Michelina Di Cesare, "Reading the Bible through Glass: The Image of Muhammad in the Sainte-Chapelle,"in *The Image of the Prophet between Ideal and Ideology: A Scholarly Investigation*, ed. Christiane Gruber and Avinoam Shalem, 187–200 (Berlin: De Gruyter, 2014), 198.

62. Peter Jackson, *The Mongols and the West, 1221–1410* (Abingdon, UK: Routledge, 2014), 58–86; Heng, *Invention of Race*, 287–98.

imagined them as the captive peoples, the apocalyptic figures of Gog and Magog of the Book of Revelation, broken out of the mountainous prison to which Alexander the Great had consigned them, to destroy Christianity.[63]

On the other hand, might the Turks emerge as the end-times foe? Symbolically significant in this second eschatological scenario was the loss of the holy city of Jerusalem, which had been accessible to Christians since the late 1220s thanks to a treaty negotiated by Emperor Frederick II (r. 1220–1250), and had come fully into their hands in 1243. The city was nonetheless vulnerable because of inadequate fortifications.[64] Khwarezmian Turks overran it in 1244, "desecrat[ing] the Christian Holy Places and the tombs of the Latin kings."[65] The soul-searching in the West provoked by this event was profound. Was Emperor Frederick II's exhausting and seemingly interminable conflict with the papacy itself a sign of the end-times? Was he the Antichrist?[66] Was the biblical prophecy fulfilled that the heathens would rampage in Jerusalem, which was God's shrine?: "O God, the heathen are come into thine inheritance; Thy holy temple have they defiled; They have laid Jerusalem on heaps. The dead bodies of thy servants have they given to be meat unto the fowls of the heaven, The flesh of thy saints unto the beasts of the earth. Their blood have they shed like water round about Jerusalem; And there was none to bury them" (Vulgate, Psalms 78:1). One could have found churchmen who thought so.[67] A few scholars may exaggerate how

63. Jackson, *Mongols and the West*, 146–48. On the changing views of Mongols and their role in apocalyptical scenarios, see Felicitas Schmieder, "Christians, Jews, Muslims—and Mongols: Fitting a Foreign People into the Western Christian Apocalyptic Scenario," *Medieval Encounters* 12 (2006): 274–95.

64. David Abulafia, *Frederick II: A Medieval Emperor* (New York: Oxford University Press, 1988), 184.

65. Peter Holt, *The Age of the Crusades: The Near East from the Eleventh Century to 1517* (London: Longman, 1986), 65–66.

66. Abulafia, *Frederick II*, 430–31.

67. Guillaume de Nangis, "Gesta sancti Ludovici," in *Recueil des historiens*

powerful this theme was in, say, the windows of the Sainte-Chapelle, as Alyce Jordan cautions, but it is certainly there.[68]

Waging war in the form of a crusade—just and holy violence—seemed a reasonable response to the devastation in the Holy Land and a way to enter once again into the mercy of God. Men in the know, such as the bishop of Beirut and the patriarch of Antioch, urged this course of action on Pope Innocent IV.[69] The occasion for French leadership was ironically auspicious, too, precisely because in a sense the king had been recalled from death to life to organize it. Louis IX had fallen desperately ill in late 1244, the year of the loss of Jerusalem. Linking the preservation of his life to the need to deliver the Holy Land, he pledged on his sickbed to lead the crusade, though some of the people around him at the time probably did not believe he would survive to fulfill his vow.[70] Others had no confidence that a vow taken in such circumstances was binding, so when the king recovered, he re-swore it in full command of his faculties and set about preparing for the war.[71] Never, as we shall now see, was the impulse to use the crusade to convert the world far from his thoughts.

---

des Gaules et de la France, ed. Martin Bouquet et al. (Paris: V. Palmé, 1840–1904), 346.

68. Alyce Jordan, *Visualizing Kingship in the Windows of the Sainte-Chapelle* (Turnhout: Brepols, 2002), 24.

69. Steven Runciman, *A History of the Crusades* (Cambridge, UK: Cambridge University Press, 1951), vol. 2, 256.

70. Jean de Joinville, *Vie de saint Louis*, ed. and trans. Jacques Monfrin (Paris: Garnier, 1995), 211–12, paragraphs 106–7.

71. Matthew Paris, *Chronica majora*, ed. Henry Luard (London: Her Majesty's Stationery Office, 1872–1883), vol. 5, 3–4.

CHAPTER ONE

The Crusade of 1248–1254

OUR EARLIEST GLIMPSE of Louis IX's hope to initiate a personal project of bringing Muslims to the Catholic faith occurs during the run-up to his first crusade. The crusade lasted from 1248 to 1254, but as we have seen, the king had already determined to go in December 1244 and immediately began preparations. These took him three and a half years.[1] Louis made truces with a number of potentially hostile European rulers and alliances with others. He created a corps of investigators known as *enquêteurs* to ferret out venal officials and their abuse of his subjects, partly to stanch the crown's loss of revenues in unchecked corruption, but mostly to cleanse his soul in the sight of God by atoning for his government's sins of commission and omission. He also induced barons who had earlier rebelled against him and been defeated to join the crusade, thus sparing France their presence while he was in *Outremer*, the lands beyond the sea. He made substantial spending cuts to give him the capacity to lend money to these barons and to redirect resources to other aspects of the planned crusade, such as the leasing of ships from purvey-

---

1. On all the matters treated in this paragraph, see Jordan, *Challenge of the Crusade*, 3–104, and Jean Richard, *Saint Louis* (Paris: Fayard, 1983), 181–204. Compare to Marie Dejoux, *Enquêtes de saint Louis: gouverner et sauver son âme* (Paris: Presses Universitaires de France, 2014).

ors in Provence and Italy. The cuts also made possible the major expansion of the Mediterranean port of embarkation, Aigues-Mortes, as well as the accumulation of supplies in Cyprus for his planned invasion of Egypt in the initial phase of the war. He persuaded the pope to authorize the French church to contribute huge sums to his enterprise; the total, almost one million pounds, was between three and four times greater than the crown's average annual revenue at the time. The success of most of these preparations nourished visions of Christian conquest in the East.

Joseph Bédier coined the term *chansons de croisade* for a number of French songs that dealt in whole or in significant part with the Crusades. He edited and translated the texts, and Pierre Aubry transcribed the corpus of music known to survive.[2] One of these *chansons* was composed during the period of Louis IX's preparations for his first crusade.[3] It is an exuberant piece, in which the songwriter fantasizes a glorious expedition culminating, as Benjamin Kedar has noted, in the conversion of the sultan of Turkey (*batisier le soldant de Turquie*) and an array of other dramatic successes in the wake of the anticipated Christian conquest.[4] Songs of this sort and this one in particular, I have argued elsewhere, captured the dominant mood and hopes of the warriors on the eve of their departure and the sentiments of the king himself.[5] If this is true, it means that men expressed the idea of converting the Muslims of Outremer as a goal prior to going to war, much as Louis's Castilian relatives did in anticipation of their so-called African crusades of the thirteenth century.[6]

2. *Chansons de croisade*, ed. Joseph Bédier and Pierre Aubry (Paris: Honoré Champion, 1909).

3. *Chansons de croisade*, 247–55.

4. Benjamin Kedar, *Crusade and Mission: European Approaches toward the Muslims* (Princeton, NJ: Princeton University Press, 1984), 161.

5. William Chester Jordan, "'Amen!' Cinq fois 'Amen!': les chansons de la croisade égyptienne de saint Louis, une source négligée d'opinion royaliste," *Médiévales* 34 (1998): 79–91 (83–87).

6. Francisco Garcia-Serrano, "Friars and Royal Authority in the Thirteenth-

An aspect of this wishful scenario was the expectation that defeated Muslim rulers and commanders would start the process of conversion by themselves going to the baptismal font, thus inspiring or insisting that their people do so as well. The successful earlier medieval conversions to Christianity in Europe—of Britons, Anglo-Saxons, Goths, western and eastern Franks, Scandinavians, and Slavs—that were recorded and repeated in countless texts, proceeded precisely in this way, at least in large measure.[7] Something similar happened after the conquest of Toledo in the late eleventh century.[8] More recently, in Valencia in the 1230s and 1240s, events that led Robert Burns to write of "the thirteenth-century dream of conversion" had confirmed the continued validity of this model.[9] Perhaps, as Robin Vose has conjectured, it was "only natural" that such dreams affected the devotees of universalistic religions like Christianity.[10]

The "obsession" that "gripped the Valencian crusaders" (Burns's language)[11] received what seemed to be unambiguous endorsement from the contemporary conversions of a few Valencian Muslim potentates out of shame for their defeat on the battlefield and, in the aftermath, as both Burns and Kedar note, the baptism of many of their subjects.[12] Similar hopes nurtured

Century Castilian Frontier," in *Authority and Spectacle in Medieval and Early Modern Europe: Essays in Honor of Teofilo F. Ruiz*, ed. Yuen-Gen Liang and Jarbel Rodriguez, 104–17 (London: Routledge, 2017), 105–6.

7. Peter Brown, *The Rise of Western Christendom: Triumph and Diversity, A.D. 200–1000*, 2nd ed. (Oxford: Blackwell, 2003), 137, 348–49, 467, etc.

8. Brian Catlos, *Muslims of Medieval Latin Christendom c. 1050–1614* (Cambridge, UK: Cambridge University Press, 2014), 23.

9. Robert Burns, *Muslims, Christians, and Jews in the Crusader Kingdom of Valencia* (Cambridge, UK: Cambridge University Press, 1984), 80, for the quotation, and more generally, 80–108. Also compare to Catlos, *Muslims of Medieval Latin Christendom*, 252.

10. Robin Vose, *Dominicans, Muslims and Jews in the Medieval Crown of Aragon* (New York: Cambridge University Press. 2009), 235–36.

11. Burns, *Muslims, Christians, and Jews*, 87.

12. Burns, *Muslims, Christians, and Jews*, 86–87; Kedar, *Crusade and Mission*, 168.

contemporary Christian missionary efforts in the thirteenth century to convert Buddhists and animists in Central Asia, according to John Tolan.[13] In Kedar's words, "Conversion of the Muslim enemy [and, one could add, of other non-Christian enemies] was an important component of the fantasy world of the western knight."[14] "Fantasy" is a favorite word among students of these matters.[15] Yet it was also a scenario, albeit repellant, imagined by Muslims fighting the crusaders, who feared that Christian victories over them would lead to waves of conversions.[16] Did moralists imagine that crusader defeats would enact the reverse process? They certainly did, as a contemporary exemplum revealing the apprehension of the Dominican moralist Stephen of Bourbon makes clear.[17] They were right to do so.

The Franciscan William of Saint-Pathus, who for several years served as the confessor for Louis IX's wife and then for the king's daughter, Blanche, was one of the most well-informed members of the court circle in the thirteenth century. He also had access to the hundreds of sworn depositions given in the king's canonization process in 1282.[18] Drawing on this store of oral and written information, he recorded his memories of and reflections on the king's life and work. Although he had a typical medieval clergyman's providential sense of history as well as unalloyed admi-

13. John Tolan, *Saracens: Islam in the Medieval European Imagination* (New York: Columbia University Press, 2002), 202–3. See also Heng, *Invention of Race*, 304–14.

14. Benjamin Kedar, "Multidirectional Conversion in the Frankish Levant," in *Varieties of Religious Conversion in the Middle Ages*, ed. James Muldoon, 190–99 (Gainesville: University Press of Florida, 1997), 194. See also Le Goff, *Saint Louis*, 160 and 174.

15. Vose, *Dominicans, Muslims and Jews*, 234.

16. Alex Mallett, *Popular Muslim Reactions to the Franks in the Levant, 1097–1291* (Farnham, UK: Ashgate, 2014), 116–17.

17. *Anecdotes historiques, légendes et apologues tirés du recueil inédit d'Étienne de Bourbon*, ed. Richard-Albert Lecoy de la Marche (Paris: Renouard, 1877), 337–38.

18. Richard, *Saint Louis*, 577.

FIGURE 1. Crusaders sparing Muslim mothers and children.
Paris, Bibliothèque nationale Française, MS fr 5716, Guillaume de
Saint-Pathus, *La Vie de saint Louis*, published by permission.

ration for Louis IX, scholars have always regarded his words as
an important and reliable source for the history of his reign, in
large part because independent documentary evidence substan-
tiates so many of the Franciscan's remarks.[19] This fact inspires
confidence even for those comments of William's for which
scholars have so far found no independent corroboration.

Thus, Kedar has suggested that there is no reason to doubt
William's report that on the eve of the war Louis IX instructed
his commanders to try to take Muslim defenders of their families
captive, if possible, rather than slay them. The king told the commanders explicitly to avoid killing their foes' wives and children.[20] Underlying this policy of relative restraint, I would argue,
were two desires. The king wished to make manifest the alleged
virtue of the Christians, but not simply to evoke appreciation in

19. Le Goff, *Saint Louis*, 337–44.
20. Kedar, *Crusade and Mission*, 165.

the beneficiaries. He saw the policy also as the initial step in proselytizing entire Muslim families. This goal was consonant with contemporary academic thinking commonly propagated in schools in France, as a thirteenth-century student's lecture notes testify.[21]

As a matter of practice, it differed wholly from the romance convention: namely, that it would be beautiful and whitish/whitening already-Christian-at-heart Muslim princesses who would yield, mesmerized, to chivalrous and victorious knights and convert.[22] The change in tint was influenced by the exegetical tradition that the Queen of Sheba, "black, *but* comely" in the Vulgate translation (Song of Songs 1:5), lost her blackness in her putative transition out of paganism.[23] The prospect of an ivory-hued princess-wife might well have informed more than one vain Christian crusader's fantasy, but the stories do not have as their sequel the conversion of the maidens' families.[24] True, a crusader might expect that his desire for a Saracen maiden was paralleled in a Muslim prince's yearning for a Christian lover, the culmination of which—marriage—could lead, in this fantasy world, to conversion of the ruler's subjects. The romance of *Floire and Blancheflor* comes to mind.[25] On the other hand, Muslim male-

21. Los Angeles, University of California–Los Angeles Library, Rouse MS 17, fols. 3v.-4r. I have treated these lecture notes, in particular the lecture on Jews (*Rubrica de judeis*), in the article "Learning about Jews in the Classroom: A Thirteenth-Century Witness, UCLA Library, Rouse MS 17," in *Envisioning Judaism: Studies in Honor of Peter Schäfer on the Occasion of His Seventieth Birthday*, ed. Ra'anan Boustan et al., vol. 2, 1247–60 (Tübingen: Mohr Siebeck, 2013).

22. Lynn Ramey, *Black Legacies: Race and the European Middle Ages* (Gainesville: University Press of Florida, 2014), 35, 54, and 63. See also Aman Nadhiri, *Saracens and Franks in 12th–15th Century European and Near Eastern Literature: Perceptions of Self and the Other* (London: Routledge, 2017), 88–89; and Heng, *Invention of Race*, 189.

23. Ramey, *Black Legacies*, 48–51.

24. Stefan Vander Elst, *The Knight, the Cross, and the Song* (Philadelphia: University of Pennsylvania Press, 2017), 159–60, 197, 223 n. 15, and 242 n. 35.

25. Lynn Ramey, *Christian, Saracen and Genre in Medieval French Literature* (New York: Routledge, 2001), 80.

Christian female coupling might lend itself to chaos instead: one thinks of *La fille du comte de Ponthieu.*[26] Romance, or at least these motifs in romance, did not provide a blueprint for practical action.

The policy that Louis IX articulated focused on converting those who could command their families to follow suit, fathers and husbands usually, and widows with small children. Kedar has raised the possibility, I think rightly, that the king recruited as many Dominicans as he did to the crusade precisely in anticipation of opportunities for proselytizing in this manner.[27] At the time, Louis IX's friend Humbert of Romans, the head of the Dominican Order in France from 1244 to 1254, would have blessed this and similar missions to Muslims enthusiastically, as even Robin Vose acknowledges.[28] This is not, however, to put into doubt Vose's broader point: namely that conversion of Muslims (or of Jews, for that matter) was never the principal focus of the Dominicans or other friars.[29] Yet, whether or not proselytizing was consistently a major goal or effort, it did attach itself importantly to the friars' mission under certain conditions. Louis IX's co-option of them was not unique; his Castilian kinsmen were also singling out the friars for this kind of activity in the wars they fought with Spanish Muslims.[30]

Of course, given Muslim marriage practices, the conversion of families by friars or anyone else raised thorny issues. Cousin-marriage was widespread in Islam and, depending on how close the cousin, the marriage partners' biological relationship could fall within the degrees prohibited by Roman canon law. On this point, canonists made an exception for husbands who converted

26. *La fille du comte de Ponthieu, conte en prose: versions du XIIIe et du XVe siècle*, ed. Clovis Brunel (Paris: Honoré Champion, 1923), 1–50.

27. Kedar, *Crusade and Mission*, 165.

28. Humbert of Romans, *Treatise on Preaching*, ed. Walter Conlon, trans. the Dominican Students of the Province of St. Joseph (Pine Beach, NJ: Newman Press, 1951), ii; Vose, *Dominicans, Muslims and Jews*, 21 and 43–48.

29. Vose, *Dominicans, Muslims and Jews*.

30. Garcia-Serrano, "Friars and Royal Authority," 105–6.

from Islam. They were not required to separate from their consanguineous spouses.[31] Polygamous marriage was different. Despite the example of Solomon and other biblical patriarchs, canonists insisted on monogamy for the converts; presumably, they were to remain in wedlock only with their first wives.[32] In the rare cases when an unmarried convert wanted to marry the widow of a crusader whom he had slain in battle or when an unmarried crusader wished to wed the converted widow of a Muslim warrior he had killed, other problems arose. Canonists addressed these in various ways, even to the point of considering whether the women before their widowhood had conspired against their husbands to get them out of the way.[33] Canonists are very clever and very thorough.

The combat on Louis IX's crusade started after the king's landing craft reached Egypt from staging areas in Cyprus in 1249.[34] The battle for the port city of Damietta ended in a total crusader victory.[35] In the wake of the seemingly miraculous triumph, according to a story told by Stephen of Bourbon that he claimed to have heard from an eyewitness, a Muslim seeking baptism approached the triumphant crusaders. They subjected his entreaty to close scrutiny (*examinato*), suspicious, one supposes, that he might be a spy or an assassin. Moreover, they would have wanted to find out whether he knew the rudiments of the Catholic faith. In the end, they honored his request. He received the sacrament

31. Benjamin Kedar, "Muslim Conversion in Canon Law," in *The Franks in the Levant, 11th to 14th Centuries*, 321–32 (Aldershot, UK: Ashgate/Variorum, 1993), 321–22.

32. Kedar, "Muslim Conversion in Canon Law," 323.

33. Kedar, "Muslim Conversion in Canon Law," 324–26.

34. In general, on the crusade, see Jean Richard, *Histoire des croisades* (Paris: Fayard, 1996), 349–66. A summary based mostly on Arabic sources may be found in Anne-Marie Eddé, "Saint Louis et la Septième Croisade vus par les auteurs arabes," *Cahiers de recherches médiévales (XIIIe-XVe s.)* 1 (1996): 65–92.

35. Richard, *Saint Louis*, 218–19.

of baptism and then joined the crusader army.[36] This incident would have reinforced the expectation among the crusaders that further successes on the battlefield would trigger additional conversions.

After a delay of several months, in part in expectation of additional crusaders, the king's army headed south. The Muslims who had retreated from Damietta had regrouped along with reinforcements. Better prepared this time, they hoped for retribution. The crusaders' loss in the new series of encounters was by no means a foregone conclusion. Scholars usually ascribe it to the rashness of one commander, the king's brother Count Robert of Artois, who made a mad dash into the town of Mansourah, leading a large contingent into what turned out to be certain death. The defeat reverberated within the Christian army; news of it spread and elated Muslims throughout the region, precipitating popular actions against native Egyptian Christians, including the desecration of Christian holy space. Arabic sources relate that "the people [in one town] went into the church of Mary with joy and pleasure, accompanied by singers and musicians, rejoicing at what had happened. They intended to demolish the church."[37] The good news of such a stunning victory was made known through sermons as had become traditional by this time, in order "to encourage a spirit of jihad among both soldiers and citizens," to borrow Jonathan Berkey's phrasing.[38] Owing to factional differences among the Muslims, however, in the longer (two-decade) afterglow of the victory the militant enthusiasm abated somewhat.[39]

36. *Anecdotes historiques . . . d'Étienne de Bourbon*, 337.

37. Holt, *Age of the Crusades*, 83.

38. *Seventh Crusade, 1244–1254: Sources and Documents*, comp. Peter Jackson (Aldershot, UK: Ashgate, 2007), 214. Jonathan Berkey, "Audience and Authority in Medieval Islam: The Case of Popular Preachers," in *Charisma and Religious Authority: Jewish, Christian, and Muslim Preaching, 1200–1500*, ed. Katherine Jansen and Miri Rubin, 105–20 (Turnhout: Brepols, 2010), 115.

39. Emmanuel Sivan, *L'Islam et la croisade: Idéologie et propaganda dans les réactions musulmanes aux croisades* (Paris: Maisonneuve, 1968), 136–39.

In the wake of the battlefield disaster at Mansourah, disengagement of the crusader army became essential. However, what started out as an uncoordinated retreat—bad enough—turned into a Christian catastrophe in which not Muslims were captured, but the king, the *raydafrance* himself (news that was also proclaimed in sermons and other media[40]), and his new convert from Damietta. According to Stephen of Bourbon, the Muslim victors tried blandishments to persuade the apostate to renounce Christianity, but this approach failed. They then, or so the story goes, struck him repeatedly, bound him to a stave, and scourged him with two hundred lashes. Stephen of Bourbon told the story because the convert continued to glorify his new faith.[41] His endurance was a lesson, an exemplum, for other Christians. However, if the information received by the contemporary English chronicler Matthew Paris, a Benedictine monk of Saint Albans, was accurate, many of the crusaders failed to exhibit the steadfastness of the neophyte, preferring to defect to Islam in the aftermath of their defeat.[42]

Louis IX's captivity, as I have remarked in other work, has fascinated scholars.[43] Arab chroniclers, perhaps influenced by Hohenstaufen propaganda, sometimes painted a hubristic image of the French king. At other times, however, they remarked the manifestation of his courage in war and his thoughtfulness, intelligence, wisdom, and refinement in captivity.[44] It is doubtful that Matthew Paris has the details right of a conversation between the sultan and the king during his captivity.[45] There had to have been

40. *Seventh Crusade, 1244–1254*, 214. Mohamad El Merheb, "Louis IX in Medieval Arabic Sources: The Saint, the King, and the Sicilian Connection," *Al-Masāq: Journal of the Medieval Mediterranean*, 28 (2016): 282–301 (297–99). (I wish to thank Professor Cecilia Gaposchkin for this reference.)

41. *Anecdotes historiques . . . d'Étienne de Bourbon*, 337–38.

42. Matthew Paris, *Chronica majora*, vol. 5, 107.

43. William Chester Jordan, "*Etiam reges*, Even Kings," *Speculum* 90 (2015): 613–34 (614–18).

44. El Merheb, "Louis IX in Medieval Arabic Sources," 297–99.

45. Matthew Paris, *Chronica majora*, vol. 5, 309–10.

meetings with all the requisite witnesses and interpreters present, because the two rulers were trying to hammer out an agreement that would lead to the ransom of the king's soldiers for money and the return of Damietta to Muslim control for Louis IX's own release.[46] However, some of the words that the monk attributed to the king sound like the private utterances of the man to his Christian companions. Consider, for example, the freely rendered statement "Why do these people not abandon their foul law? I know about their so-called holy book, and it is an instruction for depravity. I do not wish to return to France until I manage to bring these people to the faith of Christ."

These were the commonplaces of Christian polemics. They were identical with the sentiments of two of Louis IX's close friends. The first was the French Dominican Humbert of Romans, who, as earlier remarked, was head of the order in France from 1244 until 1254 and subsequently served as its master general for two decades. The second was another Dominican, Vincent of Beauvais, who wrote in a somewhat more nuanced way about Muhammed and Islam in his reworked *Speculum historiale* between 1246 and 1260.[47] The monk of Saint Albans, who reported the king's words, had carried on some diplomatic business in Norway for the French crown on the eve of the crusade.[48] He continued to have good connections, conduits of information about events at the royal court and the expedition to the East. One of the most important for our purposes, though an indirect source, was the bishop of Orléans, William of Boësses (sometimes referred to in the scholarly literature as William of

46. Richard, *Saint Louis*, 232–38.

47. Valentin Portnykh, "Short Version of Humbert of Romans' Treatise on the Preaching of the Cross: An Edition of the Latin Text," *Crusades* 15 (2016): 55–115 (90–91); Humbert of Romans, *Treatise on Preaching*, 90–91; Florence Ninitte, "Defining the Perception of Muḥammad and Islam in Vincent of Beauvais' *Speculum historiale* and Its French Translation by Jean de Vignay," *Vincent of Beauvais Newsletter* 41 (2017): 15–34 (15 and 31).

48. Richard Vaughan, *Matthew Paris* (Cambridge, UK: Cambridge University Press, 1958), 6–7 and 14.

Bussy), who accompanied Louis IX and was present at the Battle of Damietta.

Although Bishop William returned from Outremer after this victory, he visited Paris frequently and thus continued to receive information about conditions overseas, including the king's redemption from captivity.[49] He wrote to a friend, the bishop of Chichester and future saint Richard de Wych, about these events, even detailing the amount of the crusaders' ransom in one letter. (Richard had studied for the priesthood in Orléans in the early 1240s, shortly after William became bishop there.[50]) Now, in the 1250s, Bishop Richard was a correspondent of Matthew Paris, providing him with source material, especially for his *Life* of Saint Edmund of Abingdon, which the monk was writing at the time. Richard included the letter from William of Boësses about conditions on the crusade in his correspondence with Matthew, and the monk quoted it in his *Chronica majora*.[51]

Matthew clearly picked up additional bits and pieces from his other contacts about the king's expression of his feelings during his captivity. In writing them up, he sometimes situated them inaccurately, arranged them to particularly dramatic effect ("to manipulate existing feelings," as one commentator put it), or shaped them, as I am hinting, to map onto generally received opinions.[52] Nonetheless, in Benjamin Kedar's words, "Matthew Paris' imaginary 'interview' was not entirely divorced

49. *Histoire littéraire de la France*, new ed. (Paris: V. Palme, 1865–), vol. 19, 414.

50. "Richard of Chichester (Richard de Wych)," in *Oxford Dictionary of Saints*, ed. David Farmer, online at http://www.oxfordreference.com/view/10.1093/acref/9780199596607.001.0001/acref-9780199596607-e-1382.

51. Vaughan, *Matthew Paris*, 15, 161–62, and 164–65; Jules Devaux, "Petits problèmes historiques," *Annales de la Société historique et archéologique du Gâtinais* 8 (1890): 95–109 (98); *Histoire littéraire de la France*, vol. 19, 414.

52. Sophia Menache, "Written and Oral Testimonies in Medieval Chronicles: Matthew Paris and Giovanni Villani," *Medieval Chronicle* 6 (2009): 1–30 (5–10 and 16–18).

from reality."[53] It is evidence, at least, that conversion of the Muslims was still very much on King Louis IX's mind.[54]

It remained so throughout his monthlong captivity. The king's friend, fellow crusader, and biographer John of Joinville would later recall another incident in which

> a very well dressed and very handsome Saracen came to the king and presented him with pots of milk and flowers of several different kinds on behalf of the children of Nasac [either an-Nasir Daud, d. 1259, or, more likely, his father, al-Mu'azzam, d. 1227], the former [claimant to the] sultan[ate] of Egypt. He spoke in French when he presented these gifts. The king asked him where he had learned French and he said that he had been a Christian. "Be gone with you," said the king, "I'll not speak to you any more!"[55]

Louis IX's odium for the apostate from Christianity was manifest, but John of Joinville followed up on the encounter. He learned that the Muslim, a Champenois from Provins, had come to Egypt originally as a crusader, converted after his capture or desertion, married, and become wealthy. Although the former Christian acknowledged to John that he would have liked to return to the faith of his fathers, he was afraid of the consequence of a new apostasy, capital punishment. John of Joinville's admonition that hell should terrify him more did not change his mind.[56]

Louis IX detested his visitor because he was, in the king's view, a willful sinner. His relationship with the man would have altered if and only if the latter had returned to the Catholic faith. This is homologous to the framework within which one has to

53. Kedar, *Crusade and Mission*, 162.
54. Le Goff, *Saint Louis*, 789–92.
55. Jean de Joinville, *Vie de saint Louis*, 376–77, paragraphs 394–95. I quote from Caroline Smith's translation (Jean de Joinville's *Life of Saint Louis*) in *Chronicles of the Crusades* (London: Penguin, 2008). The section numbers replicate those in Jacques Monfrin's critical edition and translation into modern French. On Nasac's identity, see the notes to Monfrin's and Smith's versions.
56. Jean de Joinville, *Vie de saint Louis*, 376–79, paragraphs 395–96.

acknowledge Louis IX's well-attested animus toward Jews,[57] unchangeable so long as they remained Jews, but that saw him dedicate himself to their conversion and, along with other members of his family and entourage, sponsor them at their baptisms. This is how Geoffrey of Beaulieu, the king's longtime confessor, reported one instance: "[D]uring the feast of the blessed Denis," the patron saint of the kingdom of France, "the king was having a certain well-known Jew solemnly baptized in the church of the same blessed Denis—such that the king himself, together with the great nobles of the realm, was lifting this Jew from the sacred font."[58]

The voluntary conversion to Christianity of a man and, by implication, the women and children of his family, was the initial step, in this context, in gaining the king's respect. True, the adjustment of faith from Islam or Judaism to Christianity was not the sole factor necessary for the enrichment of relations with the king or with the Christian community in general. Plenty of Christian sinners disgusted the king and the people who shared his moral outlook. However, overcoming the hurdle of the "wrong" faith was the sine qua non for every other benefit from the crown. Hagiographers and sermonizers for centuries to come reported that Muslims or pagans who sought their enrichment—knighthood—from the king were summarily denied it if they refused to be baptized; the possibility of success, though not its certainty, remained open for converts.[59] Conversion, the king allegedly

57. Jean de Joinville, *Vie de saint Louis*, 174–77, paragraphs 51–53; William of Chartres, "On the Life and Deeds of Louis," 142–43, paragraphs 21–22.

58. Geoffrey of Beaulieu, "Here Begins the Life and Saintly Comportment of Louis, Former King of the Franks, of Pious Memory," in *The Sanctity of Louis IX: Early Lives of Saint Louis by Geoffrey of Beaulieu and William of Chartres*, ed. M. Cecilia Gaposchkin and Sean Field, trans. Larry Field (Ithaca, NY: Cornell University Press, 2014), 69–128 (117, paragraph 41). See also Guillaume de Saint-Pathus, *Vie de saint Louis*, ed. Henri-François Delaborde (Paris: Alphonse Picard et fils, 1899), 20.

59. Paris, Bibliothèque nationale de France (BnF), Collection Baluze, vol. 14,

said, opened the door to knighthood and lands in France.[60] When the king went to the port of Acre following his release from captivity, he reiterated this sentiment explicitly.

For 150 years, Acre had been a European Christian entrepôt, an emporium, most of all a "colonial outpost," in the phrase of Suzanne Akbari, although the word "colonial" carries inappropriate mental baggage, I think.[61] Perhaps "frontier outpost" would be a better phrase. Like most such entry points to an immigrant settler community, the city's population was, to borrow David Jacoby's adjective, "heterogeneous," to say the least.[62] Some of the people who arrived at the port passed through quickly on their way home to Europe or to settlements in the Holy Land. Others in the city were periodic temporary residents, the length of whose stays varied widely. A few of the temporary residents were Muslims from the hinterland.[63] Their goods, such as flax, were useful to the sustenance, convenience, and comfort of the permanent inhabitants. They or their agents presumably went back at intervals to the Muslim villages, resupplied themselves with goods, and returned to Acre, to the accursed Franks, in regular rhythms. Over the years, a few managed to master some of the lingua franca that facilitated commerce and life in the city: "People use the eloquence and idioms of diverse languages,"

fol. 2; Paris, BnF, MS. fr. 5721, fols. 38v.–39; *Mystère de saint Louis, roi de France*, ed. Francisque Michel (Westminster: Roxburghe Club, 1871), xx.

60. *Grandes chroniques de France*, ed. Jules Viard (Paris: Honoré Champion, 1920–1953), vol. 7, 155–56.

61. Suzanne Akbari, "Embodying the Historical Moment: Tombs and Idols in the *Histoire ancienne jusqu'à César*," *Journal of Medieval and Early Modern European History* 44 (2014): 617–43 (634).

62. David Jacoby, "Society, Culture, and the Arts in Crusader Acre," in *France and the Holy Land: Frankish Culture at the End of the Crusades*, ed. Daniel Weiss and Lisa Mahoney, 97–137 (Baltimore: Johns Hopkins University Press, 2004), 98–105.

63. Jacoby, "Society, Culture, and the Arts," 102.

Fulcher of Chartres noted, "in conversing back and forth. Words of different languages have become common property known to each nationality."[64]

The city was also home to residents apart from Latin Christians and Muslims. Scholars are still uncertain as to how many of these had permanently settled in Acre, were regular visitors with commercial and other interests there, or simply passed through in transit to other locations. There were certainly a few non-Latin Christians among the permanent residents.[65] There were pagans, too.[66] Perhaps the latter included animist Cumans serving as mercenaries or in flight as refugees from the Mongols, part of those "huge numbers," in Nicholas Morton's words, "of displaced people/tribes" trying to escape slaughter or bondage.[67] These were people whose cultural practices had long disturbed and intrigued Muslims, Eastern Christians, and Western Christians alike, including Louis IX's friend John of Joinville.[68] Unsurprisingly, Acre, because of the variety of ethnic, linguistic, and religious groups and the diversity of their cultural practices, was both an exciting and a fraught city. This is where Louis IX passed most of his time in the Crusader States after his release.

It did not take long, in the history of the Crusader Kingdom of Jerusalem, for Muslim traders and wholesalers to realize that they lived precariously in the middle between Christian-crusader sufferance that might lessen at any time and the distaste of many of their Islamic coreligionists.[69] Certain of our sources are prob-

64. Cited and translated in Vander Elst, *The Knight, the Cross, and the Song*, 201 n. 7.

65. Jacoby, "Society, Culture, and the Arts," 102–6: Benjamin Kedar, "Latins and Oriental Christians in the Frankish Levant, 1099–1291," in *Franks, Muslims and Oriental Christians in the Latin Levant: Studies in Frontier Acculturation*, 209–22 (Aldershot, UK: Ashgate/Variorum, 2006), 220.

66. Geoffrey of Beaulieu, "Here Begins the Life," 104, paragraph 27.

67. Nicholas Morton, "The Teutonic Knights in the Holy Land, 1190–1291," online at https://boydellandbrewer.com/medieval-herald-teutonic-knights.

68. Jean de Joinville, *Vie de saint Louis*, 438–43, paragraphs 495–98.

69. Carole Hillenbrand, *Crusades: Islamic Perspectives* (Edinburgh: Edin-

ably referring to Muslims caught in this bind, this squeeze, who came over time to think that showing regard for Louis IX might help them to bear the difficult situation in which they found themselves.[70] They also knew what he wanted in return. He had been an envious witness to the conversions of Muslims and pagan slaves to Christianity in Cyprus.[71] Kedar doubts that Louis's efforts had been the immediate impetus for these baptisms.[72] Nevertheless, he agrees that conversion was high in the king's priorities.

The very coins the king minted at Acre, Kedar agrees, deliberately spread the Christian message in Arabic-language legends and with the symbol of the cross.[73] Gold bezants bore the legend on their obverse "One God + Father Son and Holy Spirit + Struck at Acre 1251 since the Incarnation of Christ" and on their reverse "+ And of the resurrection and through Him we are saved and loved + We glorify ourselves by the choice of our Lord Jesus Christ, in whom is our salvation and our life + And our resurrection and to whom we owe our redemption and our sustenance."[74] The minting of these coins continued into the 1260s. In 1251, silver drachms were also struck bearing the legends "One God, one Faith, one Baptism" and "Father, Son and Holy Spirit: one Godhead."[75] Our sources say explicitly that early on, the king

burgh University Press, 1999), 377; Benjamin Kedar, "The Subjected Muslims of the Frankish Levant," in *The Franks in the Levant, 11th to 14th Centuries*, 135–74 (Aldershot, UK: Ashgate/Variorum, 1993), 158–59.

70. Geoffrey of Beaulieu, "Here Begins the Life," 104, paragraph 27.

71. "E breviario historiarum Landulphi de Columna, canonici Carnotensis," in *Recueil des historiens des Gaules et de la France*, ed. Martin Bouquet et al. (Paris: V. Palmé, 1840–1904), vol. 23, 192–98 (195).

72. Kedar, *Crusade and Mission*, 165 n. 19.

73. Kedar, *Crusade and Mission*, 165.

74. *Pace* Louis Blancard, *Le bésant d'or sarrazinas, pendant les croisades: étude comparée sur les monnaies d'or, arabes et d'imitation arabe, frappées en Égypte et en Syrie, aux XIIme et XIIIme siècles* (Marseilles: Barlatier-Feissat, 1880), 24, 26–27.

75. Jordan, *Challenge of the Crusade*, 132, and see also, since its appearance, *History of the Crusades*, 2nd ed., ed. Kenneth Setton (Madison: University of

offered potential converts splendid gifts (possibly including such gold and silver coins, a suggestion I owe to Robert Leonard[76]) to encourage them to adopt the Catholic faith, conversion being the key step in the process that would lead to their protection and continued support by Louis IX.[77] Kedar believes that the gifts were far more persuasive than the vague recognition that the king was in some sense a man whose influence was worth cultivating.[78] He may be correct.

Yet success in this initial phase of the conversion project was uneven. As Kedar has also remarked, certain of these putative converts took their presents and melted back into the countryside richer and still Muslim, but thereby forgoing possible future gifts. The knowledge of this trajectory endured over half a century later, as Venetian merchant Marino Sanudo attested.[79] It did so because the outlay of money was considerable and terribly inconvenient to lose. Although funds from France periodically replenished his coffers, the king's opulent gifts vied with his other self-imposed obligations, such as refortifying the Christian battlements and walls of Caesarea and Jaffa.[80] However, as Sanudo had also heard, in his enthusiasm to convert Muslims Louis IX

Wisconsin Press, 1969–1989), vol. 6, 446–47 and 468–69, with illustrations at 480–82; David Metcalf, *Coinage of the Crusades and the Latin East in the Ashmolean Museum Oxford* (London: Royal Numismatic Society/Society for the Study of the Crusades and the Latin East, 1995), 44–45 and 98–106; Alex Malloy, Irene Preston, and Arthur Seltman, *Coins of the Crusader States 1098–1291: Including the Kingdom of Jerusalem and Its Vassal States of Syria and Palestine, the Lusignan Kingdom of Cyprus (1192–1489), and the Latin Empire of Constantinople and Its Vassal States of Greece and the Archipelago*, 2nd ed. (Fairfield, CT: Berman, 2004), 118–19 and 129–40. (My thanks to Robert Leonard for these additional references.)

76. Personal email communication (16 May 2018).

77. Guillaume de Saint-Pathus, *Vie de saint Louis*, 21.

78. Kedar, *Crusade and Mission*, 164.

79. Kedar, *Crusade and Mission*, 164. See also Mallett, *Popular Muslim Reactions to the Franks*, 113.

80. Jordan, *Challenge of the Crusade*, 103–4.

was willing to bankrupt himself because he believed the divine reward, if he were successful, would be so great.[81] Such enormous outlays undoubtedly contributed to the enduring and pernicious charge, still needing refutation in the sixteenth century,[82] that Louis IX almost ruined France financially by his spending for the crusade.

The king's confessor, Geoffrey of Beaulieu, an eyewitness, also tells us that Louis IX "[f]rom his own funds . . . saw to the purchase of slaves, many Saracens and pagans, and had them baptized, and assigned provisions to them as well."[83] Although canonists, high royal officials of the Kingdom of Jerusalem, and aristocratic slave-owners differed as to whether the baptism of a slave automatically emancipated him or her,[84] the king of France appears to have sided with those who equated Christianity and free status. Baptism was a synonym for manumission. Alex Mallett regards these acts of Louis IX, effectively the new master of the Crusader Kingdom, as a species of forced conversion, for they were influenced, unfairly in his opinion, by the king's proffering of money to vulnerable people and purchasing freedom for slaves.[85] But, leaving aside liberal modern Christian and non-Christian sensitivities, which are understandable, these

81. Kedar, *Crusade and Mission*, 164.

82. Elizabeth Brown, "A Sixteenth-Century Defense of Saint Louis' Crusades: Étienne le Blanc and the Legacy of Louis IX," in *Cross Cultural Convergences in the Crusader Period: Essays Presented to Aryeh Grabois on His Sixty-Fifth Birthday*, ed. Michael Goodich, Sophia Menache, and Sylvia Schein, 21–48 (New York: Peter Lang, 1995).

83. Geoffrey of Beaulieu, "Here Begins the Life," 104, paragraph 27. One manuscript of Geoffrey's work omits this sentence, but the sentiment is in full agreement with the sentence before. (I thank the anonymous referee of this book for reminding me of the manuscript differences.) Kedar, *Crusade and Mission*, 163.

84. Kedar, "Muslim Conversion in Canon Law," 326–28; Kedar, "Subjected Muslims of the Frankish Levant," 153–54; Catlos, *Muslims of Medieval Latin Christendom*, 274.

85. Mallett, *Popular Muslim Reactions to the Franks*, 116.

methods, including the giving of gifts, did not fall into the category of force as *medieval* Christians understood the matter.[86] Commentators could and did imagine the possibility of the Crusades as wars *of* conversion, in which holy warriors would threaten battlefield opponents or those already vanquished with further violence if they refused baptism. Jonathan Riley-Smith has observed that "popes and preachers sometimes sailed close to the wind" in their recruitment efforts,[87] but this was not how the conversions were supposed to be effected.[88]

Nonetheless, in the Arabic historiographical tradition, as represented by Al-Makrizi 150 years later, this is precisely what the French king is supposed to have intimated to the Muslim ruler on the eve of the Battle of Damietta:

> You will be aware that I am the head of the Christian community. *You know also that the [Muslim] population of Andalusia pays tribute to us and gives us gifts, and we drive them before us like a herd of cattle, killing the men, widowing the women, capturing their daughters and infants, emptying their houses.* I have given you sufficient demonstration [of our strength], and the best advice I can offer. Even if you were to promise me anything on oath and to appear before the priests and monks and carry a candle before me as an act of obedience to the cross, it would not deter me from attacking you and fighting you on the land that is dearest to you. If this country falls into my hands, it will be mine as a gift. If you keep it by a victory over me, you may do as you will with me. I have told you about the armies obedient to me, filling the mountains and the plains, numerous as the stones of the

---

86. Kedar, "Muslim Conversion in Canon Law," 328–30.

87. Jonathan Riley-Smith, *Crusades, Christianity, and Islam* (New York: Columbia University Press, 2008), 15.

88. Kedar, "Muslim Conversion in Canon Law," 329; Elizabeth Siberry, *Criticism of Crusading, 1095–1274* (Oxford: Clarendon Press, 1985), 19.

earth, and poised against you like the sword of destiny. I put you on your guard against them.[89]

It is possible that Louis IX did dispatch multiple letters, some suggesting conversion, to the sultan before the attack on Damietta. In one or more of them, he likely lamented, as Matthew Paris would have it, the Egyptian ruler's adherence to Islam, at least "until he has pity on his own soul and is converted to the Lord, Who desires all men to be saved and unfurls the bosom of His mercy to all those who are converted to Him."[90] If this was the substance of the communication, Al-Makrizi's report establishes that the message suffered in transmission in the following years, as the spurious claim attributed to the king (italicized above) of having been an invincible generalissimo in Spain makes clear. The scholarship has challenged the Muslim chronicler's reliability and exaggerations a century and a half removed from the events, on other issues as well.[91] It is possible, however, as Mohamad El Merheb has asserted, that Arab historians in general transmitted distorted, often negative Sicilian/Hohenstaufen-influenced word portraits of the French king, and embellished these with literary license.[92]

Medieval Christian legends surrounding the Emperor Heraclius's recovery of the True Cross from the Persians may be of some relevance here. A version of these stories appears in Jacobus de Voragine's *Golden Legend*. They tell of the victor's offer of mercy to the vanquished Persian troops who had promised

89. *Crusade and Christendom*, 363–64. Compare the translation (*Medieval Sourcebook: Al-Makrisi: Account of the Crusade of St. Louis*, comp. Paul Halsall, online at https://sourcebooks.fordham.edu/source/makrisi.asp) of *Chronicles of the Crusades*, 542.

90. Matthew Paris, *Chronica majora*, vol. 6, 161. The translation is Peter Jackson's *Seventh Crusade, 1244–1254*, 90–91. The significance of this passage was brought to my attention by Professor Gaposchkin.

91. Kedar, "Subjected Muslims of the Frankish Levant," 162–63.

92. Compare to El Merheb, "Louis IX in Medieval Arabic Sources," 287–93.

spontaneously to convert.[93] Heraclius (referred to suggestively as "christianissimus princeps") put a condition on his mercy, however. The defeated Persians had to fulfill their promise to accept Christianity quickly or face slaughter.[94] These legends of the emperor's victory over the Romans' traditional enemy were once thought to have informed the content of the (much-restored) relic window of the Sainte-Chapelle, a claim rejected in recent scholarship.[95] Still, as Cecilia Gaposchkin has pointed out to me, the chronicler Matthew Paris twice compares Louis IX and his redemption of the relics of the Passion, treasured at the Sainte-Chapelle, with Heraclius's recovery of the True Cross.[96] If the story was in the king's mind, even absent its representation in the royal chapel's windows, it linked crusading with the voluntary conversion of the vanquished and with vengeance on those who were slow in fulfilling their promise. The threat of vengeance itself would probably have been sufficient to constitute coercion for some Christian authorities.

All this being said, observers of the thirteenth century, such as Geoffrey of Beaulieu, would have seen nothing in common between Louis IX's *actual* program of conversion in Acre and the battlefield threats that soldiers might make ("convert or be slain—and even if you offer to, if you are slow, I might slay you

93. Jacobus de Voragine, *The Golden Legend: Readings on the Saints*, trans. William Granger Ryan (Princeton, NJ: Princeton University Press, 1993 [2012]), 555, and Stephan Borgehammar, "Heraclius Learns Humility: Two Early Latin Accounts Composed for the Celebration of *Exaltatio Crucis*," *Millennium* 6 (2009): 145–201 (145).

94. Borgehammar, "Heraclius Learns Humility," 184–85.

95. Jordan, *Visualizing Kingship*, 58–63. For older views, see *Vitraux de Notre-Dame et de la Sainte-Chapelle de Paris*, comp. Marcel Aubert et al. (Paris: Caisse nationale des monuments historiques, 1959), 296–303.

96. Matthew Paris, *Chronica majora*, vol. 4, 90–92. M. Cecilia Gaposchkin, "Making Capetian the Cross of Christ: A Paper in Honor of Peggy Brown," paper presented at "Paradigms and Personae in the Medieval World: A Symposium in Honor of Elizabeth A. R. Brownp" Graduate Center, City University of New York, 16 March 2018, 2 (unpublished, cited with the author's permission), and personal conversation, 16 March 2018.

anyway"). Nor would Geoffrey have seen any similarity with the savage actions of malefactors back in Europe who forced Jews, most notoriously in the Rhineland in 1096, to accept baptism.[97] We also simply have no evidence of which I am aware or can recall of the king's attitude toward or treatment of those who promised to accept baptism yet were slow to do so or changed their minds—backslid completely before undergoing the rite. Of events in Acre in the 1250s, Geoffrey simply wrote "[h]ow piously [the king] received Saracens who came to the faith. Moreover, during this time many Saracens came to him to adopt Christianity, whom he welcomed happily and had baptized and carefully instructed in the faith of Christ. He supported them at his own expense, *brought them back to France* [my emphasis] with him, and assigned provisions to them and to their wives and children for as long as they lived."[98]

"Brought them back to France"—where did the idea that a Christian king should bring Muslims or converts back to his domains come from? One possibility is that Louis IX knew of King Richard I of England's transport of a few Muslims to his Norman lands after the Third Crusade. This small group, seemingly adult males who were brought into Richard's retinue for reasons that escape me, were lodged/employed at Domfront (Orne) and the nearby forest of Le Passais, about thirteen kilometers away. He provided them with appropriate clothing, and at least one, "Gibelin le Sarrasin," received funds, 50 s., to purchase a horse.[99] John Gillingham does not appear to regard Richard's Muslims as converts to Christianity, but Gibelin, to my knowledge, is not a given name among Near Eastern adherents of Islam.[100] (There

97. Robert Chazan, *The Jews of Medieval Western Christendom, 1000–1500* (Cambridge, UK: Cambridge University Press, 2006), 178.

98. Geoffrey of Beaulieu, "Here Begins the Life," 104, paragraph 27. Kedar, *Crusade and Mission*, 164.

99. Louis Duval, "Domfront aux XIIe et XIIIe siècles," *Bulletin de la Société historique et archéologique de l'Orne* 8 (1889): 530–77 (539–40); John Gillingham, *Richard I* (New Haven, CT: Yale University Press, 1999), 295.

100. Gillingham, *Richard I*, 295.

was one village, once a crusader enclave, known as Gebelin or Bethgebelin.[101]) Of course, it may have been the crusaders' garbled version of the Muslim's true name. Nonetheless, Gibelin and variant spellings did find a place in the name pool of Latin Christians. A famous bearer of it was Gibelin of Arles, a late eleventh-/ early twelfth-century prelate who served as archbishop of Arles, papal legate, and, for the last four years of his career and life, 1108–1112, Latin Patriarch of Jerusalem.[102] Consequently, Gibelin would not have been an inappropriate Christian name for a Muslim convert in King Richard's entourage when he returned from the Third Crusade. Moreover, given the Lionheart's lingering reputation in the Holy Land, it would not be surprising if Louis IX heard stories about Richard and his Muslims or Muslim converts, maybe even his providing them with clothing and a horse or horses after he took them back to Europe.

If we step back a moment, how ought we properly to interpret these assertions, reports, and snippets of data in the narrative sources in relation to the unfolding of events after the king's release from captivity? As I read the texts summarized and discussed above, it is possible to identify, simplifying a bit, three groups or waves of converts to Christianity in Acre. First, there were relatively elite Muslims such as military commanders and common soldiers in their units who intimated or feigned a willingness to convert beginning in 1253. Why 1253? After the treaty following the loss at Mansourah, there was a prolonged peace between the crusaders and the Egyptians.[103] The king paid the ransom for his captured soldiers and arranged for the return of Damietta to Egyptian control.[104] The sultan, on the contrary, was slow in releasing Christian prisoners, in part because of dif-

101. Ronnie Ellenblum, *Frankish Rural Settlement in the Latin Kingdom of Jerusalem* (Cambridge, UK: Cambridge University Press, 1998), 142–43.

102. Runciman, *History of the Crusades*, vol. 2, 84–85.

103. *Seventh Crusade, 1244–1254*, 206.

104. Richard, *Saint Louis*, 235 and 237.

ferences that had arisen between him and his own Muslim enemies and led to internecine war.[105] There was, of course, apprehension in Egypt that, once back in Christian hands and
reoutfitted, the former captives would strengthen the crusader
army dangerously, a sentiment expressed pointedly by many
Muslims, it was reported, when the prisoners were finally released.[106] This was no will-o'-the-wisp fear. The prisoners, some
held since battles six years before Louis IX's defeat at Mansourah, numbered in the thousands.[107]

The king and his advisers in Acre knew of and wanted to ex-
ploit the divide among their enemies, but they too were appre-
hensive.[108] There had been a sufficient number of small infrac-
tions by rogue soldiers on both sides for either to justify
renouncing the peace. The crusaders conjectured that if they did
so, the Christian prisoners would be slaughtered—and indeed,
an Arabic source boasts (exaggeratedly?) of the thousands
slain.[109] The French king dispatched a mission to the sultan to
remind him of his obligation, but it was not until the Egyptians
got the upper hand over their own Muslim foes that the release
of the remaining prisoners began in earnest.[110] Bands of Muslim
irregulars, the remnants of forces fighting one another, then
began in 1252 and 1253 to harry Christian settlements.[111] It was
these numerous mostly small but bloody encounters that provided by 1253 a significant pool of captive Muslim warriors, including emirs (commanders), some of whom—shamed and

105. Richard, *Saint Louis*, 231, 241–43, and 245–46; *Seventh Crusade, 1244–
1254*, 206.

106. William of Chartres, "On the Life and Deeds of Louis," 137, paragraph 9.

107. William of Chartres, "On the Life and Deeds of Louis," 137, paragraph 9;
Richard, *Saint Louis*, 233; *Seventh Crusade, 1244–1254*, 206 and 208 n. 11.

108. *Seventh Crusade, 1244–1254*, 206.

109. *Seventh Crusade, 1244–1254*, 160; Charles Stanton, *Medieval Maritime
Warfare* (Barnsley, UK: Pen and Sword Maritime, 2015), 104.

110. Richard, *Saint Louis*, 239.

111. Jean de Joinville, *Vie de saint Louis*, 466–71 and 486–91, paragraphs
541–42, 545, and 574–78; Richard, *Saint Louis*, 247–48.

dispirited and also having suffered in recent fierce battles with other Muslims—expressed their willingness to convert and brought some of their soldiers with them.[112] It was a pattern known before.[113]

The whole process moved rapidly and perhaps superficially because, as the chronicler Primat tells us, the emirs pledged themselves to fight in future skirmishes on the crusaders' side under an Arab-speaking Christian commander,[114] and the king had a pressing need for additional troops. A few of the Dominican friars in his entourage knew Arabic.[115] Again according to Primat, they listened to the emirs' stories and proceeded to catechize them.[116] Local Arabic-speaking clergy were accustomed to serve as dragomans and would have been helpful throughout the course of these encounters.[117] In a number of instances, the new converts were really crypto-converts, waiting for an opportunity to abandon Acre before their scheduled departure to France.[118] They took a dangerous chance by returning, with their gifts and perhaps reoutfitted for war, to nearby areas under Islamic control, hoping against hope to be welcomed back to the fold.[119] If they were not as persuasive as they expected to be in explaining that they had merely feigned their conversions, they could easily have experienced the fate of the convert of Damietta.[120]

The use of Christians as mercenaries in Muslim armies and Muslims as mercenaries in Christian armies is a well-attested

112. Primat, "Chronique," in *Recueil des historiens des Gaules et de la France*, 24 vols, ed. Martin Bouquet et al. (Paris: V. Palmé, 1840–1904), 14–15; Guillaume de Saint-Pathus, *Vie de saint Louis*, 21; Kedar, *Crusade and Mission*, 163–64.

113. Hillenbrand, *Crusades: Islamic Perspectives*, 377.

114. Primat, "Chronique," 14–15; Kedar, *Crusade and Mission*, 163–64.

115. Jean de Joinville, *Vie de saint Louis*, 224, 406–7, and 414–17, paragraphs 134, 444, and 458; Vose, *Dominicans, Muslims and Jews*, 43 and 230.

116. Primat. "Chronique," 14.

117. Hillenbrand, *Crusades: Islamic Perspectives*, 333; Kedar, *Crusade and Mission*, 163.

118. Mallett, *Popular Muslim Reactions to the Franks*, 118.

119. Kedar, "Multidirectional Conversion," 191.

120. Kedar, *Crusade and Mission*, 164 n. 15.

phenomenon in the medieval Mediterranean.[121] Louis IX's converts were not mercenaries in the strict sense, of course, but the point is that local Christian commanders could have informed the king that using people of a different faith in their armies was a tricky but an often-employed practice and could work to the crusaders' advantage. In any event, while some deserted, a number of the converts—commanders and ordinary soldiers—are said to have remained loyal to the French king or did not wish to be shamed before their former coreligionists. Along, perhaps, with a few civilians, the least able-bodied among the military men, those who could not contribute to defending Acre and other Christian holdings, sailed for France in 1253. This was the first wave of converts.

Those captive warriors who were battle-worthy and remained steadfast in their new religion stayed behind and fought when called upon to do so. Subsequent captives who converted, however, experienced different treatment. The French king and his advisers, having come to recognize the duplicity of some of the alleged conversions, provided additional instruction for them in the Christian faith. Only then did they go to the baptismal font. Moreover, except for doling out spending money, referred to as alms, Louis IX did not bestow substantial gifts on these converts before their departure for France. Rather, his men made promises in royal letters patent to them. A chancery had recently been established, along with the temporary royal mint and scriptorium.[122] The letters patent were sealed there with a new seal (the old one having been lost).

121. Hussein Fancy, *The Mercenary Mediterranean: Sovereignty, Religion, and Violence in the Medieval Crown of Aragon* (Chicago: University of Chicago Press, 2016).

122. Étienne Cartier, "Remarques," *Revue numismatique* 12 (1847): 124–50 (140); Jaroslav Folda, *Crusader Art in the Holy Land, from the Third Crusade to the Fall of Acre, 1187–1291* (Cambridge, UK: Cambridge University Press, 2005), 243–48, 269, 282–95, 359–60; Arthur Giry, *Manuel de diplomatique* (Paris: Hachette, 1894), 753.

The Holy Roman Emperor Frederick II had died in 1250. With his heir apparent, King Conrad IV of Germany, consumed by the continuing struggle with the papacy and thus unable to prosecute his additional claim to the kingship of Jerusalem (as Conrad II), it was Louis IX who had settled into the royal castle in Acre, an emphatic symbolic statement of his intent to rule and to govern.[123] The letters issuing from the revitalized government center attested, Matthew Paris records, that his converts would receive the full rewards of their baptism when Louis returned home: "They carried letters patent of the king of the Franks, [stipulating] that they would be supported by royal alms until he came to his own lands, whereupon he would provide for them more fully" ("Attulerant autem regis Francorum literas patentes, ut de elemosinis regis sustentarentur, donec ipse veniret in partes proprias, et tunc plenius eisdem provideret").[124]

If the conversion of vanquished military men might be understandable given the precedents, why would any other Muslims in Acre or Christian-dominated settlements in the Holy Land convert under such precarious conditions, the possibly untrustworthy promises of future substantial rewards in France? Moreover, how did their relatives, one-time friends, and other coreligionists who refused to yield to the king's offer regard them? Perhaps their vulnerability was already great if they were of "low social standing" (Kedar's words), women who were stereotypically regarded as exposed (widows or spurned second, third, and fourth wives of elite converts), orphans, pagans, slaves, and the sick, including the casualties among them physically disabled in the fighting or in fear of becoming the collateral damage of war.[125] Represented disproportionately in this second wave of

123. Louis de Mas Latrie, *Histoire de l'île de Chypre sous le règne des princes de la maison de Lusignan*, 3 vols. (Paris: Imprimerie impériale, 1852–1861), vol. 1, 359.

124. Matthew Paris, *Chronica majora*, vol. 5, 425.

125. Matthew Paris, *Chronica majora*, vol. 5, 425, and the sources marshaled in Hillenbrand, *Crusades: Islamic Perspectives*, 359. See also Kedar, "Multidirec-

converts, their immigration conformed to the simple, harsh reality that they had insufficient resources to flee and establish themselves elsewhere in the Holy Land safe from militant Muslims or vengeance-seeking Frankish Christians.

I place the date of the departure of the surviving military converts—those who had fulfilled their personal vow to fight for the king as long as he was in the Holy Land and many of the more vulnerable civilians and wounded soldiers—in 1254. They would have sailed in the thirteen or fourteen ships accompanying Louis IX when he left on 25 April.[126] The king's ship alone had 800 passengers, and many other ships plying the Mediterranean and serving the crusaders and common travelers carried up to 1,100, 1,500, even 2,000 passengers, not counting steeds and supplies.[127] Geoffrey of Beaulieu speaks of the immigrants who came *with him*, the king, back to France.[128] Almost from the moment they boarded the ships they would have had reason to wonder, as they may have before, whether their choice was the right one. Off Cyprus, the flotilla came close to running aground and wrecking in a brutal gale.[129] Louis IX prostrated himself in prayer before the Host, in expectation of his imminent death.[130] To whom did the converts pray?

tional Conversion," 191–93 and 196; and Yvonne Friedman, "Women in Captivity and Their Ransom during the Crusader Period," in *Cross Cultural Convergences in the Crusader Period: Essays Presented to Aryeh Grabois on His Sixty-Fifth Birthday*, ed. Michael Goodich, Sophia Menache, and Sylvia Schein, 75–87 (New York: Peter Lang, 1995).

126. Jean de Joinville, *Vie de saint Louis*, 512–13, paragraph 617 and n. 617a.

127. Edward Peters, "There and Back Again: Crusaders in Motion, 1096–1291," *Crusades* 5 (2006): 157–71 (161 and 166); Stanton, *Medieval Maritime Warfare*, 101; Benjamin Kedar, "Passenger List of a Crusader Ship, 1250: Towards the History of the Popular Element on the Seventh Crusade," *Studi medievali* 13 (1972): 267–79 (269–70).

128. Geoffrey of Beaulieu, "Here Begins the Life," 104, paragraph 27.

129. Primat, "Chronique," 15.

130. Jean de Joinville, *Vie de saint Louis*, 512–17, paragraphs 618–22; Geoffrey of Beaulieu, "Here Begins the Life," 107–8, paragraph 30.

The third wave of converts was composed of those insuffi-
ciently advanced in the catechism before the king departed.
Those who finished their instruction relatively soon after he left
underwent baptism in Acre and then took ship for France in the
summer months of heavy sea transit. Others, requiring further
instruction, also sailed before the winter season but finished the
process of conversion following their arrival in France. Agents in
the pay of Geoffrey of Sergines, the commander of the French
contingent the king established in the Crusader Kingdom for
continuing defense, probably organized all this.[131] Geoffrey was
or has been remembered principally as a devout warrior knight,
a point stressed in the contemporary poet Rutebeuf's work, most
comprehensively in "La Complainte de monseigneur Geoffroy de
Sergines" but in other poems as well.[132] Nevertheless, to assert,
as I do, that in the absence of the king he had executive supervi-
sion of the initial steps in conveying the last wave of converts to
France seems reasonable.

Contemporary narrative sources also refer to Geoffrey as
Louis IX's administrative official (*gubernator, gouverneeur*) and
lord (*seigneur*) of Acre.[133] Even Rutebeuf alludes in the "Complainte" to the knight's concern for the poor ("Ses povres voisins
ama bien"),[134] and most of these last converts and would-be converts had to have been poor to begin with. The truce, better kept
after the king's departure and the decline of irregular forces,
helped to dry up the number of elite Muslim commanders and
the troops captured with them. Even if it had not, the chaos in
subsequent years occasioned by internecine strife on the Christian side between the Pisans and the Genoese crippled the cru-

131. Richard, *Saint Louis*, 266–67.

132. *Oeuvres complètes de Rutebeuf*, vol. 1, 411–18; see also vol. 1, 430 ll. 169–
71, 447 ll. 90–91, 449 l. 168, 501 ll. 125–28; Xavier Hélary, "Les rois de France et
la Terre sainte: De la croisade de Tunis à la chute d'Acre (1270–1291)," *Annuaire-
Bulletin de la Société de l'histoire de France* (2005), 21–104 (41–43).

133. Guillaume de Nangis, "Gesta sancti Ludovici," 386 and 389; Primat,
"Chronique," 15.

134. *Oeuvres complètes de Rutebeuf*, vol. 1, 416 l. 77.

saders' capacity to defeat their Muslim foes on the battlefield.[135] Consequently, the last converts consisted of poor people: not destitute, perhaps, but at best only a step above abject poverty because of the alms they received before they arrived in France. Louis IX's words, as reported by chronicler William of Nangis, implicitly put into Geoffrey of Sergines's hands the care of these converts until they left the Holy Land. Indeed, the full array of matters pertinent to the crown fell to the knight. Everyone knew this. Everyone was to comply with what he ordered: "praecipiens [rex] ut omnes ei in reipublicae negotiis obedirent."[136] Nevertheless, it was only in France that the immigrants were to receive substantial regular grants from the government, funds intended to assure their well-being.

Why did Louis IX not let these converts remain in the Holy Land? Why did he not channel their grants through Geoffrey of Sergines, to whom he would soon be sending approximately 4,000 l. each year for the latter's needs?[137] Why did he not present them with some of the agricultural tools he had brought with him for the Frankish settlers whom he had once hoped to induce to settle in the Crusader Kingdom in the aftermath of his expected victories?[138] These questions are simple to answer. Louis IX and his fellow *old* Christians envisaged the genuine and permanent conversion of the whole world. The abandonment of neophytes in the faith in the Holy Land would have consigned the latter to continued proximity and contact with thousands of Muslims. Some of the converts, as I suggested above, probably had relatives or former friends who had chosen not to respond to the king's blandishments and baptism. Separating them from their quondam coreligionists in general and their Muslim families and friends, in particular—and their utter deracination—

135. Richard, *Saint Louis*, 515–17.
136. Guillaume de Nangis, "Gesta sancti Ludovici," 386, and see also 389.
137. Richard, *Saint Louis*, 267.
138. Matthew Paris, *Chronica majora*, vol. 6, 163; Kedar, "Passenger List of a Crusader Ship," 275.

made it easier for them to resist both the temptation to backslide and the recriminations of the Islamic faithful.

It was Geoffrey of Sergines and his staff, then, who would have arranged passage in the summer and early fall of 1254 for the new Christians. They would have done so also for their catechizers (friars, probably) and for guards, this last group intended to prevent escapes by those among the converts weakening in their resolution at planned or unexpected stops along the way or on disembarkation in Provence or France proper. After reaching the border crossings into French territory along the lower Rhône or Mediterranean littoral (from Beaucaire to Aigues-Mortes to Béziers) and empowered by letters patent from the king, the escorts would have made easy contact with men monitoring sea traffic for the royal government. These men served in the regional administration, that is, under the auspices of the *sénéchaux* of Beaucaire-Nîmes and Carcassonne-Béziers.[139]

The nexus Beaucaire–Aigues-Mortes was considerably nearer than Béziers and probably preferred as an entry point. It had other virtues, too. Beaucaire had a certain aura in the romantic drama of conversion. It provided the setting in which the songfable *Aucassin et Nicolette* reached its climax with the union of its Christian prince, Aucassin, and his converted Saracen princess and former childhood crush, Nicolette.[140] Aigues-Mortes, meanwhile, was Louis IX's very own port, purpose-built as an embarkation and disembarkation point for crusaders.[141] The latest escorts, like those on earlier ships, would have been directed by the

139. Robert Michel, *L'administration royale dans la sénéchaussée de Beaucaire au temps de saint Louis* (Paris: Alphonse Picard et fils, 1910), 322 and 350 n. 13.

140. *Aucassin et Nicolette, chantefable du deuxième siècle*, trans. Alexandre Bida and Gaston Paris (Paris: Hachette, 1878), 101.

141. William Chester Jordan, "Supplying Aigues-Mortes for the Crusade of 1248: The Problem of Restructuring Trade," in *Order and Innovation in the Middle Ages: Essays in Honor of Joseph R. Strayer*, ed. William Jordan, Bruce McNab, and Teofilo Ruiz, 165–72 (Princeton, NJ: Princeton University Press, 1976).

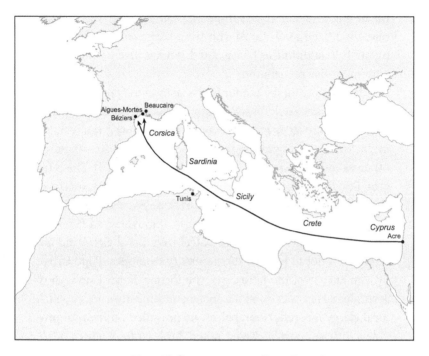

MAP 1. Trans-Mediterranean routes (Acre–France).
Prepared by Dr. Merle Eisenberg.

monitors of sea traffic to the *sénéchaux*'s headquarters, where the former would make certain the immigrants received the resources needed to continue their travels. No doubt, a few of the functionaries who had accompanied the king forewarned local authorities that more immigrants would likely soon arrive and need to go north. For these journeys, I believe that they would also have had the help of guides/guards hired with funds allocated by the *sénéchaux*, for in general these officials had wide powers to act on the king's behalf.[142] The sequence I have reconstructed is consistent with all the information provided by the chroniclers Geoffrey of Beaulieu, Primat, William of Saint-Pathus, and William of Nangis. It also coheres with what Matthew Paris remarked about

142. Michel, *Administration royale*, 26.

the immigrants to France comprising some people who were already baptized and others who were still awaiting the sacrament.[143] In addition, as I have noted, it maps nicely onto existing administrative procedures.

After managing the exodus of the last wave of converts, Geoffrey of Sergines could devote more or less full time to trying to protect the crusader lands. On occasion, however, the residual impact of the immigration intruded on his time. It stimulated other would-be converts to seek refuge in the city.[144] The refugees' first thought, we learn from a papal letter of 1264, was to go to the local churches to seek help, but these Saracens (and Jews, according to the pope) were mostly impoverished.[145] They needed sustenance while being catechized. Local clergy did not or claimed not to possess the necessary resources. Pope Urban IV, the author of the letter, was the former Latin Patriarch of Jerusalem. He understood the enormous difficulties under which local clergy labored. Nonetheless, he prevailed on them to provide a little support, as Kedar noted, "at least for a few days."[146] The pope saw to it that Muslims of standing got more resources.[147] Had he not and had this fact become well known, it would have discouraged other elite Muslims from apostatizing. A small but steady stream of would-be converts seems to have come to Acre while Louis ruled in France and thereafter until 1291.[148]

The refugees referred to by Pope Urban IV in 1264 would have been better served by applying to Geoffrey of Sergines for help, at least if they wanted to go to France. In one case, if my inter-

143. Matthew Paris, *Chronica majora*, vol. 5, 309–10; Kedar, *Crusade and Mission*, 163.

144. David Jacoby, "Society, Culture, and the Arts in Crusader Acre," in *France and the Holy Land: Frankish Culture at the End of the Crusades*, ed. Daniel Weiss and Lisa Mahoney, 97–137 (Baltimore: Johns Hopkins University Press, 2004), 103 and 126 nn. 43 and 45.

145. Kedar, *Crusade and Mission*, 215 no. 3.

146. Kedar, *Crusade and Mission*, 151–52.

147. Kedar, *Crusade and Mission*, 152.

148. Kedar, *Crusade and Mission*, 152–54.

pretation of the evidence is correct (I am arguing back from sources generated in France), a mother and daughter arrived in Acre around 1268 in hope of baptism and immigration. The daughter, eventually christened Margaret, always thereafter appears in the French sources as a *nova baptizata* to distinguish her from the original converts, those who had sailed away in 1253 and 1254.[149] We shall have occasion to return to Margaret and her mother's case in the next chapter. Apparently a father with his child came to Acre seeking baptism at the same time and successfully resettled in France as well.[150] As we shall later see, it is very likely that he made the decision to convert and go to France conjointly with the future Margaret and her mother; as we shall also see, it is unlikely that his catechism was complete before they all departed.

Now comes the fundamental question. On the matter of conversion in Acre and crusader-dominated localities thereabouts, something, of course, happened in the mid-1250s involving Louis IX. Yet, is most of the reconstruction merely a house of straw inspired by a hagiographical conceit, as many historians (those who have not simply ignored them) have considered the stories about Muslims being baptized in numbers? Are these tales of Louis IX's efforts deliberate fabrications? If this is too scornful, are they absurd exaggerations meant to make an allegedly saintly Christian king seem even more holy?

Retelling the stories certainly appealed to the saint-makers and saint promoters. Pope Boniface VIII referred to the conversions in his bull of canonization of Louis IX, as did the liturgists studied by Cecilia Gaposchkin who were the architects of the king's veneration in prose, verse, and chant.[151] Even though there

---

149. *Recueil des historiens des Gaules et de la France*, 24 vols, ed. Martin Bouquet et al. (Paris: V. Palmé, 1840–1904), vol. 22, 664 and 749.

150. *Recueil des historiens*, vol. 22, 749.

151. "Pope Boniface VIII's Bull *Gloria laus* (11 August 1297)," in *The Sanctity of Louis IX: Early Lives of Saint Louis by Geoffrey of Beaulieu and William of*

do not appear to be any contemporary or near-contemporary depictions of Louis IX's presence at the baptism of Muslim apostates while in Outremer,[152] people under the spell of the hagiography attributed his patronage to art objects that evoked the conversion project. Most famously, this was the case with the "baptistère de saint Louis," which no hard evidence ties to the king.[153] The *baptistère* is a thirteenth- or, more likely, fourteenth-century Muslim-wrought basin of Near Eastern origin.[154] Its possible provenance is Acre, according to Jaroslav Folda.[155] It also became the French royal baptismal font in the early modern period after it found its way to Europe, no one knows when or how.[156] Yet an early admirer must have thought that the time of

Chartres, ed. M. Cecilia Gaposchkin and Sean Field, trans. Larry Field, 160–72 (Ithaca, NY: Cornell University Press, 2014), 167; *Blessed Louis, the Most Glorious of Kings: Texts Relating to the Cult of Saint Louis of France*, ed. M. Cecilia Gaposchkin, trans. M. Celia Gaposchkin and Phyllis Katz (Notre Dame, IN: University of Notre Dame Press, 2012), 71, 117, and 181.

152. In sifting through the *Grande chroniques* images assembled in a separate volume by Anne D. Hedeman, I could find no such depictions. Hedeman very kindly (personal communication, 1 February 2018) verified that one unpublished image (*The Royal Image: Illustrations of Grandes chroniques de France, 1274–1422* [Berkeley: University of California Press, 1991], 212, "Louis IX gives provisions") is no exception. Although where this image appears in the chronological sequence of Louis IX's life a scene of his time in Acre would be appropriate, it does not depict the baptism of any apostates or the giving of provisions to them. The description reads "Standing Saint Louis with arms crossed at the left in red/orange houce before fleur-de-lis-draped throne. Two advisors behind. A group of monks kneel [I assume before him]. The foremost monk wears a white cape over a dark robe and the rest are in dark robes."

153. David Rice, "The Blazons of the 'Baptistère de Saint Louis,'" *Bulletin of the School of Oriental and African Studies* 13 (1950): 367–80 (368); Rachel Ward, "The 'Baptistère de Saint Louis'—A Mamluk Basin Made for Export to Europe," in *Islam and the Italian Renaissance*, 113–32 (London: Warburg Institute Colloquia, 1999); Sophie Makariou, "Baptistère de saint Louis," in *Les arts de l'Islam au musée du Louvre*, ed. Sophie Makariou, 282–88 (Paris: Hazan and Musée du Louvre, 2012), 282.

154. Folda, *Crusader Art in the Holy Land*, 478.

155. Folda, *Crusader Art in the Holy Land*, 478.

156. James Allan, "Muhammad ibn al-Zain: Craftsman in Cups, Thrones and Window Grilles?" *Levant* 28 (1996): 199–208; Makariou, "Baptistère de saint

FIGURE 2. This French royal baptismal basin (le baptistère dite de saint Louis) is a work of Islamic art attributed (by legend) to Louis IX's patronage. Mamluk Egypt, 1320–1340. Muhammad Ibn al-Zayn (14th century CE). Location: Louvre, Paris, France. From the Treasury of the Sainte Chapelle at the chateau of Vincennes. Copper with gold, silver, and black paste incrustations, h. 22.2; diam. 50.2 cm. Inv. LP 16. Photo: Hughes Dubois. Copyright © Musée du Louvre, Dist. RMN–Grand Palais/Hughes Dubois/Art Resource, NY.

its fabrication or when it became the possession of Frenchmen was more or less contemporary with Louis IX, that its Muslim craftsmanship and provenance were suggestive, and that its extraordinary beauty was appropriate to a royal patron or purchaser. The theory may not have achieved full articulation until the eighteenth century,[157] but it is not likely that it sprang up full-grown. Why not imagine the magnificent basin's first use as a font for the saint's infant converts in Outremer? His subjects were fond of attributing to him many other fascinating appropriations of the East, with more or less evidence, from the Carmelite Order to basset hounds.[158] How appropriate, it would

Louis," 282–88; David Rice, *Le Baptistère de saint Louis* (Paris: Éditions du Chêne, 1951), 9.

157. Makariou, "Baptistère de saint Louis," 282.

158. On the Carmelite legend, which has a substantial claim to truth, see Andrew Jotischky, *The Carmelites and Antiquity: Mendicants and Their Pasts*

seem, to incorporate such an artefact as the sumptuous Saracen basin into the French ceremony of royal baptism.

In the same way and for centuries preachers and other enthusiasts, drawing on the hagiography, almost fetishized the king's pious obsession to bring Saracen converts to France and make them wealthy—and to do so without resorting to intimidation or violence.[159] Yet, speaking skeptically, could very many Muslims really have chosen to resettle in the land of the Franks without the threat of physical force or its use (enchainment)? Consonant with his elite status as an emir's son, ambassador, poet, and memoirist, the Arab-Syrian "gentleman" (Philip Hitti's word) Usāma b. Munqidh imagined that, for a Muslim, the prospect of dwelling in France was repugnant; it denoted a condition inferior to that suffered by prisoners of war.[160] His was not an idle comparison. Usāma's familiarity with prisoners of war arose from his observation of the awful experiences of both Muslim captives, some of whom he ransomed from crusaders, and Chris-

---

in the Middle Ages (Oxford, UK: Oxford University Press, 2002), 34 and 245. The legend is quaintly depicted with Louis (haloed) in a boat with Carmelite travelers on a body of water, collapsing the Mediterranean and the Seine together, between Outremer and Paris: Angers, Université Catholique de l'Ouest, imprimé (1516), non coté [1], Heures à l'usage des Carmes, fol. 59, "Saint Louis ramenant les Carmes de Terre sainte à Paris." I owe this reference to Professor Gaposchkin. On the far less defensible claim of Louis IX's personal introduction of a Near Eastern variety of big gray dog that was bred with the Saint Hubert (bloodhound) to produce the French basset hound, see Yoland Grosjean, "Basset bleu de Gascogne and French Bassets—Hunting Dogs," online at http://yoland.tripod.com/bassets3 .html.

159. Paris, Bibliothèque nationale de France, Collection Baluze, vol. 14, fol. 2. Thomas Worcester, "The Classical Sermon," in *Preaching, Sermon and Cultural Change in the Long Eighteenth Century*, ed. Joris van Eijnatten, 133–72 (Leiden: Brill, 2009), 163; M. Cecilia Gaposchkin, "The Place of the Crusades in the Sanctification of Saint Louis," in *Crusades: Medieval Worlds in Conflict*, ed. Thomas F. Madden, James Naus, and Vincent Ryan, 195–209 (Burlington, VT: Ashgate, 2010).

160. Usāmah Ibn Munqidh, *An Arab-Syrian Gentleman and Warrior in the Period of the Crusades* (New York: Columbia University Press, 1929), 161; Holt, *Age of the Crusades*, 36.

tian captives, whose sufferings he knew of first-hand.[161] If this sentiment was common, can it be that the descriptions of Louis IX's conversion project and particularly of its successes are anything but tropes one imputes to the conventional literary practices of the authors of saints' lives?

True, Geoffrey of Beaulieu wrote shortly after Louis IX died in 1270 and thus more than two decades before the formal canonization in 1297. However, he did so in the interest of making the case for the king's sanctity.[162] Matthew Paris died in 1259, more than a decade before the king. Although far from uncritical of Louis IX, he too had a very positive overall opinion of him.[163] Of Primat of Saint-Denis, scholars know little. He composed his work in the 1270s and therefore did not refer to Louis IX as "saint," but he was writing in the monastery where the king's bones lay buried and where his cult was beginning to flourish. Saint-Denis was an institution whose entire historiographical output was oriented toward celebrating the monarchy and, at the time, Louis IX in particular.[164] William of Nangis was also a monk of Saint-Denis. More or less the official royal historiographer, he wrote in the years on either side of the king's canonization.[165] William of Saint-Pathus was a Franciscan, confessor to both Queen Margaret and Princess Blanche (Louis IX's daughter) and an ardent promoter of the king's veneration.[166] In the absence of other evidence, then, skepticism is justifiable as to the

161. Usāmah Ibn Munqidh, *Arab-Syrian Gentleman*, 110–12; Hillenbrand, *Crusades: Islamic Perspectives*, 549–56.

162. *The Sanctity of Louis IX: Early Lives of Saint Louis by Geoffrey of Beaulieu and William of Chartres*, ed. M. Cecilia Gaposchkin and Sean Field, trans. Larry Field (Ithaca, NY: Cornell University Press, 2014), 32–33.

163. Matthew Paris, *Chronica majora*, vol. 4, 203.

164. Gabrielle Spiegel, *The Chronicle Tradition of Saint-Denis* (Brookline, MA: Classical Folia Editions, 1978), 89–92.

165. Spiegel, *Chronicle Tradition*, 98–108.

166. M. Cecilia Gaposchkin, *The Making of Saint Louis: Kingship, Sanctity, and Crusade in the Later Middle Ages* (Ithaca, NY: Cornell University Press, 2008), 38.

spin these men may have given to the king's deeds in general, let alone his alleged success in converting Muslims and pagans. Does it wholly or largely taint the information they provide? What one needs fundamentally to make the case for trusting the narrative evidence is substantial documentary proof. Happily, this exists—as it turns out, in abundance.

CHAPTER TWO

The Resettlement of
the Converts

IN THE SEVENTEENTH CENTURY Antoine Vyon d'Hérouval,
a contemporary and scholarly correspondent of Louis IX's great-
est biographer, Louis-Sébastien Le Nain de Tillemont, excerpted
sections of the French royal fiscal accounts on payments the
crown made to converts in the thirteenth century.[1] Most of the
records from which he made his transcriptions perished in the
next century in the great fire at the Treasury, the *Chambre des
comptes*, on the night of 26/27 October 1737.[2] Fortunately, scholars can compare Vyon d'Hérouval's work with early modern copies of some of the records, thirteenth-century copies and notes
preparatory to the official enrollments, and still-surviving frag-
ments of the originals that somehow escaped the inferno. The
comparison demonstrates that he reproduced the originals
faithfully. Some of the excerpts refer to converts from Judaism,
and scholars since Tillemont, who had Vyon's copies, have taken

---

1. Alexandre Bruel, "Notes de Vyon d'Hérouval sur les baptisés et les convers
et sur les enquêteurs royaux au temps de saint Louis et de ses successeurs (1234–
1334)," *Bibliothèque de l'École des chartes*, sixth series, 3 (1867): 609–21.

2. John Baldwin, *The Government of Philip Augustus* (Berkeley: University
of California Press, 1986), 406.

nearly all of them as such.[3] This has been a misstep, in particular
for the period 1253–1255. Even the otherwise very astute Théophile Cochard, who did distinguish Jewish from Muslim converts in Vyon's extracts, erroneously typed all the Muslim converts as orphaned infants.[4] This is not to say that there were no
orphans among the converts, as we shall see.

Why must the records for 1253–1255 refer to Christian converts from Islam rather than from Judaism? The reason is tragic
but straightforward. However poorly drafted an order was "dis-
ciplining" French Jews that the king sent from the Holy Land in
1253, administrators attempted to carry it out in his absence. In
that order, he called for the expulsion from France of those Jews
who were not living by the honest labor of their own hands. To
put it the other way around, he targeted Jews living from the
profits of illicit moneylending, usury, which, as we know, since
the Ordinance of Melun of 1230 was any interest payment at all.
This was standard policy throughout the king's reign.[5] Yet officials in France in 1253 seem to have assumed that all or most
Jews were making money at least in part from usury and trying
to hide their activities or using stratagems to evade the law. Perhaps it is also the case that these officials had no strong interest
in taking the time to separate law-abiding Jews from lawbreakers. Either way, contemporaries remarked how officials drove
Jews out of the realm indiscriminately in response to the king's
order and in the absence of his monitoring to secure the proper
execution of the mandate: "The Jews were pursued throughout

3. Louis-Sébastien Le Nain de Tillemont, *Vie de saint Louis, roi de France*,
6 vols, ed. J. de Gaulle (Paris: J. Renouard, 1847–1851), vol. 5, 296–98; François
de Mézeray, *Histoire de France depuis Faramond jusqu'au règne de Louis le
Juste*, 2nd ed. (Paris: Denys Thierry et al., 1685), vol. 2, 279; Margaret Labarge,
"Saint Louis et les juifs," in *Siècle de saint Louis*, ed. Régine Pernoud, 267–74
(Paris: Hachette, 1970), 273; and all the way to Jordan, *Challenge of the Crusade*,
156.

4. Théophile Cochard, *La juiverie d'Orléans du VIe au XVe siècle* (Orléans:
Georges Michau, 1895), 59.

5. Juliette Sibon, *Chasser les juifs pour régner* (Paris: Perrin, 2016), 61–89.

the kingdom of France and (by the king's order) thrown out" ("Judaei fugati sunt per totum regnum Franciae, et [per praeceptum domini regis] ejecti").[6] Louis IX did confirm the order when he returned from crusade, while making clear that it was limited to and only enforceable against Jews for whom there was proof of usury. Here he was adhering to ecclesiastical opinion that opposed blanket expulsion.[7] The word went out that those Jews against whom his men could prove no crime might return. In time, many did so and obtained compensation for their losses.[8] None of this occurred before the king had reassumed the reins of governance in France after the crusade.

Everything was different for the immigrant converts. The fiscal account recording royal expenditures for the Ascension to All Saints term 1253, a year before the king's arrival back in Paris and while the Jews were fleeing the country, documents outlays for immigrant converts, who were then arriving in France *from overseas*: "pro expensis conversorum de partibus transmarinis cviii solid. vi den."[9] The extracts provided by Vyon d'Hérouval from the accounts for the fiscal term for Ascension 1255 also speak of moneys given to the baptized and to slaves who had recently arrived *from Outremer*, obviously also not Jews: "pro denariis traditis baptisatis et sclavis qui ultimo venerunt de ultra mare X libr."[10] The recently arrived slaves, at the time still unbaptized, were evidently awaiting the sacrament, but they needed money to live on before baptism.

Jews and a fortiori Jewish converts, many of whom spoke lovingly of France even in difficult periods in their experience as

6. "E chronico Normanniae," *Recueil des historiens des Gaules et de la France*, 24 vols, ed. Martin Bouquet et al. (Paris: V. Palmé, 1840–1904), vol. 23, 212–22 (215); "E chronico Sanctae Catharinae de Monte Rotomagi," *Recueil des historiens*, vol. 23, 402; Jordan, *French Monarchy and the Jews*, 148.

7. John Hood, *Aquinas and the Jews* (Philadelphia: University of Pennsylvania Press, 1995), 1–18.

8. Jordan, *French Monarchy and the Jews*, 148–50.

9. Bruel, "Notes de Vyon d'Hérouval," 617.

10. Bruel, "Notes de Vyon d'Hérouval," 617.

their motherland and fatherland,[11] were able to communicate with their neighbors and perhaps buy shelter and protection from the king's men in 1253 and until the ruler's return in 1254. They were scarcely strangers to the areas where they chose to reside and whose culture they shared in many ways.[12] They knew good hiding places. On the contrary, Muslim and pagan converts (whether slave or free, prior to baptism in Acre and France) were fully separated from native Frenchmen by habits and speech. Only providing them money directly and keeping close watch over them could assure that the king's plan for them had the remotest chance to succeed.

The first problem was where to settle the immigrants. Jewish converts offer a nice comparison. As French men and women and native speakers of the French language in one dialect or another, Jewish converts to Christianity in the 1220s, 1230s, and 1240s may have chosen to relocate away from the local Jewry, street of the Jews, or place of the Jews after baptism. This was a minor physical change for most of them, though not necessarily a minor emotional change. Because of their evident Frenchness—in work habits, gestures, language, and shared entertainments in the central squares of the towns—there does not appear to have been much concern on their neighbors' part in Louis IX's reign that they would backslide into Judaism, although this sensibility may have eroded in the fourteenth century.[13] Nothing could be further from the experience of converted Muslims and pagans in 1253, 1254 and 1255, and the fiscal accounts confirm this. Dis-

11. Jordan, *French Monarchy and the Jews*, 237.

12. Kirsten Fudeman, *Vernacular Voices: Language and Identity in Medieval French Jewish Communities* (Philadelphia: University of Pennsylvania Press, 2010), 13 and 22; Susan Einbinder, *Beautiful Death: Jewish Poetry and Martyrdom in Medieval France* (Princeton, NJ: Princeton University Press, 2002), 133–34.

13. Jessica Elliott, "Jews 'Feigning Devotion.'" : Christian Representations of Converted Jews in French Chronicles before and after the Expulsion of 1306," in *Jews and Christians in Thirteenth-Century France*, ed. Elisheva Baumgarten and Judah Galinsky, 169–82 (New York: Palgrave Macmillan, 2015).

placement was total. To get into their heads, one must try to imagine, to borrow a phrase from a modern study of immigrant life, "their vulnerable state of ignorance."[14] They had no immediate local knowledge of the kingdom in which they had arrived (everything they "knew" was based on hearsay), and they had little reason at the time, if ever, to love France. Moreover, the Near Eastern lingua franca a few of the immigrants spoke was not French. Acquiring genuine competency in the language of northern France—where, as we shall see, we can confine our focus—took time.

What might facilitate the acquisition of the language? Early on, before Louis IX returned, but certainly with his knowledge and consent, administrators in France decided *not* to establish and place the new Christians in a House of Saracen or Pagan Converts, comparable to the English crown's exactly contemporary *Domus Conversorum* for Jewish converts and their families.[15] The French may have suspected, just as historians have speculated, that communal living, although intended to be temporary, inhibited the integration of the English Jewish converts into mainstream society.[16] Nor did the group housing provided both for *béguines* and for reformed prostitutes, that is to say, for single women, not families, offer a useful alternative. Indeed,

14. Beth Lew-Williams, *The Chinese Must Go: Violence, Exclusion, and the Making of the Alien in America* (Cambridge, MA: Harvard University Press, 2018), 93.

15. Robert Stacey, "The Conversion of Jews to Christianity in Thirteenth-Century England," *Speculum* 67 (1992): 263–83 (273–83).

16. Stacey, "Conversion of Jews," 275 and 282–83; followed by Anna Sapir Abulafia, *Christian-Jewish Relations, 1000–1300: Jews in the Service of Medieval Christendom* (London: Routledge, 2011), 99. See also Reva Berman Brown and Sean McCartney, "Living in Limbo: The Experience of Jewish Converts in Medieval England," in *Christianizing Peoples and Converting Individuals*, ed. Guyda Armstrong and Ian Wood, 169–91 (Turnhout: Brepols, 2000), 183–84; John Tolan, "Royal Policy and Conversion of Jews to Christianity in Thirteenth-Century Europe," in *Contesting Inter-Religious Conversion in the Medieval World*, ed. Yaniv Fox and Yosi Yisraeli, 96–111 (London: Routledge, 2017), 104–5.

group living, however arranged, would have been a setting conducive to the continued general use of Arabic among the former Muslims or of Central Asian languages among the former pagans. Failure to learn French in such an environment or substantial and frustrating difficulties in the language among the immigrants could also contribute to nostalgia and regret for the lost cultural practices of the Near East and, for the non-Muslims, for the traditions of tribal life that had so recently governed their existence.

The French government could have opted to segregate all the immigrants in a single expansive area where they could farm and have their own residences, workplaces, markets, and communal ovens and wells. Or the king could have had groups of them concentrated in a few neighborhoods and a few hospices of some sort, as Cochard mistakenly hypothesized.[17] Or, finally, he might have founded an entirely new town, as princes like his brother Alphonse of Poitiers ("a bastide founder of unparalleled energy") did for strategic and economic reasons,[18] then prodded the church to provide, partly at his expense, a parish church or churches and the like. Such a policy would have adapted Emperor Frederick II's more or less recent resettlement of thousands of Sicilian Muslims, who had been widely dispersed on the island and often in conflict with the government, to mainland Italy. He commenced these deportations in 1224 and continued them for two more decades, planting individuals and families in Lucera in order to bring peace to the island and give his administrators efficient oversight of them on the Italian peninsula.[19] However, by this strategy the emperor was seeking to contain potential enemies *who remained Muslims*. Although there is evidence of a few "voluntary" baptisms toward the end of the colony's violent

17. Cochard, *La juiverie d'Orléans*, 60–61.
18. Adrian Randolph, "The Bastides of Southwest France," *Art Bulletin* 77 (1995): 290–307 (293 and 303).
19. Abulafia, *Frederick II*, 146–48; Julie Taylor, *Muslims in Medieval Italy: The Colony at Lucera* (Oxford: Lexington Books, 2003).

disappearance in 1300,[20] in general Frederick II and his successors' program was subject to the same criticism as group housing. It was inappropriate for nurturing immigrant converts, who needed to adjust themselves to their newfound faith and learn the language of their new neighbors.

Therefore, almost certainly motivated by a concern that concentrated settlement would work against the converts' adjustment and encourage backsliding, Louis IX and his advisers chose a radically new approach: namely, to distribute the new Christians throughout the northern part of the kingdom of France, in the belief that the old faith of an immigrant minority would fade away when living among and intermarrying with a majority Catholic population. Scattering itself was not a new tactic: in late Antiquity, Christian (Roman provincial) captives of the Sasanians were dispersed among the Zoroastrian population of Iran in expectation that their adherence to Christianity would weaken. This event was unknown to Louis IX.[21] In any event, conversion in the French case *preceded* scattering and intermarriage; it did not derive from it.

Vyon d'Hérouval's excerpts provide evidence of families planted in the towns and hinterlands (microregions, for short) of Bourges, Évreux, Orléans, Péronne, Saint-Quentin, and Tours in 1253.[22] Although he did not use the word, Cochard, it is clear, saw the administrative attractiveness of the regional settlement.[23] In Louis IX's time one reckoned an urban hinterland variously from one to seven leagues (approximately 5.5 km to 38.5 km) in radius from the town's central square; five was a conventional standard, for example, in the Orléanais, a microregion

20. Taylor, *Muslims in Medieval Italy*, 72, 108, 190. See also Catlos, *Muslims of Medieval Latin Christendom*, 126–27.

21. Compare to Richard E. Payne, *A State of Mixture: Christians, Zoroastrians, and Iranian Political Culture in Late Antiquity* (Oakland: University of California Press, 2015), 65–68.

22. Bruel, "Notes de Vyon d'Hérouval," 612–13. See also Cochard, *La juiverie d'Orléans*, 60.

23. Cochard, *La juiverie d'Orléans*, 59.

mentioned above.[24] Additional evidence for 1255, both from
Vyon d'Hérouval's notes and from fragmentary originals, allows
one to add similar microregions around Amiens, Chauny, Compiègne, Laon, and Noyon, along with further information on
Orléans.[25] Evidence from 1256 confirms the converts' continued
settlement in and around Amiens, Compiègne, Laon, Péronne,
and Tours, as well as other settlements established in Coutances,
Paris, Poissy, Pont de l'Arche, Pontoise, and Rouen and their environs.[26] A court case from 1260 evokes their presence in Senlis.[27] Later evidence concerning Hesdin, Sens, Saint-Denis (in
the Paris microregion), and Saint-Omer strongly suggests that
they were additional locales of *baptisati* settlement.[28]

What no records—original, near-contemporary, or in early
modern transcriptions of mid-thirteenth-century texts—suggest
is that the southern part of the kingdom where they first disembarked experienced an influx of the immigrants for long-term
resettlement. The south was too close to Spain and the southern
Mediterranean rim with their large Islamic populations, too
tempting to Muslim converts who might have a change of heart
and mind toward the Christian faith. Louis IX, who, through his

24. For the Orléanais, see Paris, Bibliothèque nationale de France, MS fr.
14580, "Anciennes coutumes d'Orliens," fol. 18. In general, see Jean Brissaud, *A
History of French Public Law*, trans. James W. Garner (Boston: Little, Brown,
1915), 250 n. 3.

25. Bruel, "Notes de Vyon d'Hérouval," 612–13; *Recueil des historiens*, vol. 22,
742. See also Cochard, *La juiverie d'Orléans*, 60.

26. Bruel, "Notes de Vyon d'Hérouval," 613–14; *Recueil des historiens*, vol. 21,
365–66. See also Cochard, *La juiverie d'Orléans*, 60.

27. *Olim, ou Registres des arrêts rendus par la Cour du roi*, 3 vols, ed. Arthur
Beugnot (Paris: Imprimerie Royale, 1839–1848), vol. 1, 482 no. 17.

28. *Inventaire des titres de Nevers de l'abbé de Marolles*, comp. Georges de
Soultrait (Nevers: Paulin Fay, 1873), col. 293; *Recueil des historiens*, vol. 20, 635;
Atlas historique de Saint-Denis: Des origines au XVIIIe siècle, comp. Michaël
Wyss et al. (Paris: Editions de la Maison des Sciences de l'Homme, 1996), 145;
Compte général du receveur d'Artois pour 1303–1304, ed. Bernard Delmaire (Brus-
sels: Académie Royale de Belgique, 1977), nos. 369, 2078, 3351, and 3365; Alain
Derville, *Saint-Omer des origines au début du XIVe siècle* (Lille: Presses Univer-
sitaires de Lille, 1995), 128 n. 11.

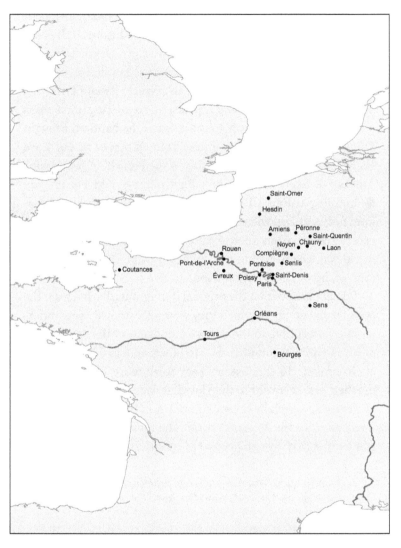

MAP 2. Sites of settlement in northern France.
Prepared by Dr. Merle Eisenberg.

Castilian relatives, knew much about policies in Spain, would likely have heard about the contemporary frustrations the crown experienced there in preventing converts' backsliding, which it blamed on the close proximity of practicing Muslims.[29] It is not until almost a century later, in 1350 to be precise, that one can find a descendant of one of the converted families living in a southern town: in this instance, Beaucaire. People knew the background of this Raymond Amfossi (my rendering into French of *Amffocii*). He belonged "to the stock of the baptized brought *a long time ago* [emphasis mine] from *Outremer* by our Lord Louis of sacred memory, late king of the French" ("Raymundus Amffocii de Bellicadro, de stipite Baptizatorum, adductorum jam dudum de partibus Ultramarinis per sanctae memoriae dominum nostrum Ludovicum quondam regem Francorum").[30] The excerpt comes from a letter of remission, signifying that Raymond was a convicted felon who had obtained a pardon[31]—but even so, he was a *Christian* felon.

I do not believe that the original immigrants, barred from the Mediterranean life to which they were accustomed, were differentially susceptible to the disease pathogens of the north, most of which could be found in the Mediterranean and Near Eastern environment. To this extent, they were more fortunate than northerners who went to the Holy Land and fell victim to types of diseases, especially fevers, unknown in the natural environment north of the Massif Central. The most common estimate proffered is that over 30 percent of crusaders died on their expe-

---

29. Kathryn Miller, *Guardians of Islam: Religious Authority and Muslim Communities of Late Medieval Spain* (New York: Columbia University Press, 2008), 174.

30. This is Kedar's translation (*Crusade and Mission*, 164) of a passage transcribed by Charles du Fresne Du Cange, *Glossarium mediae et infimae Latinitatis*, 10 vols. (Niort: L. Favre, 1883–1887), vol. 1, 582, under "baptizati." See also Cochard, *La juiverie d'Orléans*, 59 n. 2.

31. Michel François, "Notes sur les lettres de rémission transcrites dans les registres du Trésor des chartes," *Bibliothèque de l'Ecole des chartes* 103 (1942): 317–24 (318).

ditions, and anyone who has studied the evidence knows that disease was a—perhaps the—dominant factor in the high mortality. James Powell, for example, estimated that noncombatants who traveled with the crusaders to Damietta in the earlier thirteenth-century crusade, 1213–1221, suffered a mortality rate from disease of 20 percent.[32]

Food was another matter. By the time the immigrants reached the north, they would have been routinely ingesting the new diet with its butter and lard, as opposed to olive oil, together with hitherto less familiar northern varieties of grains, such as "millet, oats and rye" that only farmers of uplands, as in northwestern Iberia, cultivated in the south.[33] Lamb the two cultures shared, but ox-beef was far more common in the north. Pork was ubiquitous—and the cultural "shock" of consuming it may have been significant. All of this suggests that there would have been some psychological stress in adopting new foodways and that there were inevitably cases of diarrhea while the immigrants were traveling north. For people who were already weak or sick, severe diarrhea and accompanying dehydration could have been quite debilitating, with "high fever, vomiting, or bloody stools," even death. Modestly healthy people make regional dietary adjustments quickly, however, and despite a brief initial period of discomfort, "this illness in travelers is usually not severe."[34]

It was neither the impact of new diseases nor the effect of new foods that was most surprising to the new arrivals. It was the cold of late fall and winter in northern France. The government anticipated the problem. The immigrants were dressed in clothes appropriate to the climate and workmanship of the Eastern

32. James Powell, *Anatomy of a Crusade, 1213–1221* (Philadelphia: University of Pennsylvania Press, 1986), 169–71.

33. Damián Fernández, *Aristocrats and Statehood in Western Iberia, 300–600 C.E.* (Philadelphia: University of Pennsylvania Press, 2017), 92.

34. The quotations are from the US National Institutes of Health, "Travelers' Diarrhea," online at https://consensus.nih.gov/1985/1985TravelersDiarrhea048 html.htm.

Mediterranean littoral when they first disembarked in Provence and Languedoc. The styles, in themselves, may have provoked curiosity and even suspicion among some Provençal and Languedocian natives when they encountered the new arrivals. The familiarity of these Christians with Spanish Catholics' negative perceptions of converts arrayed in Muslim-style dress may have informed this sentiment.[35] In particular, contemporary European Christians associated striped cloth, common in the Near East, with their Muslim enemies, depicted them in it, and disdained it. The Carmelite friars had discovered this when they arrived in France from the Holy Land to set up their earliest houses in Europe only a few years before the arrival of Louis IX's converts. The friars received a very cool reception, Michel Pastoureau has argued, because the striped habit they wore evoked deviltry and stereotypes of Muslim dress. Christians in France were indignant with men who would voluntarily array themselves in stripes.[36]

However, the immigrants may have been wearing clothing of Near Eastern manufacture but European style, if Louis IX's people had provided it as alms in the Holy Land. The Minstrel of Reims tells us that when the king first came to Acre he bought new clothing for all of the troops released with him, because their apparel was threadbare.[37] It would not have been odd to do the same for poorly arrayed converts. Upon their arrival in France, however, the immigrants needed supplementary clothing for an

35. On these negative perceptions and various arguments of converted Muslims to counter them, see Olivia Remie Constable, *To Live Like a Moor: Christian Perceptions of Muslim Identity in Medieval and Early Modern Spain*, ed. Robin Vose (Philadelphia: University of Pennsylvania Press, 2018), 15–62.

36. Michel Pastoureau, *The Devil's Cloth: A History of Stripes and Striped Cloth*, trans. Jody Gladding (New York: Columbia University Press, 2001), 12. For a depiction, see the cover of this book.

37. *Récits d'un Ménestrel de Reims*, paragraph 396: "The king left for Acre; and, as the Christians had just been released from captivity and had nothing to wear, the king had them all newly dressed according to their station." (I borrow from the soon-to-be-published English translation by Samuel Rosenberg.)

additional reason, the harsh climate where they were going to settle. One confirms this from one of Tillemont's citations, an entry from a fiscal account of 1253 "pro robis duorum converso-rum et pro burris," that is, for robes and cloaks for two converts.[38] Unfortunately, the great *érudit* erroneously thought this referred to Jewish converts, and no scholar since his time has associated the entry with the immigrants from Acre. Yet the wording is re-vealing. The clothing provided the converts was heavy cold-weather apparel. The cloaks mentioned in the fiscal records, *burri*, were garments that were pleated, padded, or furred, tech-niques providing for added warmth.[39]

The Rouennais, to concentrate on just one of the microre-gions in which converts settled, is on the same latitude as Win-nipeg, Canada. Unless they had come to the port as refugees from climatically harsher mountainous or high-plains regions, the converts arriving in northern France for the first time had never really been cold. Judging by modern measurements, Acre's cold-est average temperature in January, the chilliest month, was ap-proximately 14° centigrade/57° Fahrenheit and rarely, if ever, fell as low as 11°C/52°F. January was also the coldest month in the northern French communities, like those of the Rouennais, where the average temperatures ranged from 3–4°C/37–39°F but were potentially several degrees lower, depending on the proxim-ity of moderating bodies of water. Prevailing winds off the Atlan-tic Ocean and the Channel transformed the uncomfortable chill and sleety rain into vectors of bitter numbing cold.

The necessity of providing winter clothes for immigrant adults and children from the Near Eastern littoral in a timely

---

38. Le Nain de Tillemont, *Vie de saint Louis*, vol. 5, 296.

39. R. E. Latham, *Revised Medieval Latin Word-List* (London: Oxford Uni-versity Press, 1965), under "birrus"; J. F. Niermeyer, *Mediae Latinitatis, lexicon minus* (Leiden: E. J. Brill, 1976), under "burra." Compare to OF *bourru*, meaning "furred" (*Lexique de l'Ancien Français*, comp. Frédéric Godefroy [Paris: H. Wel-ter, 1901], 61) and *borre*, signifying "stuffing" (Alan Hindley, Frederick Langley, and Brian Levy, comps., *Old French-English Dictionary* [Cambridge, UK: Cam-bridge University Press, 2000], 87).

manner was therefore obvious. The practice in the case before us drew on and was therefore an extension of Louis IX's yearly orders to distribute abundant clothing to the poor *at the onset of winter* ("in introitu hiemis"), as a French preacher, recalling the king's acts of devotion, would describe it.[40] The practice, of course, found its deeper inspiration in Jesus's injunction to the righteous to clothe the naked (among the least of his followers), whereby they also clothed him (Matt. 25:35–40). Lepers, like "the least" in the parable, also received annual donations of winter clothing at Louis IX's behest. Allegedly, those afflicted with the disease were hypersensitive to the cold, a trope elaborated in the popular contemporary French *Life* of Saint Julian the Hospitaller. Its near-closing scenes have him and his wife offering to warm the sufferer's body with their own, when the Lord visits them in the guise of a leper and complains that he is colder than ice ("je suis plus froiz que glace").[41] As Gustave Flaubert, a native of Rouen, reminded readers of the *Trois Contes*, one of which retold Julian's *legendum*, he remembered the story from its representation in the stained glass of a church where he grew up ("Et voilà l'histoire de saint Julien l'Hospitalier, telle à peu près qu'on la trouve, sur un vitrail d'église, dans mon pays").[42]

Modern research suggests that this cultural perception of lepers as particularly vulnerable to cold weather was an accurate observation of those suffering the disease. In certain cases, lepers are supersensitive to low temperatures; in others, because of nerve deformation, they have chronic insensitivity to cold and are therefore in peril of suffering unwitting frostbite.[43] In both

40. Paris, BnF, Collection Baluze, vol. 14, fol. 4v.

41. *Old French Prose Legend of Saint Julian the Hospitaller*, ed. Carolyn Swan (Tübingen: Niemeyer, 1977), lines 1189–1329. One awaits the publication of the translation of this text by Brianna Gustafson (ABD, Princeton University).

42. Gustave Flaubert, "La légende de saint Julien l'Hospitalier," in *Trois contes*, new ed., 89–164 (Paris: Bibliothèque-Charpentier, 1908), 164.

43. Govind Malaviya, "Review: Sensory Perception in Leprosy-Neurophysiological Correlates," *International Journal of Leprosy and Other Mycobacterial Diseases* 71 (2003): 119–24.

cases, one could say that lepers are and were singular victims of low temperatures. Every time the cold weather approached, therefore, many poor people and lepers in Louis IX's realm were thought to need special help, the poor because their poverty prevented the replacement of their tattered and threadbare clothing, the lepers because of their bodily vulnerability even when they possessed clothing that might have been minimally sufficient for healthy persons. At Louis IX's orders, they all received wood for their hearths, heavy woolen and leathern cloaks, and new shoes as royal alms or, in the words of the anonymous preacher, "Item omni anno in introitu hiemis de lignis, de vestibus de burello et pellitiis et sotularibus in maxima quantitate."

The practice and vision of philanthropy just described thus co-opted vulnerable convert immigrants. The provision of clothing was not a one-time occurrence but annual, as with the poor and lepers. Direct evidence of such distributions ongoing in 1256 survives in the wax tablets used for temporary record-keeping at the *Chambre des comptes*; it exists for former Muslim families dwelling in the microregions of or centering on Compiègne, Coutances, Paris, Péronne, Pont de l'Arche, and Rouen.[44] The families received the clothing (*rob[a]e*) at one of the fiscal terms of and in tandem with the delivery of their pensions. The appropriate term, logically, was Ascension, because the following term of All Saints, 1 November, was often too late in the year in the north. The weather would most likely have already changed dramatically.

Based on modern recordkeeping, October is by far the rainiest month in the Rouennais (Upper Normandy), November the second-rainiest, and December the third (97.1 mm, 83.3 mm, and 76.1 mm [3.8 inches, 3.3 inches, and 3.0 inches], respectively). Warm summer rains are about 30 percent less heavy.[45]

44. *Comptes sur tablettes de cire de Jean Sarrazin, chambellan de Saint Louis*, ed. Elisabeth Lalou (Louvain: Brepols, 2003), 94 (sections 221a and 221c); *Recueil des historiens*, vol. 21, 365–66.

45. "Regions of France," online at http://www.regions-of-france.com/regions/upper_normandy/weather/.

Meanwhile, average temperatures there also dive precipitously around the turn of October to November: September's average of 14.5° centigrade/58.1° Fahrenheit yields to October's 10.9°C/ 51.6°F and November's 6.4°C/43.5°F.[46] The change is somewhat less dramatic in the other *climata* with microregions of convert settlement, but still very significant.[47] Equally pertinent, winds increase their average velocity by 1.6 kilometers/1 mile per hour in October and November after the consistently gentler breezes of the late spring and summer months (May through September), even in the less severe climate of the microregion of convert settlement centered on Caen (Lower Normandy).[48] The immigrants, in other words, needed good warm clothing before the harsh late fall and winter weather set in. It is not surprising, therefore, that the evidence of the wax tablets identifies the Ascension term explicitly as the most frequent distribution date.[49]

The available evidence gives a great deal more information beyond where the government settled the converts and, inferentially, did not settle them, and the environments to which they had to adjust. It explains how they got to where they lived. In the case of the Orléanais, which was probably typical, it was the *prévôt* of Lorris, one of seventeen local administrators of the district known as the *bailliage* of Orléans, who brought the recent converts to the microregion: "[p]ro baptisatis ducendis Aurelia[nu]m per praepositum Lorriaci."[50] Royal *prévôts* in general resided in towns, saw to the protection of crown property and the collection of rents and tolls, monitored sales and exchanges of lands and rights, and the like.[51] They distributed

46. "Regions of France."

47. In general, follow the prompts on "Regions of France."

48. See https://www.timeanddate.com/weather/france/caen/climate.

49. *Comptes sur tablettes de cire de Jean Sarrazin*, 94 (sections 221a and 221c); *Recueil des historiens*, vol. 21, 365–66.

50. Bruel, "Notes de Vyon d'Hérouval," 612; Louis d'Illiers, *Histoire d'Orléans*, new ed. (Orléans: Lodé, 1954), 51; Cochard, *La juiverie d'Orléans*, 60.

51. James Fesler, "French Field Administration: The Beginnings," *Comparative Studies in Society and History* 5 (1962–1963): 76–111 (81–82).

clothing allotments and arranged housing in a timely fashion so that it would be ready for occupancy when the converts arrived. If our sources refer routinely to expenditures for the immigrants in the interval between their landing in France and their permanent resettlement, they refer also over and over again to the funds the crown disbursed to lease dwellings for them—"pro locagio domorum," "pro locatione domorum," and "por [or pour] leurs mesons."[52] One finds this leasing attested in and around Amiens, Compiègne, Laon, Orléans, and Tours in 1255 and 1256.[53] The role of the *prévôt* in securing the leases for the housing units is explicit in evidence from All Saints 1256 for Amiens.[54] There are scattered additional references at other dates or from otherwise undated fragmentary thirteenth-century records for the Amienois as well as for the Rouennais, the latter identifying the new settlers explicitly as "des sarrazins convertis a la foi chretienne."[55]

Within four years of the arrival of the first immigrants and their taking up residence in new homes, a disaster affected all of northern France and England but hit Normandy particularly hard: famine and sustained high mortality, the consequence of horrendous weather, root-stock damage, and high livestock,

52. Bruel, "Notes de Vyon d'Hérouval," 613; Charles Beaurepaire, "De la Vicomté de l'Eau de Rouen," *Recueil des travaux de la Société libre d'agriculture, sciences, arts et belles-lettres de l'Eure*," third series, 3 (1854): 81–600 (440–41). Some of the information on the Orléanais rentals is in Paris, BnF, Collection Moreau, vol. 173 fol. 31, but is incorrectly dated 1251. The *bailli* in whose account it appears is Mathieu de Beaune, who served in Orléans in the years 1254–1256, not before, not after. I want to thank Mr. Andrew Collings, at the time of writing a PhD candidate at Princeton University, for providing me a photograph of the section of the manuscript in which the transcription of this account appears and other transcriptions from the Collection Moreau.

53. Bruel, "Notes de Vyon d'Hérouval," 613; *Recueil des historiens*, vol. 22, 742.

54. *Recueil des historiens*, vol. 22, 742.

55. Bruel, "Notes de Vyon d'Hérouval," 614–15; *Recueil des historiens*, vol. 22, 748; Beaurepaire, "De la Vicomté de l'Eau de Rouen," 440–41. I have verified Beaurepaire's readings: Paris, Bnf, MS fr. 5966, fol. 79 v., online at http://gallica .bnf.fr/ark:/12148/btv1b9060747s/f89.image.r=Rouen.

grain, and wine prices.[56] Louis IX, who liked the comparison, may have projected himself as a new Joseph the Patriarch helping the Israelites, also migrants, who had come begging to Egypt in a time of dearth (Gen. 41–42).[57] He might also have imagined himself as a new Boaz, the rich man who had looked out for Ruth gathering remnants in his harvested fields according to the scriptural book of her name, a story lavishly illustrated and moralized in one of the royal bibles.[58] In either case, he acted with dispatch to provide huge supplementary resources to the duchy, in the form of cash, to people distressed by the three-year food shortages (1257–1259) and those helping them cope. And in this period the king also visited several of the places that were hard-hit, including some of the microregions in which the converts had been settled: the Évrecin, the Rouennais, and Pont de l'Arche and its hinterland. Whether the converts suffered directly from the famine or not, they would, in this early period of their residence in France, have seen much misery all around them. They would have observed conditions in the countryside that motivated the king to impose radical measures to assure the survival of paupers by giving them a privileged opportunity to glean on all royal estates in Normandy.[59]

56. "Notes sur quelques manuscrits du Musée britannique," 187; William Chester Jordan, *From Servitude to Freedom: Manumission in the Sénonais in the Thirteenth Century* (Philadelphia: University of Pennsylvania Press, 1986), 50–54; William Chester Jordan, *The Great Famine: Northern Europe in the Early Fourteenth Century* (Princeton, NJ: Princeton University Press, 1996), 243 n. 161; William Chester Jordan, "The Gleaners," in *Boundaries in the Medieval and Wider World: Essays in Honour of Paul Freedman*, ed. Thomas Barton, Susan McDonough, Sara McDougall, and Matthew Wranovix, 201–20 (Turnhout: Brepols, 2017), 215; Derek Keene, "Crisis Management in London's Food Supply, 1250–1500," in *Commercial Activity, Markets and Entrepreneurs in the Middle Ages: Essays in Honour of Richard Britnell*, ed. Ben Dodds and Christian Liddy, 45–62 (Woodbridge, UK: Boydell, 2011), 50–57.

57. William Chester Jordan, "The Psalter of Saint Louis (BN MS Lat. 10525): The Program of the Seventy-Eight Full-Page Illustrations," *ACTA* 7 (1980): 65–91.

58. Jordan, "Gleaners," 210–17.

59. Jordan, "Gleaners," 214–17.

For the immigrants, the times were, after the uncertainties and strains of the initial period of resettlement, an inauspicious new phase in their life in France. The uncertainties, it turns out, were not at an end. As if the famine were an insufficient horror, a brutal winter windstorm that destroyed homes, uprooted trees, and damaged ships struck the province in 1258 while hunger was still besetting the inhabitants: "Ventus vehemens in Octavis Sanctorum Innocentium [6 January] qui multa mala domibus et nemoribus et in mari fecit."[60] What kind of place was this unforgiving frigid clime? Why had the king sent them here?

A similar storm in 1260, a year after the famine's end, devastated parts of northern France, knocking out half the prime housing stock, "well built and attractive homes," in Crépy-en-Laonnois ("per quam tempestatem bene ceciderunt in eadem villa triginta domus bone et pulchre, quas reficere vel reparare non possunt").[61] If other parts of the Laonnois, a microregion, as we know, of convert settlement, were as badly affected, many recent immigrants would probably have suffered displacement. On the one hand, as with the famine, these calamities may have stimulated them to rue their choice to come to France. On the other, the converts would also have perceived, at least from the royal program to deal with the famine, that the country's ruler was not slow to come to the aid of his people. The king's subjects were, as one observer put it, the apple of his eye.

Despite natural disasters, there was no hiatus in the funds remitted to the converts. The general expression "for expenses" ("pro expensis") or "for money dispensed" ("pro denariis traditis")[62] must at times have also covered the lifetime pensions, term-by-term payments to the newly settled adult male converts and widowed heads of households. This was the practice in respect to the treatment of Jewish converts, and it continued long

60. "E chronico sanctae Catharinae de Monte Rotomagi," 404.
61. *Layettes du Trésor des chartes*, ed. Alexandre Teulet et al., 5 vols. (Paris: H. Plon, 1863–1909), vol. 3, 554 no. 4644.
62. Bruel, "Notes de Vyon d'Hérouval," 617.

after Louis IX's death, until 1350 according to Tillemont, although he cites no source for this assertion.[63] The Rouennais evidence is very specific. It speaks of the Saracen converts having *gages* at a rate of such-and-such per day ("il ont de gages chascun jor"), along with the term-by-term payments of the rents for the residences allocated to them ("et combien l'an pour leur mesons assigniez").[64] That the recipients were adults, not infants as Cochard believed, and that they were receiving the pensions for entire households, not merely for themselves, is explicit in some evidence that Cochard did not know about.[65] The crown cared for orphans until they took up residence with childless or small families whose adult or adults were capable of caring for them. One Jordan the Scribe (*Jordein ecriven, Jordein scriba*) saw to the needs of two such orphans for a total of at least 31 weeks in 1256 until homes were made available to them.[66] Let us recall that the converted families might count physically disabled members among them or be headed by overburdened single parents—in other words, be incapable of accepting orphans.

The Rouennais pensions listed were the equivalent of 4 d., 5 d., 6 d., 7 d., and 8 d. per day (so approximately 6 l. to 12 l. per year). The variations must reflect the size of each recipient's natural family and any orphans living in the same household. Of course, the cost of living varied over time. Therefore, pensions received increases from time to time—"pro crès" and "pro le crès pagae"—on Louis IX's direct orders, as, for example, in 1256: "Rex concessit baptisatis de cressance, cuique xii. denarios, vigilia beati Laurentii" (the eve of Saint Lawrence's Day being 9 August).[67] The household of two latecomer immigrants intro-

63. Le Nain de Tillemont, *Vie de saint Louis*, vol. 5, 296; Jordan, *French Monarchy and the Jews*, 150.

64. Beaurepaire, "De la Vicomté de l'Eau de Rouen," 440–41.

65. For Cochard's view, see *La juiverie d'Orléans*, 59.

66. *Comptes sur tablettes de cire de Jean Sarrazin*, 84–85 (sections 200 and 202).

67. *Comptes sur tablettes de cire de Jean Sarrazin*, 94 (section 221c); *Recueil des historiens*, vol. 21, 366.

duced in the previous chapter, *nova* Margaret and her mother, had a very modest pension of 4 d. per day in 1268: "Margareta, nova baptizata, et ejus mater iiii d. per diem."[68] Much had changed by 1285, when the most recent "augmentation" brought the pension to 14 d. per day and better housing, "Margareta, nova baptizata, pro augmentatione guagiorum suorum, xiiii [d.] Pro augmentatione locationis domus suae iii s. iii d."[69] What happened to evoke this response?

The Rouen evidence contributes to answering this question. The leases for houses there occupied by the converts cost the crown 2 s., 4 s., 5 s., 6 s., and 8 s. per each accounting term, which was approximately six months long in Normandy, marked by the feasts of Easter and Michaelmas, 29 September.[70] Calculated on an annual basis they varied, then, from 4 s. to 16 s. There was nothing unusual in this, especially for the leasing of houses as opposed to stores and workshops; 62 percent of all rents in thirteenth-century Rouen, according to Alain Sadourney's calculations, were less than 1 l. per year.[71] The fundamental differences reflect the sizes of the families and thus the size of the housing units, but presumably they also register to some degree the real estate market, where prices varied by location and the quality of the dwellings. Thus, one Rouennais convert who received a large pension of seven pennies per day to help support his big family lived in a low-rent district where his residence leased for only 2 s. per half year.[72] Incidentally, this evidence of differential rents for the housing markets further confirms that in these microregions local officials *usually* distributed the con-

68. *Recueil des historiens*, vol. 22, 749.

69. The published record has "xiiii s.," but this is absurd and I have corrected to pence; *Recueil des historiens*, vol. 22, 664.

70. Joseph Strayer, *The Administration of Normandy under Saint Louis* (Cambridge, MA: Mediaeval Academy of America, 1932), 37–38.

71. Alain Sadourny, "Les rentes à Rouen au XIIIe siècle," *Annales de Normandie* 21 (1971): 99–108 (101). On the limitations of Sadourny's figures, however, see, Davis, *Holy Bureaucrat*, 235 n. 56.

72. Beaurepaire, "De la Vicomté de l'Eau de Rouen," 440.

verts in dwellings spread over various villages and in various parishes in the larger towns of settlement. A family of converts did not *typically* have other converts for neighbors, but French Christians. The separation that commenced in the Holy Land by taking the converts out of the Crusader Kingdom in order to forestall backsliding came to perfection in France.

Typically, usually—but it was different for *nova* Margaret. The pension allotted to her in 1268 was, as we have seen, the equivalent of 4 d. per day. Her mother was living with her. Logically her mother should have received the pension as the head of household. Margaret, however, assumed this role. The reasonable conclusion is that her mother was incapable of doing so because of mental or serious physical disability, one of those vulnerable people perhaps made so by the collateral damage of war. Living in the same neighborhood, judging from the juxtaposition of the entry for his pension in the fiscal records, was the other latecomer immigrant and his son. His pension was the equivalent of 6 d. per day. He is named Martin in the record, which, given the fact that he was dwelling in Tours, leads me to believe that he completed his catechism in France, was baptized in the cathedral, and took the name of its patron saint. Until he was a Christian, he could not marry another Christian (native or convert) and would have had to keep up a separate household with his child. "Martinus baptisatus, et ejus liber, vi d. Par. per diem, xxxviii s. ix d." Once his conversion was complete, the impediment disappeared.

I have found no subsequent record of Martin, but I conjecture that he, a widower with a child, and *nova* Margaret, an unmarried woman with a disabled mother, came to France together. I believe authorities permitted them to live in near proximity in Tours (a radical anomaly, given the overall nature of the system) because they had told the authorities of their intent to marry when this became legally possible. The new household, increasing over time with additional children, required an augmented pension and augmented housing. By 1285, nineteen years later, if this scenario is accurate, *nova* Margaret's mother was probably dead (she is no longer mentioned), and it was not likely that the household would continue to grow. *Nova* Margaret's childbearing years were probably over, and in any case, it was she who was drawing the pension. If she had married Martin and he had still been living, then he would have done so.

In the five cases in the Rouennais discussed above, the funds for the pensions and leased properties drew on the revenues that the crown collected through the Viscounty of the Water of Rouen, whose territorial reach, jurisdictionally speaking, mapped well onto the city limits.[73] The revenues gathered by this office consisted of the tolls and other charges the royal government levied on marine and riverine traffic along the lower Seine, Rouen being the principal node of collection.[74] The Exchequer of Normandy paid the converts' pensions and the rents for leasing their residences at each of its terms (*à chascun eschiquier*), that is, at the Easter and Michaelmas disbursements.[75]

To judge from evidence from other fiscal records, each microregion had someone to whom the crown had delegated authority to look after the converts. The system was similar in certain respects to that of monasteries that were under the special protection of one or another aristocrat or institution and of religious orders under the special oversight of cardinal-protectors.[76] More directly relevant, however, were the *enquêteurs*, special investigators, often Franciscan or Dominican friars, whom the king appointed, beginning on the eve of his first crusade, to hear grievances from victims of administrative wrongdoing and to provide redress.[77] Louis IX authorized new commissions on his return from Outremer.

73. Beaurepaire, "De la Vicomté de l'Eau de Rouen," 440–41; Strayer, *Administration of Normandy*, 81–83.

74. Strayer, *Administration of Normandy*, 82.

75. Beaurepaire, "De la Vicomté de l'Eau de Rouen," 440–41.

76. Frederic Cheyette, "The Royal Safeguard in Medieval France," *Studia Gratiana* 15 (1972): 631–52; Louis Lekai, *The Cistercians: Ideals and Reality* (Kent, OH: Kent State University Press, 1977), 74.

77. Jordan, *Challenge of the Crusade*, 51–58 and 153–54.

As I see it, these ombudsmen, to use an anachronistic but quite apt job title, would be the individuals to whom converts could complain and hope for a sympathetic hearing if they felt harassed, bullied, or threatened, in particular by local authorities. Knowledgeable of, indeed obsessed with, the frequency and danger of even more-or-less honest administrators' intimidation of those whom they were ostensibly charged with protecting[78]— and probably guessing that the converts, immigrants ignorant of local behavioral norms, might be seen as tempting targets for exploitation and abuse—the king had provided the ombudsmen for them as a special recourse.

By definition, the *prévôts* discussed above, sergeants (law officers), or similar local administrators, such as mayors, could not be ombudsmen, for it was all of the former who had to be monitored.[79] For the same reason, not even the itinerant royal functionaries, such as the curiously named Cape, who was active in the 1250s and was one of many who saw to the distribution of the converts' pensions,[80] could hold the job of ombudsman. Yet the very existence of the ombudsmen may have confused local officials. In particular, did the king's brief to them to protect the immigrant converts compromise the jurisdictional powers of existing authorities? Those authorities in general, by custom and sometimes by charter, possessed extensive criminal, civil, and gracious jurisdiction and enforcement powers (the last to register private contracts). They wanted it confirmed that these pertained to the converts whom the king had settled among them just as they did to native Christians. The mayor of Senlis and

78. William Chester Jordan, "Anti-Corruption Campaigns in Thirteenth-Century Europe," *Journal of Medieval History* 35 (2009): 204–19 (208–14).

79. On the mayors, see William Chester Jordan, "Communal Administration in France, 1257–1270: Problems Discovered and Solutions Imposed," *Revue belge de philologie et d'histoire* 59 (1981): 292–313 (306–9).

80. For 1256, see, for example, *Comptes sur tablettes de cire de Jean Sarrazin*, 94 (section 221c); *Recueil des historiens*, vol. 21, 363–65; "Dissertation sur les dépenses et les recettes ordinaires de saint Louis." *Recueil des historiens*, vol. 21, liii–lxxvii (lxv).

several other mayors of the king's "good towns" petitioned *Parlement* for clarification of the answerability to them of converts assigned residences in their bailiwicks. The High Court confirmed this fact definitively in 1260, writing that the mayors "should exercise justice over the baptized dwelling in their towns, when they commit crimes that fall under their jurisdiction" ("habeant justitiam de baptizatis in villis suis manentibus, quando delinquunt, in hiis tamen in quibus justicia pertinet ad ipsos").[81]

Still, the crown regarded ombudsmen as necessary. After all, even honest *prévôts*, sergeants, and mayors could be unduly harsh on immigrants, a more than occasional scenario—then and now.[82] Moreover, in 1261, a year after the confirmation of the towns' jurisdiction, royal authorities uncovered the fact that the very mayor of Senlis who had joined with his brother administrators in seeking clarification of their power was dishonest. He tried to bribe an incorruptible *bailli* and was caught.[83] Dishonesty was something of a habit among the mayors and municipal judges of Senlis. A few years afterward (1264), following the revelation of a depraved judgment (*pravum judicium*) inflicted on a fellow citizen of Senlis by the mayor and the town councilors of the cathedral city, they were ousted from their offices, fined 400 l. *tournois*, and banned by *Parlement* from municipal administration for five years.[84] Men appointed or elected to offices with high-level police powers were supposed to be righteous. This was the hope, but it was no guarantee against the abuse of those powers.

It is characteristic that Auguste-Arthur Beugnot, the editor of the *Olim*, the records of *Parlement*, misinterpreted the High

81. *Olim*, vol. 1, 482 no. 17; Du Cange, *Glossarium mediae et infimae Latinitatis*, vol. 1, 582, under "baptizati."

82. William Chester Jordan, *From England to France: Felony and Exile in the High Middle Ages* (Princeton, NJ: Princeton University Press, 2015), 95–96.

83. Paris, Archives Nationales, 1028A, fol. 52v. I owe this reference to Mr. Andrew Collings.

84. *Olim*, vol. 1, 587–88 no. 10.

Court's 1260 decision confirming the converts' necessity to answer to local justice. He thought the decision to confirm the competence of local officials over *baptisati* who broke the law concerned converted *Jews*. In a revealing endnote, he declared that "by *baptizati* one should understand Jews who had received baptism, but who were still not considered genuine Christians. Judaism," he continued, "was not truly effaced among them until the third generation."[85] He thus perpetuated an error in 1842 that went back as far as Tillemont in the seventeenth century. Historians of Jewish-Christian relations—James Parkes and I among them, I am sorry to say—once interpreted this case as evidence of the government abandoning Jewish converts to local officials and perhaps unintentionally inducing the latter to treat converts more harshly.[86] Edgar Boutaric, under Beugnot's influence and implicitly "improving" the text, simply added the word *juifs* in brackets to his 1863 paraphrase of the case in his more systematic coverage of the acts of *Parlement*.[87] In truth, the case cannot be about jurisdiction over converted Jews. Local officials' jurisdiction over them had been settled law for centuries.

The new-Christian immigrants were, in a metaphor to which I have already alluded, the apple of Louis IX's eye. I borrow the biblical metaphor William of Chartres employed in describing the king's care for his subjects, "ut omnes quasi pupillam oculi conservaret."[88] "Apple of his eye" is not an idle scriptural metaphor for Louis IX's solicitude for his subjects, in particular the converts from the Near East. It occurs, for example, in the description of God's love for Jacob/Israel in Deuteronomy 32:10: "He found him in a desert land, in a place of horror, and of vast

85. *Olim*, vol. 1, 1033 n. 27.

86. Le Nain de Tillemont, *Vie de saint Louis*, vol. 5, 297; James Parkes, *The Jew in the Medieval Community: A Study of His Political and Economic Situation*, 2nd ed. (New York: Hermon Press, 1976), 143; Jordan, *French Monarchy and the Jews*, 150.

87. *Actes du Parlement de Paris*, 2 vols., ed. Edgar Boutaric (Paris: Henri Plon, 1863–1867), vol. 1, 42 no. 479.

88. William of Chartres. "On the Life and Deeds of Louis," 139, paragraph 12.

wilderness: he led him about, and taught him: and he kept him as the apple of his eye" ("invenit eum in terra deserta in loco horroris et vastae solitudinis circumduxit eum et docuit et custodivit quasi pupillam oculi sui"). It also occurs in Zechariah 2:8: "For thus saith the Lord of hosts: After the glory he hath sent me to the nations that have robbed you: for he that toucheth you, toucheth the apple of my eye" ("quia haec dicit Dominus exercituum post gloriam misit me ad gentes quae spoliaverunt vos qui enim tetigerit vos tangit pupillam oculi eius").[89] The converts' protectors, the ombudsmen, were the operative element in this allusion, the sentinels who made good on Jesus's hope, "I was a stranger, and you took me in" (Matt. 25:35). One might call upon the ombudsmen at those moments, to imagine a few instances, when the converts misunderstood an idiom in their quest to master French and thereby offended a native interlocutor or transgressed an ill-understood local ordinance or custom. The unjustifiable denial of apprenticeships or other employment would be another cause to turn to them. If converts had disputes with their neighbors, suffered abuse because they failed to execute social or religious practices correctly, or just needed reassurance that consuming pork and drinking wine were not sinful, they might ask for help from the ombudsmen.

One such ombudsman who bore a revealing honorific title was *Magister Dyonisius*. Master Denis looked after the converts dwelling in the Orléanais.[90] The medieval term *magister*, like its thirteenth-century French vernacular translation *maistre* or *mestre*, is a signal to us that Denis was a literate man, not necessarily a university graduate but esteemed for his expertise in one or more of the practical, spiritual, or scholarly arts.[91] He was

89. The two other scriptural passages with the phrase as traditionally translated are Psalms 17:8 and Proverbs 7:2.

90. Bruel, "Notes de Vyon d'Hérouval," 614–15.

91. Niermeyer, *Mediae Latinitatis, lexicon minus*, under "magister"; Latham, *Revised Medieval Latin Word-List*, under "magister"; Hindley, Langley, and Levy, *Old French-English Dictionary*, under "maistre¹" and "mestre."

almost certainly a churchman, as the editor of Vyon d'Hérouval's notes supposes,[92] like so many of the *enquêteurs* whose office his paralleled. He and the other ombudsmen were therefore men who had an emphatic professional interest in seeing that the king's project of bringing non-Christians to the Catholic faith succeeded. Denis may have been a monk or canon,[93] even a cathedral canon, but there is no justification for the editor's supposition that his "mastership" signifies that he presided over some sort of group home for the converts.[94] Recall that the sources regularly speak of the leasing or the assignment of individual *houses* in the plural.[95]

The possibility that Master Denis was a canon of the Cathedral of the Holy Cross in Orléans is an attractive one.[96] Medievalists may relish the imaginative use of the disciplined imagination, given the unevenness of the source base available to them. Indeed, this may be what attracted them in part to devote their careers to the study of the Middle Ages. Nevertheless, on occasion the invigorating challenge presented by the loss of this piece or that genre of evidence does not outweigh the misfortune of the loss. This is especially the case with respect to evidence on the settled families of the Orléanais. The bishop of Orléans, William of Boësses, whom we met in the previous chapter, had been present at the dedication of the Sainte-Chapelle in 1248. He had subsequently accompanied Louis IX on crusade, witnessed the victory at Damietta, and passed along first-hand information, as

92. Bruel, "Notes de Vyon d'Hérouval," 614. See also Cochard, *La juiverie d'Orléans*, 60–61.

93. Compare to Cochard, *La juiverie d'Orléans*, 61.

94. Bruel, "Notes de Vyon d'Hérouval," 614.

95. Beaurepaire, "De la Vicomté de l'Eau de Rouen," 440–41; Bruel, "Notes de Vyon d'Hérouval," 613. I am following Bruel's transcription *domorum* (plural) for the rentals in the Orléanais, rather than *domus* (singular) in the transcription in Paris, BnF, Collection Moreau, vol. 173 fol. 31.

96. On the dedication of the cathedral, see Thomas Head, *Hagiography and the Cult of Saints: The Diocese of Orléans, 800–1200* (Cambridge, UK: Cambridge University Press, 1990), 292.

well as hearsay about the expedition gleaned from synods he attended in Paris in 1252 and 1253, to his correspondents upon his return to France.[97]

We also know that the conversion of the world was on William's mind when he returned from Outremer. Almost his first major task was to ally himself with the continuing effort to eradicate the so-called Albigensian heresy and bring the dissenters back to the Catholic fold, although the details of his activities are unknown.[98] Equally to the point, in the 1250s (he died in 1258), he wrote a *Life* of Louis IX, whom he much admired and continued to have occasions to meet after the king came back from overseas. Both, for example, were in Paris in 1256, the bishop at yet another synod there.[99] He also served the king in an inquest in *Parlement* in 1257.[100] Jacques Severt, the early seventeenth-century savant, referred to this *Life* in his 1628 ecclesiastical history of the alleged primacy of the archiepiscopal see of Lyon and its relations with other French bishoprics, including Orléans: "Qui Guilelmus sanctissimi Principis vitam conscripsit."[101] Severt had apparently not seen the *Life* himself, and so he lamented that there was no copy of it to be found in the recently published (1615) *Annales ecclesiae aurelianensis* of Charles Saussey—"Haec [vita] non in Sausseyo."[102] The *Annales* was the major history of the bishops of Orléans and the fundamental compilation of texts pertaining to them.[103] The *Life* has not surfaced since Severt's

97. *Histoire littéraire de la France*, vol. 19, 414.

98. *Histoire littéraire de la France*, vol. 19, 414.

99. *Histoire littéraire de la France*, vol. 19, 414–15.

100. Pierre-Anne Forcadet, "Les premiers juges de la Cour du roi au XIIIe siècle," *Revue historique de droit français et étranger* 94 (2016): 189–273 (227).

101. Jacques Severt, *Chronologia historica*, 2nd ed. (Lyon: Simon Rigaud, 1628), part 3, 171.

102. Severt, *Chronologia historica*.

103. Charles Saussey chronicles William of Boësses' episcopal career in the *Annales ecclesiae aurelianensis saeculis et libris sexdecim* (Paris: Hieronymus Drouart, 1615) on pages 520–24. Transcriptions of most of the original sources appear in the body of the *Annales*; others follow the *Annales* section per se, pages 747–78.

time. I presume that besides information duplicated in other biographies, the admiring prelate would have had a number of original things to say about matters particular to his personal relations with Louis IX. Might he have mentioned or at least alluded to the families that the crown had settled in the Orléannais? Would he have reported to the king on the converts' adjustment to their new environment in their first few years in the area? Might he have provided precious information on the ombudsman, Denis, especially if the master was one of his cathedral canons? Might he even have recommended him for the post?

Despite the misfortune of having lost William of Boësses's *Life* of Louis IX and its (likely) information on the Orléannais, we are lucky to have some compensatory evidence for the settled families of other microregions, including the Rouennais and Paris, in the first few years after immigration to France. The heads of five Rouennais households who lived in the city proper are interesting in part because we know their Christian names. A scribe recorded them in French as *Aalart, Bedoin, Marguer, Suseyre*, and *Jacqueline*.[104] The Norman French spellings of some of them may look a little strange at first glance, but the names are not. Male crusaders christened *Aalart, Alart*, or *Alard* (from the Latin *Alardus*) appear in the database assembled by Jonathan Riley-Smith and his colleagues.[105] In addition, the name appears for characters in the *chansons de gestes*, including the *Roman d'Aquin* and *Renaut de Montauban*.[106] That a convert bore the name would not have struck anyone as particularly strange, and one can infer that a Christian *Alard* sponsored the man at the baptismal font in Outremer. *Bedoin* is merely an al-

104. Beaurepaire, "De la Vicomté de l'Eau de Rouen," 440–41.

105. Jonathan Riley-Smith, Jonathan Phillips, Alan Murray, Guy Perry, and Nicholas Morton, "A Database of Crusaders to the Holy Land, 1095–1149," https://www.hrionline.ac.uk/crusaders/, under "Alard."

106. *Le roman d'Aquin*, ed. F. Joüon des Longrais (Nantes: Société des Bibliophile Bretons, 1880), 51, section 18, line 1299; *Renaut de Montauban*, ed. Philippe Verelst (Ghent: Romanica Gandensia, 1988), 83.

ternative spelling of *Baudoin* (Baldwin), a common northern French and Franco-Flemish aristocratic name, and one, given that five kings of Jerusalem bore it, particularly associated with the Eastern Crusades. *Marguer*, like its alternative in Normandy, *Marguerin*,[107] is a masculine form of Margaret (*Marguerite* in French; *Margareta* in Latin). It may not be too much of a stretch to imagine Louis IX's queen, Margaret of Provence, who was with him in Acre, as one of his sponsors. An inverse parallel among the immigrant converts was the christening of a girl who settled in Artois as *Roberte* (with diminutive or pet names *Roberie* and *Robine*), presumably in honor of the king's brother, fallen at Mansourah. Another such parallel, dated 1264, involved a Jewish female convert sponsored by Lord *Raymbaud* (*Raymbaudus*) of Esparron in the Dauphiné, who took the baptismal name *Raymbaude* (*Raymbauda*) from her sponsor.[108]

The two female names in the Rouennais are *Jacqueline* and *Suseyre*. The first needs no parsing. Either a Christian woman of the same name or a man named Jacques stood as a godparent for her. *Suseyre* seems odder, but it is a sounding-out of the French form of Medieval Latin *Cesarie* (Classical Latin, *Caesaria*). The

107. For several examples, see "Le 'Livre' ou 'Cartulaire' de la Nation de Normandie de l'Université de Paris," ed. Henri Omont, *Société de l'histoire de Normandie: Mélanges* 8 (1917): 8–114 (12 and 80); Louis Moréri, *Le grand dictionnaire historique, ou Le mélange curieux de l'histoire sacrée et profane*, 10 vols. (Paris: Les libraires associés, 1759), vol. 7, 229–30; "Rôles normands et français et autres pièces tirées des archives de Londres par Bréquigny en 1764, 1765 et 1766," ed. Léon Puiseux, *Mémoires de la Société des antiquaires de Normandie* 23 (1858): 1–307 (165 no. 344, incorrectly indexed at 302); *Leonis X. Pontificis Maximi Regesta*, ed. Joseph Hergenroether (Freiburg im Breisgau: Herder, 1884), 216; Charles Beaurepaire, *Archives départementales antérieures à 1790, Seine-Inférieure: archives ecclésiastiques—série G (nos. 8515–8962)* (Rouen: Julien Lecerf, 1900), 107 (G8801); FranceArchives at https://francearchives.fr/facomponent/a743cff69d13d832678b2ab079df8b037624497e and at https://francearchives.fr/facomponent/ed1f9949cbc448f60fbe895989c5fc4c738c2a22; and Geneanet at https://pt.geneanet.org/archives/releves/search_etat_civil_raw.php?clef=dep_47&ref=franorf27cauvervi_m&sens=tableau&lang=pt&sort_field=code_lieu14&sort_order=asc.

108. Jordan, *French Monarchy and the Jews*, 297 n. 58.

Italian form, *Cesarina*, and the Portuguese form, *Cesária*, are
still in use. The most famous Caesaria had a reputation for holiness. She was the sister of the Late Antique saint Bishop Cae-
sarius of Arles, and an abbess in her own right.[109] They were
buried in close proximity and their cults flourished together.[110]
A nun who adopted her name, whom scholars refer to as Saint
Caesaria II or the Younger, succeeded her as abbess.[111] I suspect
that an indigenous Mediterranean Christian bearing the name
and serving or living in the Holy Land acted as one of this convert's sponsors.[112]

The baptismal names of a few other immigrant converts in
France in this period appear in the wax tablets.[113] Among those
living in Paris were a Bartholomew, a Bertrand, and a Dreux
(*Droco*).[114] Their names appear along with those of two other
unnamed adult converts and two unnamed children in a fiscal
record of 1256.[115] There are references to other *baptisati* (un-

109. *Sainted Women of the Dark Ages*, ed. and trans. Jo Ann McNamara and
John Halborg (Durham, NC: Duke University Press, 1992), 112–14.

110. Jane Tibbetts Schulenberg, "Women's Monasteries and Sacred Space:
The Promotion of Saints' Cults and Miracles," in *Gender and Christianity in
Medieval Europe*, ed. Lisa Bitel and Felice Lifshitz, 68–86 (Philadelphia: Univer-
sity of Pennsylvania Press, 2008), 73.

111. *Sainted Women of the Dark Ages*, 112–14.

112. Less likely, I think, though a possibility suggested to me, is that the convert may have undergone baptism in Caesarea, which Louis IX refortified during
his time on crusade: see Jean de Joinville, *Vie de saint Louis*, 422–23 and 436–39,
paragraphs 470, 493, and 495; and Geoffrey of Beaulieu, "Here Begins the Life,"
103, paragraph 26. The fact that scribes, like one of those for John of Joinville's
Life of Saint Louis, occasionally render the toponym with initial S instead of the
more common C perhaps enhances the plausibility of this suggestion; Jean de
Joinville, *Vie de saint Louis*, 224–25 and 422–23, paragraphs 135 and 470.

113. *Comptes sur tablettes de cire de Jean Sarrazin*, 61–64, 71, 84–85, 87, 94,
97, 102, 106–7, and 110 (sections 54e, 54j, 54l, 55, 125a, 200, 202, 209, 221c, 274,
343a, 353, 358, and 370a); *Recueil des historiens*, vol. 21, 323, 325–26, 355, 358,
366, 381; Michael Lower, "Conversion and Saint Louis's Last Crusade," *Journal
of Ecclesiastical History* 58 (2007): 211–31 (222); Kedar, *Crusade and Mission*,
164, esp. n. 16.

114. *Comptes sur tablettes de cire de Jean Sarrazin*, 61 (section 54e).

115. *Comptes sur tablettes de cire de Jean Sarrazin*, 63, 84, 85, and 94 (sections
54 l, 200, 202, and 221c).

numbered) in this record.[116] Unlike Benjamin Kedar and Elisa-beth Lalou, the recent editor of the wax tablets, I hesitate to identify *Berteran Mareschal* and *T.* or *Th. clericus* as *baptisati*. Their names appear in sections on *baptisati* and in many other sections of the accounts as well,[117] but where the association with the converts seem closest, it may be because the men served as disbursers of funds to them without being converts themselves. However, if Kedar and Lalou are correct, one would have to add these men and their families to the number of converts in the capital. Two other Parisians attested by name in later records were Guy (*Guillot*) and Stephen.[118] There was another Bar-tholomew, another Dreux, and a Nicholas who had settled in the *bailliage* of Senlis and a Vincent in or near Compiègne. Dreux of Senlis, like Guy and Stephen of Paris, was alive at least as late as 1285. Bartholomew and Nicholas of Senlis were dead by that date, and Vincent of Compiègne by 1295.[119]

What we know about Dreux of Paris turns out to be especially important. The name was common in the contemporary French aristocracy, as in the line of Dreux of Mello, and had already been in use long before in the Carolingian royal family.[120] It was also a saint's name: that of a twelfth-century northern hermit, whose ever-increasing physical deformities assaulted the visual sensi-bilities of his neighbors and occasioned his retreat into a cell of the local church of Sebourg in his *patria*, the hotbed of crusader enthusiasm, the Franco-Flemish borderlands.[121] It is a curiosity that Sebourg (or Sébourc) was the identifier often used for King

116. *Comptes sur tablettes de cire de Jean Sarrazin*, 64, 102, and 106 (sections 55, 343a, and 353).

117. *Comptes sur tablettes de cire de Jean Sarrazin*, 61–63, 71, 87, 94, 97, 106–7, and 110 (sections 54e, 54j, 54l, 125a, 209, 221c, 274, 353, 358, and 370a).

118. *Recueil des historiens*, vol. 22, 627.

119. *Recueil des historiens*, vol. 22, 630 and 762.

120. On Bishop Drogo of Metz, half-brother of Emperor Louis the Pious, see Helmut Reimitz, *History, Frankish Identity and the Framing of Western Ethnic-ity, 550–850* (Cambridge, UK: Cambridge University Press, 2015), 432.

121. Louis Dancoisne, *Numismatique béthunoise* (Arras: Alphonse Brissy, 1859), 145–51. See also the charming word portrait of Saint Dreux (alt. Droco,

Baldwin II of Jerusalem and of the eponymous crusader hero, based loosely on the king's exploits, of the epic *Baudouin de Sébourc*.[122] Fortuitously or not, Dreux was a very good name for a convert from the Holy Land.

The wax tablets show that the crown authorized the payment of 10 l. in July 1256 for Dreux of Paris's wedding: "Droco baptisatus, Sanctum Germanum, ad nuptias faciendas."[123] *Ten pounds.* The expenditure for the five houses for converted families in Rouen, whose leases the crown paid at Easter and Michaelmas, came to a combined total of 70 s. per year, or 3 l. 10 s. Ten pounds, in other words, allowed for a sensational wedding party. Whom did Dreux of Paris marry, and why was there such an expensive wedding? Let us return briefly to the narrative sources. William of Saint-Pathus noted expressly that Louis IX had "enriched" certain Muslims, elite military commanders who felt shame at their capture and then converted and whom the king had "brought back to France."[124] William adds that these men married Christian women of their new country, as the king had hoped.[125]

From conversations while in Cyprus or the Holy Land, if not by some other means, Louis could have heard that Byzantine officials in the period before the Frankish conquest of 1204 had had similar hopes. They commended the marriage of Christian women, including widows, to such men as these commanders, "Saracen prisoners" who underwent baptism, in order to solidify the latter's commitment to their new faith and to fighting for it. Indeed, this was a sentiment hoary with age and, for a time (perhaps as late as the tenth century), found a place in official Byzantine government legislation, despite ecclesiastical reservations about the compulsion of Christian widows inherent in the impe-

---

Drogo, and Druon) in Joan Cruz, *Saints for the Sick* (Charlotte, NC: TAN Books, 2010), 32.

122. Vander Elst, *The Knight, the Cross and the Song*, 160–66.

123. *Comptes sur tablettes de cire de Jean Sarrazin*, 86 (section 204); *Recueil des historiens*, vol. 21, 355; Kedar, *Crusade and Mission*, 164.

124. Guillaume de Saint-Pathus, *Vie de saint Louis*, 21.

125. Guillaume de Saint-Pathus, *Vie de saint Louis*, 21.

rial policy.[126] If Louis IX found inspiration in the knowledge of the earlier Byzantine practice, he did so while apparently eschewing the use of any coercive measures, contrary to Catholic canon law. One might think that the king's bestowal of wealth on the men and the expectation among the French women who married them of coming under the king's special solicitude—bragging rights, if ever there were any—were regarded as sufficient encouragement to potential spouses.

However that may be, as Kedar long ago pointed out, Dreux of Paris was one such man.[127] There is evidence of a royal increase ("pro *crès*")[128] in the monetary allowance for his household and/or his service. He had a residence in Paris located in the shadow of Saint-Germain, in this case Saint Germain-l'Auxerrois. The other Saint-Germain, Saint Germain-des-Prés, had its distinctive bailiwick whose jurisdiction the monks zealously defended and whose inhabitants the royal government considered "strangers to the [walled] city" of Paris.[129] It is unlikely the king would have tried to settle a family of converts there. Saint Germain-l'Auxerrois's neighborhood, on the contrary, was scarcely a five-minute walk to the royal palace and the crown's magnificent Sainte-Chapelle. This fact is itself a sign of this convert's importance to the king. Moreover, the neighborhood was an elegant one of handsome residences, the favored quarter of the administrative elite in the thirteenth century as well as of wealthy Italian bankers on assignment in Paris.[130] There were

126. John Haldon, *The Empire That Would Not Die: The Paradox of Eastern Roman Survival, 640–740* (Cambridge, MA: Harvard University Press, 2016), 117 and 321 n. 153.

127. Kedar, *Crusade and Mission*, 164.

128. *Comptes sur tablettes de cire de Jean Sarrazin*, 94 (section 221c).

129. *Registre criminel de Saint-Germain-des-Prés*, in *Histoire des justices des anciennes églises et communautés de Paris*, ed. Louis Tanon, 413–54 (Paris: L. Larose et Forcel, 1883), 413–54; Raymond Cazelles, "'La condition du Parisien vers 1300," *Bulletin de la Société de l'histoire de Paris et de l'Île de France* 93 (1966): 49–50 (49).

130. Anne Massoni, "Saint-Germain-l'Auxerrois de Paris à la fin du moyen âge," *Bulletin de la Société de l'histoire de Paris et de l'Île de France* 141 (2014):

also almost no Jews in the neighborhood.[131] From the perspective of any native Christian living in the city, Dreux's residence was located in an upscale and fashionable district.

The convert's splendid July wedding had its sequel in September in another fine royal gift to him, a *roncin* worth 8 l.[132] *Roncin* is ordinarily translated "packhorse," so it was not a saddle horse (*pallefridus*), which went for 10 l. to 28 l. at the time or even substantially more, or a carriage horse (*equus*), which then went for 9 l. to 14 l.[133] I would speculate that Dreux of Paris already owned these even costlier animals, the result of royal benefactions. However, the packhorse had a singular purpose; it was not merely a gift. It arrived just as Dreux became something akin to a roving emissary by serving the king as a liaison to other converts in northern parts, including Coutances, Paris, Rouen, and their hinterlands. He made sure that they received the emoluments due them (for which having a good packhorse was a great asset), and those converts he encountered could in Dreux himself lay eyes on evidence that they could thrive in this society.[134] Dreux of Paris was the model convert, and the king showed him off. Here, if anywhere, was early evidence of the king's success, as far as he and his circle of advisers might have interpreted it. Whether it was sufficient evidence is yet to be explored.

17–33 (25–30); Sharon Farmer, *The Silk Industries of Medieval Paris: Artisanal Migration, Technological Innovation, and Gendered Experience* (Philadelphia: University of Pennsylvania Press, 2017), 151 and 284 n. 31.

131. Farmer, *Silk Industries of Medieval Paris*, 150–51.

132. *Comptes sur tablettes de cire de Jean Sarrazin*, 88 (section 212); *Recueil des historiens*, vol. 21, 358.

133. *Comptes sur tablettes de cire de Jean Sarrazin*, 87–88 (sections 209–212); *Recueil des historiens*, vol. 21, 357–58.

134. *Comptes sur tablettes de cire de Jean Sarrazin*, 94 (section 221a); *Recueil des historiens*, vol. 21, 365.

CHAPTER THREE

Living in France

THIS CHAPTER COMMENCES with a difficult issue, but one ultimately related to the question of success raised at the end of the last: taken together, how many Muslim and pagan converts actually immigrated to France? All the chroniclers and thirteenth-century biographers of Louis IX who write about the conversion project appear to imply that the overwhelming proportion of converts were from Islam. One of them, William of Saint-Pathus, writing of those baptized on crusade, says the number of Saracens was forty or more.[1] Another, Primat of Saint-Denis, stressing those Muslims who fought for Louis IX in general (or promised to), counted five hundred.[2] A number of the first wave of converts abandoned the king in the Holy Land when they had the opportunity to do so. Benjamin Kedar therefore prefers the lower number.[3] In most chronicles and medieval biographies of Louis IX, however (Geoffrey of Beaulieu's "Here Begins the Life and Saintly Comportment of Louis, For-

1. Guillaume de Saint-Pathus, *Vie de saint Louis*, 21.
2. Primat, "Chronique," 14.
3. Kedar, *Crusade and Mission*, 163–64; this seems at variance with his recognition of the appeal of conversion to Muslims of "low social standing"; Kedar, "Multidirectional Conversion," 191–93 and 196. See also Lower, "Conversion and Saint Louis's Last Crusade," 222.

mer King of the Franks, of Pious Memory" is the exception), the principal interest is not in ordinary, vulnerable Muslims such as the elderly, widows, and orphans, let alone slaves and pagans. Instead, they followed those whose conversions, even if impermanent, had a spectacular element about them—*men* who had commanded Muslim contingents, survivors who failed in battle, surrendered, and apostatized; *men* who had local standing—not others.

Yet the documentary evidence—Vyon d'Hérouval's excerpts, fragmentary original accounts that supplement his data, and the Rouennais material, which incorporated details of the converts' settlement into a contemporary version of its regional custumal—tells a different story. In 1253, authorities settled twenty-five immigrant converts, heads of households, in and around Bourges.[4] By 1255, the Laonnois had settled fourteen more, the Noyonnais eleven, and the Orléanais at least twenty-five.[5] The wax tablets that record Dreux of Paris's celebrity wedding and the gift of a *roncin* in 1256 list four additional converted heads of household in his bailiwick of Paris.[6] Moreover, there were seventeen in the Amienois and fifty-six more residing in the Touraine in the same year.[7]

We have already seen that the Rouennais evidence contributes information on five households. Other evidence, however, confirms that there were in fact thirteen families originally settled in the microregion. Reference is made for the year 1308 to the sons of thirteen converts in the Rouennais "whom Louis had formerly brought from Outremer": "Filii XIII baptizatorum de Rhotomago, quos Ludovicus quondam adduxit [de] Ultramare."[8]

---

4. Bruel, "Notes de Vyon d'Hérouval," 613.

5. Ibid., 612–13.

6. *Comptes sur tablettes de cire de Jean Sarrazin*, 61, 63, 84, 85, and 94 (sections 54e, 54l, 200, 202, and 221c); *Recueil des historiens*, vol. 21, 323, 325–26, 355, 358, 366, and 381.

7. Bruel, "Notes de Vyon d'Hérouval," 613–14.

8. *Comptes sur tablettes de cire de la chambre aux deniers de Philippe III le*

In the section of the wax tablets covering alms for Christmas 1308, where this entry appears, the record notes their receiving 17 l. 12 s., divided among them. (Were they so poor at the time that they were living hand to mouth? We shall return to this question.) Five of them were then listed together because their house rents and pensions were paid from the Viscounty of the Water of Rouen, the direct geographical jurisdiction of which was, as remarked earlier, more or less coextensive with the city limits. This in turn suggests that officials distributed them through different parishes of the city of Rouen itself, while the other eight families settled in the hinterland and received support from separate sources of royal revenue. Of the five families in the city proper, two were headed by women, who had to be widows or, less likely, spinsters.[9] One wonders (and shudders, given the often-precarious conditions of women in medieval French society) if the proportion of female-headed households among converts from Islam elsewhere in the kingdom was really close to 40 percent.

In any case, the total number of households in eight microregions of northern France is 166, an average of slightly more than twenty per district. Even using a small multiplier for average household size (say, three, lower than for two-parent families unaffected by war and long-distance migration) would still mean that one is talking about 498 immigrants. Of course, this aggregate figure does not include other towns and hinterlands for which the fiscal and other records expressly note the settlement of converts from overseas or payments to them without providing precise figures for the number of households they occupied in the early years of settlement, the mid-1250s. Such is the case for thirteen more microregions around Chauny, Compiègne, Coutances, Évreux, Hesdin, Péronne, Poissy, Pontoise, Pont de

---

Hardi et de Philippe IV le Bel (1282–1309), ed. Elisabeth Lalou (Paris: Boccard, 1994), 817 no. 131; Farmer, *Silk Industries of Medieval Paris*, 287 n. 101.

9. Beaurepaire, "De la Vicomté de l'Eau de Rouen," 440–41.

l'Arche, Saint-Omer, Saint-Quentin, Senlis, and Sens.[10] If the number of households averaged twenty for each of these districts, as it does in the present reckoning for the eight for which we do have figures (my working hypothesis), one would have to add another two-hundred-plus dispersed families of converts, or approximately six hundred individuals. The total would therefore exceed one thousand persons immigrating in the years 1253 and 1254.

One cannot stress enough how rich the information is on which this preliminary estimate is based; yet, more can be said. Let me return briefly to the evidence on Paris. The residence in the capital's Saint Germain-l'Auxerrois bailiwick of the convert Dreux of Paris is explicit for 1256. Fortuitously, from the same fragmentary records that mention him, we know that a few other converts, incorporated in the calculations made above, were also living in the area. Fiscal records from the same year tell us further that the crown designated at least five men to disburse funds to converts settled in other neighborhoods around the city.[11] Later evidence for Saint-Denis in the Paris microregion shows that there was an additional family of converts there. This signifies that there were additional but unnumbered convert households in other parishes of the capital and its hinterland, whose numbers need to be added to the total of one-thousand-plus computed above.

To continue along this line of thought, would it be productive to search for additional immigrant converts who resided in other royal administrative, castle, and market towns of the north?[12] Half of the microregions where converts are known to have been settled coincided with the chief towns of major administrative centers, *bailliages*, including Paris, and their environs: Amiens,

10. Bruel, "Notes de Vyon d'Hérouval," 612–13.

11. *Comptes sur tablettes de cire de Jean Sarrazin*, 94 (sections 221a and 221c); *Recueil des historiens*, vol. 21, 365–66.

12. Cochard (*La juiverie d'Orléans*, 59 n. 3) noted the mix of settlers in regional administrative centers and non-centers.

Bourges, Coutances (Le Cotentin), Orléans, Paris, Rouen, Saint-Omer, Saint-Quentin (Vermandois), Senlis, and Tours.[13] It makes sense that the king and his advisers would work through the *baillis*, who would mobilize their subordinates—*vîcomtes* in Normandy and *prévôts* elsewhere—to arrange for the new arrivals. It would certainly be worthwhile to continue the search for records from the mid-1250s pertaining to other chief administrative towns in the northern *bailliages*: Arcques (Caux), Bayeux, Caen, Étampes, Gisors, Mantes, Pont-Audemer, Verneuil. In the same spirit, it would be worth trying to find additional evidence for the same period for microregions centered on important castle and market towns in the north that did not serve as the *baillis'* headquarters. After all, Chauny, Compiègne, Évreux, Laon, Noyon, Péronne, Poissy (the king's birthplace), Pontoise, Pont de l'Arche, and Saint-Denis were sites of settlement but not chief towns of the *bailliages* in which they were situated. Other similar locations, requiring further investigation beyond what I have been able to accomplish, would include at the very least Abbeville, Alençon, Auxerre, Beaumont-sur-Oise, Beauvais, Blois, Chartres, Falaise, Ham, Meaux, Melun, Soissons, Vendôme, and Vernon.

As *rues des juifs*, *juiveries*, their Medieval Latin equivalents, and the like often indicate historic sites of Jewish settlement in France, toponyms with the element *Saracen* need consideration for the same possibility. It has long bothered scholars, including Jean Benoît Désiré Cochet, that northern France even had such toponyms in the Middle Ages: "Mais comment comprendre cette qualification en deçà de la Loire et de la Seine, et même jusqu'en Belgique, où les Sarrasins n'ont jamais pénétré?"[14] One explanation offered is that this usage is another example of medieval

13. The name of the *bailliage*, where it differs from the name of the administrative center, is in parentheses.

14. Jean Benoît Désiré Cochet, *La Seine-Inférieure et archéologique* (Paris: Derache, 1864), 173 n. 1.

playfulness.[15] This possibility, which was hardly uncommon in other contexts, should definitely give one pause before identifying every place with such an element in its toponym as evidence of the settlement of a Muslim convert to Christianity.

It should also restrain the easy identification of people bearing the epithet "Saracen" or "Moor" as Muslim converts. Similar caution is called for in identifying such people as brown-skinned: that is, as taking either word as a marker of foreignness or racial otherness, despite Marie-Thérèse Morlet's emphatic assertion that these epithets "pas de doute" point to a dark complexion.[16] In fact, one can doubt. Take "Saracen." The word might just as well have described a buckwheat farmer, if it is true that Norman adventurers introduced the plant (Modern French, *sarrasin*) upon their return from the wars of conquest in southern peninsular Italy and Sicily in the eleventh and twelfth centuries.[17] It might also have evoked a herbalist who used birthwort vine, a meaning of *sarrasin* attested in Old French, in medical treatment.[18] Alternatively, perhaps it goes back to a baker or hawker of quiche, OF *sarrasson*, "fromage cuit avec des oeufs," or simply a cheesemonger's product, "Sarrasson, fleetings or hasty curds, scumd from the whey of a new milk cheese."[19]

Further caution is also called for since, as a toponym, "Saracen" may stand in for "infidel," "idolater," or "Northman," as it

15. Michel Roblin, *Le terroir de Paris aux époques gallo-romane et franque* (Paris: A. et J. Picard, 1951), 81.

16. Compare to Marie-Thérèse Morlet, *Étude d'anthroponymie picarde: les noms de personne en Haute Picardie aux XIIIe, XIVe, XVe siècles* (Amiens: Musée de Picardie, 1967), 187. She applies the phrase to epithets based on OF *more*/ML *maurus*, and then extends it to Saracen ("Avec la même valeur").

17. Michel Giard, *Dictionnaire du Cotentin* ([Brest]: Le Télégramme, 2012), 181.

18. Hindley, Langley, and Levy, *Old French-English Dictionary*, under "sarrasine"; *Lexique de l'Ancien Français*, under "sarasine."

19. *Lexique de l'Ancien Français*, under "sarrasson." Compare to *Leechdoms, Wortcunning, and Starcraft of Early England: Being a Collection of Documents, for the Most Part Never before Printed, Illustrating the History of Science in This Country before the Norman Conquest*, 3 vols., comp. Thomas Cockayne (London: Longman, Green/Longman, Roberts, and Green, 1864–1866), vol. 2, 385.

does occasionally in medieval apologetics and stories.[20] Sites
bearing the word may thus take their names from the fact that
they earlier served as pagan Viking forts and staging areas.[21]
Châtel Sarrazin in medieval Évreux, *Le Buisson Sarrazin* (recalling a fortified gateway) in the Chartrain, *Fossés-Sarrazins* in
Berry, and *La Cave Sarrazine* in the Gâtinais might be examples
of the former; and *La Butte aux Sarrasins* in Normandy, *Le
Champ des Sarrasins* near Paris, and *Le Camp des Sarrasins*
near Compiègne, examples of the latter in the same period.[22]
That this is the only credible explanation, however, may be too
strong, given how frequent and varied such medieval toponyms
are. They include *Le Tombeau des Sarrasins*, *La Grotte aux
Sarrasins*, and the hamlet of *Le Sarrasin* near Conteville, all in
Normandy; *Sarzé*, *Sarzin*, *Sarrasinière*, and *Sarrazin* in Berry;
Sarrazin in the Touraine; and *La Fontaine des Sarrasins* close
onto Sermaize in the Île-de-France, just to name a few.[23]

20. Debra Strickland, *Saracens, Demons, and Jews: Making Monsters in Medieval Art* (Princeton, NJ: Princeton University Press, 2003), 165. Compare to
Rachel Fulton Brown, *Mary and the Art of Prayer: The Hours of the Virgin in
Medieval Christian Life and Thought* (New York: Columbia University Press,
2018), 34.

21. Cochet, *La Seine-Inférieure*, 174 and 173–74 n. 1. Compare to Reginald
Griffith, *Sir Perceval of Galles: A Study of the Sources of the Legend* (Chicago:
University of Chicago Press, 1911), 91 n. 3.

22. Roblin, *Le terroir de Paris*, 205; *Les noms de lieux in Eure-et-Loir (microtoponymie)*, vol. 4: *Canton de Courville (28 1 12)* (Chartres: Société archéologique d'Eure-et-Loir, 1995), 39 no. 456; Maxime Legrand, "Les ruines
romaines et les mosaïques de Souzy-la-Briche," *Annales de la Société historique
et archéologique du Gâtinais* 3 (1885): 85–121 (90 and 120 note); Daniel Bernard,
Légendaire du Berry: au coeur de l'imaginaire populaire (Saint-Cyr-sur-Loire:
Alan Sutton, 2005), 97; Cochet, *La Seine-Inférieure*, 174 and 173–74 n. 1; Jean
Benoît Désiré Cochet, *Répertoire archéologique du département de la Seine-
Inférieure* (Paris: Imprimerie nationale, 1871), col. 122. See also Alphonse Roserot, *Dictionnaire topographique du département de la Haute-Marne* (Paris: Imprimerie nationale, 1903), 30, 39, and 163; and Félix Liénard, *Dictionnaire
topographique du département de la Meuse* (Paris: Imprimerie nationale, 1872),
217.

23. Cochet, *La Seine-Inférieure*, 173–74 n. 1. (Sermaize is wrongly identified
with the Marne town that did not receive the name until the mid-nineteenth
century; the proper Sermaize is in the Île-de-France.) See also Louis de la Tram-

I am not suggesting that one should expect converted Muslims or pagans to have been present, let alone documentable, in all the towns and *banlieux* listed in the previous paragraphs or that the settlement of converted Muslims is indicated by every or any personal or place name with the element "Saracen." The extent of settlement, after all, depended foremost on the number of immigrants in the high tide of conversion, 1253–1254. The most generous estimate would still mean that there were too few families to necessitate settling them in every possible location. Moreover, certain locations that might otherwise have been appropriate sites may not have had housing vacancies in the then-current state of the local real estate markets. A winter hurricane, not unlike the devastating storms of Christmas 1999 in Normandy and elsewhere in western Europe, famously recalled for having displaced thousands of people and uprooted millions of trees continent-wide,[24] struck the province on the octave of Epiphany in 1252, the eve of the first arrivals of converts from the Holy Land. It leveled houses, uprooted trees, and caused widespread flooding and an enormous loss of human life and livestock ("ventus fuit vehemens in octavis Epiphaniae, unde facta est domorum subversio, arborum eradicatio, maris inundatio et gentium et pecudum maxima submersio").[25] This would have

---

blais, "De la signification et de la convenance des noms de lieux des en Berry, et particulièrement dans le département de l'Indre," *Compte rendu des travaux de la Société du Berry* 13 (1866): 330–66 (362); Bernard, *Légendaire du Berry,* 97; J.-X. Carré de Busserolle, *Dictionnaire géographique, historique et biographique d'Indre-et-Loire et de l'ancienne province de Touraine,* 6 vols., Mémoires de la Société archéologique de Touraine, 27–32 (Tours: Rouillé-Ladevièze, 1878–1884), vol. 6, 15; and *Mémoires et notes de M. Auguste Le Prevost pour servirr à l'histoire du département de l'Eure,* 3 vols., ed. Léopold Delisle and Louis Passy (Évreux: Auguste Hérissey, 1862–1869), vol. 1, 539. See also Roserot, *Dictionnaire topographique du département de la Haute-Marne,* 163; and Liénard, *Dictionnaire topographique du département de la Meuse,* 217.

24. Rayond Pearce, David Lloyd, and David McDonnell, "The Post-Christmas 'French' Storms of 1999," *Weather* 56 (2001): 81–91; and Douglas Hoyt, "A Chronology of Notable Weather Events," online at http://www.breadandbutterscience.com/climatehistory.pdf.

25. "E chronico Normanniae," 214–15.

limited the availability of housing and, thus, the settlement of immigrants in the hardest-hit places.

Consequently, I would argue for a few more microregions of settlement at most, and only in those hit relatively less hard by the storm and, as a further consequence, only a modest possible increase in the estimate of converts. A few dozen additional families/households would not add more than approximately three times that number of individuals to the total immigrant-convert population. My estimate of the number of families or households, all things considered and crude as it may be, would then have to be adjusted upward slightly to about five hundred total (and thus 1,500 individuals). Still, a more systematic investigation seems called for, if only to seek to establish the plausibility of this estimate. There are, one suspects, discoveries for scholars yet to make.

There is one more reason to think that this might be so. In my 1979 study of the French king's rulership, *Louis IX and the Challenge of the Crusade*, I described patterns in his travels in the run-up to his first crusade. In particular, he made a circuit of the royal domain in early 1248 in order to represent his bond with the realm on the very eve of his departure. Accompanying these travels were acts of justice and largesse that deepened the bond.[26] At the time of this early research, I could not discern a similar nice neat tour before Louis IX's last crusade, although the king, who had spent much of the years 1266–1268 in and around Paris and his nearby residences, traveled a great deal more in 1269 and 1270 before heading to the south. I concluded that this, too, constituted a circuit of sorts in which "Louis reached out to districts which had rarely seen him," and I interpreted this endeavor as similar to the desire that he had in 1248 to emphasize the royal majesty "as a symbol of unity."[27]

I still believe that this is true, but it is only part of the story. In 1268, the king visited Évreux and Gisors on business that

26. Jordan, *Challenge of the Crusade*, 105–10.
27. Jordan, *Challenge of the Crusade*, 147.

related primarily to administrative matters.[28] At Évreux, he was in preliminary negotiations with the chapter about a bishop to succeed Raoul of Chevry, who seems to have been gravely ill and had perhaps made his intent to resign known to the king. In any event, Bishop Raoul died the next year and Louis IX put forward his own candidate, Mathieu of Vendôme, the abbot of Saint-Denis (who declined), and then Philippe of Cahors, a high royal administrator in orders, who was elected. This was an important matter. The king may have preferred to have a bishop as co-regent during the upcoming crusade he was planning for 1270, but he wanted Mathieu, whether he agreed to stand for election to the see of Évreux or not. Bishop Philippe was designated as the abbot's replacement as co-regent if the latter were to die or be incapacitated.[29] Besides discussing the nomination, the king also informed local churchmen that he intended to found a Dominican church when he returned from crusade, at which time he would possess, with his expenses reduced, the disposable capital to do so.[30] As for Gisors, history had made the town's jurisdictional status a bit of a nightmare, with disputes coming to the *Parlement* of Paris in the 1260s.[31] It is likely that as the crusade neared, Louis wished to put his personal imprimatur directly on the settlements decreed in the High Court.

During his stays in Évreux and Gisors, the king could also learn about the families of converts living in the two microregions of which these towns were the centers. He may have met individuals from these families, an inference highly probable, since the visits to the towns appear to have been sufficiently revelatory to prompt similar trips elsewhere. The year 1269 and

28. *Recueil des historiens*, vol. 21, 422.

29. On these matters, see William Chester Jordan, *A Tale of Two Monasteries: Westminster and Saint-Denis in the Thirteenth Century* (Princeton, NJ: Princeton University Press, 2009), 131.

30. I discuss these matters fully in my study of Philippe of Cahors (in progress).

31. *Olim*, vol. 1, 566–67, 656–57, and 791 nos. 3, 17, and 4, respectively, and 1040 n. 55.

early 1270 took him to Coutances, Pontoise, Saint-Omer, Sens, Rouen, and Tours, all of which were also centers of convert settlement.[32] During this period, he made visits as well to a number of other towns that were the administrative centers of northern *bailliages*: Mantes, Pont-Audemer, and Verneuil.[33] He included many major castle and market towns: Beaumont-sur-Oise, Chartres, Ham, Meaux, Melun, Vendôme, and Vernon.[34] In some cases, he had not made trips to these localities in over forty years (Vendôme) or ever before (Ham).[35] The (hypothesized) presence of converted families may have been a stimulus for some of this inclusiveness.

Ham is a particularly interesting case in this regard, for the commune of Athies would have fallen within its microregion if the crown had chosen to settle immigrants in and around the castle town. That commune's fiscal account for 1259–1260, presented to the masters of the King's Court in 1260, shows that one of the few sources of income the town fathers collected in that year was the leasing of houses. The total amount was 4 l. 2 s. "more or less" ("l'un en plus, l'autre mains"), comparable to the sums the crown was paying elsewhere to house the converts. Other towns, such as Compiègne in its accounting for 1261–1262, recorded rents that they received for small numbers of houses as line-item income.[36] Why set these rents apart in their accounts? The tantalizing entries in the records for Athies and Compiègne do not specify whether the crown was leasing the houses or who was occupying them. The only hint that the party making the disbursement had clout was the stipulation in the Athies record that the commune maintain the houses in good repair: "li louaiés des maisons: IIII liv. et II sols, l'un en plus, l'autre mains, et suer

32. *Recueil des historiens*, vol. 21, 422–23.
33. *Recueil des historiens*, vol. 21, 422–23.
34. *Recueil des historiens*, vol. 21, 422–23.
35. Jordan, *Challenge of the Crusade*, 147.
36. *Documents sur les relations de la royauté avec les villes en France de 1180 à 1314*, ed. Arthur Giry (Paris: A. Picard, 1885), 91 no. 1.

chou il les convint retenir de carpentrie et de couverture."[37] From the accounts of the *commanderie* of Saint-Denis, which record expenditures to keep the lodgings of the "Saracen" family living there in fit condition, one can infer that pressure on lessors was effective: "Pro domo Sarraceni reparare, xii s." (1288–1289); "Pro domo Sarraceni reparare . . . xxxviii s. iiii d." (1290–1291).[38]

I am less inclined to believe that this was done outside the royal domain, the territories under the immediate rule of the king. Despite their generally good relations, I think it improbable that Louis IX sought to impose on great territorial lords such as the count of Champagne or the duke of Burgundy, almost sovereign princes, the financial burden associated with the crown's immigrant converts.[39] I also doubt that any were settled in the appanages of Anjou, Maine, and Poitou: that is, the vast northern lands governed by the two young men (Alphonse of Poitiers and Charles of Anjou), who accompanied their brother Louis IX on crusade.[40] After their release from captivity both had returned home following disputes with the king about how best to salvage the mission.[41] All of this was before the conversions in Acre began in earnest and long before the first waves of converts and potential converts arrived in France. They were also preoccupied with other matters once they got to France: Alphonse was ill (he temporarily went blind), and Charles became involved in the War of the Flemish Succession.[42] Moreover, the king, being sensitive to his brothers' jurisdictional rights, would have avoided settling

37. *Layettes du Trésor des chartes*, vol. 3, 532 no. 4613.

38. *Atlas historique de Saint-Denis*, 145.

39. On the governance of the great territorial fiefs and their relation to the crown, see Jordan, *Challenge of the Crusade*, 40–41.

40. On these lands and the system of government, see Charles Wood, *The French Apanagess and the Capetian Monarchy 1224–1328* (Cambridge, MA: Harvard University Press, 1966).

41. Jean de Joinville, *Vie de saint Louis*, 382–83, 392–93, and 402–5, paragraphs 405, 422–23, 438, and 442.

42. Jordan, *Challenge of the Crusade*, 117 and 124–25.

immigrants in their appanages. The settlement, in this sense, was the king's project. It was his wholly.

The one clear exception to restricting settlement to the royal domain concerned the appanage lands of Robert of Artois, the king's other brother, who had died at Mansourah. His territories were under the king's guard, and Robert's widow administered them on a daily basis through comital functionaries in her infant son's name.[43] Under the circumstances Louis IX felt comfortable in having converted families settled there as a tribute to the memory of his brother. In the late 1250s, he frequently made gifts in honor of Robert. In Chartres in August 1259, the king endowed the altar dedicated to All Angels and Virgins for his own soul, the souls of his wife and parents, "of his brother, late count of Artois, and of all those who perished in Egypt and other places in Outremer while we were there."[44] The accounts of the receiver of Artois and other manuscript evidence show "Saracens" (original settlers well along in age and their descendants) in dwellings on lease in Saint-Omer and Hesdin down to the early fourteenth century.[45]

In the mid-1990s when the late Alain Derville, a fine historian, came across some of this evidence of settlement, he was surprised and did not recall or did not credit Louis IX's conversion project. He decided that the usage "house of the Saracen" that he found in one manuscript had a rather different origin and one that could explain all other references to Muslim immigrants in the county of Artois as well. For him it evoked the antics of the adventuresome knights of the region. After all, he wrote, many

43. Jean de Joinville, *Vie de saint Louis*, 317–18, paragraph 290.

44. *Cartulaire de Notre-Dame de Chartres*, 3 vols., ed. Eugène de Lépinois and Lucien Merlet (Chartres: Garnier, 1862–1865), vol. 2, 171: "quondam comitis Attrebatensis, et eorum omnium qui in Egypto et alias in transmarinis partibus nobis ibidem existentibus decesserunt." Lépinois, *Histoire de Chartres*, 2 vols. (Chartres: Garnier, 1854–1858), vol. 1, 144.

45. *Compte général du receveur d'Artois*, nos. 369, 2078, 3351, and 3365; Derville, *Saint-Omer*, 128 n. 11.

young male aristocrats of Artois left the northern fogs (*brumes*) of their native land in the last third or so of the thirteenth century in the company of Robert II of Artois to join the forces of his uncle, Charles of Anjou, and his successors in the wars of southern Italy and Sicily. After their sunny escapades—"équipées ensoleillées"—what would "ces hommes des brumes" bring back to Artois if not a few Neapolitan Saracens, whose dwellings were known familiarly as Saracen houses?[46] Were these Saracens slaves? Derville did not discuss their status, though he implied some sort of patronal power (inhering in the aristocrats) over them. In his discussion he rightly construed the locative phrase in the manuscript he quoted, "De là la maison dite du Sarrasin sur la Vieux Marché" ("from there [to] the house called 'the Saracen's' [abutting] the Old Market").[47] In other words, the building was once the habitation of a Saracen family, no longer living there in 1305, but the memory of whose residence persisted. Leaving aside for a moment Count Robert II of Artois, youthful sundrenched warriors would hardly have settled Saracen families in individual houses. Derville would have had a stronger case if there were evidence that the newcomers had living space for themselves (as servants, say) in the castles or urban residences (*hôtels*) of their putative patrons.

The weakness of Derville's argument becomes even clearer when looking at the other evidence that he referred to but did not discuss. There were at least two other dwellings in the county of Artois in 1303 still occupied by converted Saracens and their descendants. Their heads of household were receiving pensions. It comes as no surprise that one was called Robert, which is to say, he had received the name of Louis IX's brother at his christening. His pension was of an amount similar to those documented for converts from Outremer living in the royal domain, in this case 6 d. *parisis* per day: "Pour les gages Robert qui fu

46. Derville, *Saint-Omer*, 128.
47. Derville, *Saint-Omer*, 128 n. 11.

sarrazins, pour le terme desus dit, 6 d. par."[48] The other head of household—also unsurprisingly—was Roberta (*Roberte*), also after the saint-king's brother. Because this *sarrazine/sarrasine* also went by her pet names, *Roberie* and *Robine* (diminutives of *Roberte*), I think it likely she was baptized as an infant or very young child in the mid-1250s. As head of her household fifty years later, her pension was 6 d. per day as well.[49]

Surprised that a woman would be receiving this payment, the editor of the accounts, Bernard Delmaire, suggested that the enrolling clerk had erred and that *Roberte* was a mistake for *Robert*.[50] This is quite improbable, for the clerk was consistent. The feminine form of the name always comes with the feminine form of the noun Saracen ("qui fu sarrazine [*or* sarrasine]"). The masculine form of the name accompanies Saracen only in the masculine.[51] Although Louis Duval considered this Roberta to be the same person as another Roberta (*Roberte*) who appears in the contemporary records, this too is dubious. This other was the goddaughter (*filleule*) of Count Robert II.[52] Referred to in this way, she was probably still quite young around 1300. Her presence in Artois could well be a case of a girl abducted or rescued from southern Italy and brought to France, in the manner suggested by Derville. Whoever was responsible, the name Roberta would then honor her abductor/rescuer, if he were a Robert, or Count Robert II, and/or the memory of Saint Louis's brother and Robert II's father.

What is abundantly clear, however, despite some uncertainty on a few details, is that the original converts' households and lineages persisted in the royal domain and the appanage of Artois over a significant length of time. Other evidence about pensions and related disbursements, including housing subsidies,

48. *Compte général du receveur d'Artois*, no. 369.
49. *Compte général du receveur d'Artois*, no. 3351.
50. *Compte général du receveur d'Artois*, 283.
51. *Compte général du receveur d'Artois*, 22, 197, and 283.
52. Duval, "Domfront aux XIIe et XIIIe siècles," 576.

confirms it further.[53] And why not? After all, the payments were scheduled to last, in Geoffrey of Beaulieu's words, "for as long as they lived,"[54] "they" being the immigrant male and female heads of household and the underage males brought from Outremer, once they headed households of their own. Moreover, the continuity of these convert lineages is expressly noted in several places. Also recorded is the leasing of living spaces, always, to repeat, in the plural. The Amienois, the Évrecin, the Laonnois, the Noyonnais, the Orléanais, the Sénonais, the environs of Compiègne, Péronne, and Saint-Denis, the *prévôté* of Paris, and the *bailliages* of Bourges, Saint-Quentin, Rouen, Senlis, and Tours provide examples.[55] A typical entry in the accounts, like that for Sens at All Saints 1285, reads "Thirteen baptized ones, 6 s. 6 d. per day, [total] 44 l. 10 s. 6 d. And for the leasing of their houses, for the third payment [four months], 45 s. 4 d." ("Baptizati tredecim, vi s. vi d. per diem, xliiii l. x s. vi d. Et pro locagio domorum suarum, pro tertio, xlv s. iiii d.")[56]

The system was not open-ended, however, and as we have seen, considerations of gender complicated it. Male heads of household (by definition, adults) received pensions and housing subsidies from the time they settled in France. So did widows and spinsters who were heads of households when they first settled in the kingdom (Jacqueline and Suseyre of Rouen, for example, and *nova* Margaret of Tours).[57] Married women at the time of

53. In addition to specific evidence on localities, see the summary entries in the royal accounts for All Saints 1285; *Recueil des historiens*, vol. 22, 662 and 665.

54. Geoffrey of Beaulieu, "Here Begins the Life," 104, paragraph 27; Kedar, *Crusade and Mission*, 164.

55. *Recueil des historiens*, vol. 22, 625, 627, 629–31, 632–36, 665, 742, 748–49, 751, 759, and 762; Bruel, "Notes de Vyon d'Hérouval," 613–14; Rouen, Archives Départementales (AD): Seine-Maritime, G 1107, Cahier of copies of the accounts of the Viscounty of [the Water] of Rouen, fols. 1 v., 2 v., 4–4 v., 6–6 v., 7 v.–8, and 9 v. I wish to thank Mr. Troy Tice, PhD candidate in History, Princeton University, for securing me digital photographs of this manuscript.

56. *Recueil des historiens*, vol. 22, 635.

57. Beaurepaire, "De la Vicomté de l'Eau de Rouen," 440–41; *Recueil des historiens*, vol. 22, 664 and 749.

settlement who outlived their husbands and did not remarry—two are documented in the *bailliage* of Senlis and one in Compiègne—began receiving pensions immediately upon widowhood, but recalibrated according to changed family size. Thus, in 1285 in the *bailliage* of Senlis the convert Bartholomew's widow received the equivalent of 12 d. per day; the widow of Nicholas the convert in the same year and the same *bailliage* and the widow of Vincent, living in Compiègne in 1295, each received only 4 d.[58] Underage girls born Muslim or pagan in Outremer who married native Christians when they came of age in France lost eligibility for subsidies. However, if they did not marry (and did not profess as nuns), they would someday presumably have become heads of households themselves and begun to receive pensions and related subsidies from that point on. Male children born Muslim or pagan, baptized, and brought from Outremer became eligible for lifetime pensions and housing subsidies when they established separate households in France.

Let us imagine a three-year-old boy arriving in France in 1253, marrying at age twenty-five in 1275, and living another thirty years. By his death at age fifty-five in 1305, he and his father (or widowed mother) before him would have been receiving a pension and other subsidies for fifty-two years. Such an imagined person would have been dying just around the time the whole of Louis IX's project was winding down. When the generations of the converts died out entirely, the system of subsidies came to an end, and with it the now-unnecessary ombudsman structure. Male and female descendants of the converts, descendants who had never been Muslim or pagan, were not eligible for pensions or housing subsidies.

So much for inference. One may observe the playing out of this scenario in documents preserved in a copy of the accounts of the Viscounty of the Water of Rouen in the very early fourteenth century, while Pierre Saimel (1298–1302) and Pierre de

58. *Recueil des historiens*, vol. 22, 630 and 762.

Hangest (1303–1320) were *baillis* of Rouen.[59] The earliest entries in these notes (1301), from Saimel's time, finds the converts or their descendants, those born in Outremer, receiving collectively, in the usual language used for such entries everywhere, 19 d. per day as well as subsidies in the form of house leases for them and their families.[60] Babies born in Outremer in 1251 or 1252 would have been about 50 years old in 1301; their children, born in France, as old as thirty or so. As these young people moved out and established households of their own, they ceased, as we have surmised, to benefit from the pensions granted to heads of household who had been born abroad, and the expense of the pensions themselves declined as the original households shrank in size. The next entry reflects these changes.[61] The collective pensions decreased to 9 d. par. per day plus the leasing of houses at 9 s. (down from 19 s.), the abatement of leasing costs indicating the dissolution of one or more households.

This situation remained stable for approximately one year.[62] Then the crown's expenditures fell once again, this time to 4.5 d. ("iv d. ob.") per day. The expenditure for leasing houses "pro baptisatis" also fell, to 4 s. 6 d.[63] Clearly, however, a few of the converts' children—specifically, seven—were beginning to have a hard time, and at the next term they received small supplementary grants ("pro vadiis liberorum septem baptizatorum") of 2 s. 9 d. in all, per day.[64] This was the general situation for the next three terms (another year and a half).[65] There was, however, a decline in the cost to the crown of leasing houses from 4 s. 6 d. to 4 s. in the ultimate entry in the records for the converts.[66]

59. Rouen, AD: Seine-Maritime, G 1107, Cahier of copies of the accounts of the Viscounty of [the Water] of Rouen; front and back covers and elsewhere for the names of the *baillis*.

60. Ibid., fol. 1 v.

61. Ibid., fol. 2 v.

62. Ibid., fols. 4–4 v.

63. Ibid., fol. 6.

64. Ibid., fols. 6 v.–7.

65. Ibid., fols. 7 v., 8–8 v., 9 v.

66. Ibid., fol. 9 v.

I have already referred to the entry on the wax tablets of royal alms bestowed on descendants of the Rouennais converts in 1308. What we see in the evidence addressed in the previous paragraph is that the difficult financial situation that year, however it arose, was already affecting some of these descendants at the turn of the century. These people had fallen into poverty or perhaps had special needs, much like scholars and *béguines*. Earlier, as evidence demonstrates for the Paris region in the Candlemas and All Saints terms of 1285, bursaries (expenses "pro bursis") were available to some of the converts' descendants.[67] They appear in records together with accounts of monies given to students and to inmates of Louis IX's foundation, the *béguinage* of Paris. In other words, the converts' offspring, born in France, came to have access to the same varieties of alms available to any other poor or needy Christians. However, one may surmise that the story by which they or their advocates—ombudsmen *après la lettre*—hoped to curry favor ("do not forget that these are the descendants of those who came from Outremer with the king of holy memory") may have succeeded to the extent that they received a more sympathetic, if not more generous, hearing.

The converts, in terms of occupations, were probably a varied lot as they grew used to their circumstances. It would be easiest to suppose most of them learned how to farm in the northern climes, practiced as artisans in crafts they knew from Acre or learned *de novo* in France, and served the communities in which they settled as butchers, laundresses, common laborers, cooks, and servants. Having been travelers themselves and, after a while, coming to the realization that it was extremely common for immigrants living in France to use their residences as small inns (one might say as bed-and-breakfasts),[68] they might do the

67. *Recueil des historiens*, vol. 22, 665 and 759.

68. Kathryn Reyerson, "Medieval Hospitality: Innkeepers and the Infrastructure of Trade in Montpellier during the Middle Ages," *Proceedings of the Western Society for French History* 24 (1997): 38–51 (40–42).

same. A small medieval hostel or tavern with the name or *ensei-gne* (banner) *Aux Saracens* may recall such an establishment, or would this, too, be mere playfulness?

Immigrant boys who grew to adulthood in France and achieved fluency in French could serve in the administration. A Jean Saracen (*Johan Sarrasin*) appears in the records for 1309 as a policeman, who walked his beat in the *prévôté* of Paris. It is possible that he was a descendant of one of the king's immigrants who settled in the city.[69] This low-status employee was no relation to the high-ranking Christian Treasury clerk of the same name who served in Louis IX's government until the latter's death and received rich rewards from him.[70]

Better documented is *Gobert Sarraceni* (the genitive denoting a surname). He was active as a collector of royal revenues in the late thirteenth and early fourteenth centuries. He appears more than once as *Gobertus Sarraceni de Lauduno*, that is, "from Laon," as if to draw attention to the town, a center of convert settlement, and thereby to signal it as the place of origin of an official so named.[71] He was to his French neighbors back home *Gobert Sarrasin* and to the people from whom he collected revenue *Gobert de Laon*. He worked in tandem with *Odardus Sarraceni*, who, if I am right, was his kinsman.[72] Since the path of administrative service to social integration was open to converts

69. "Liste des sergents du Châtelet de Paris en 1309," ed. Marius Barroux, *Bulletin de la Société de l'histoire de Paris et de l'Île de France* 20 (1893): 36–38 (38).

70. *Comptes sur tablettes de cire de Jean Sarrazin*, 18; Cazelles, "La réunion au domaine royal de la voirie de Paris (1270–1363),"*Bulletin de la Société de l'histoire de Paris et de l'Île de France* 90 (1963): 45–60 (46–47).

71. *Inventaire d'anciens comptes royaux dressé par Robert Mignon sous le règne de Philippe de Valois*, ed. Charles-Victor Langlois (Paris: Imprimerie nationale, 1899), 143 and 205 nos. 1123 and 1648; (also in Jules Havet, "Compte du Trésor du Louvre [Toussaint 1296]," *Bibliothèque de l'Ecole des chartes* 45 [1884]: 237–99 [259 and 267 no. 321]).

72. *Comptes du Trésor (1296, 1313, 1384,1477)*, ed. Robert Fawtier (Paris: Imprimerie nationale, 1930), 6 and 11 nos. 124 and 253 (also in Havet, "Compte du Trésor du Louvre," 267 no. 446).

from Judaism as well, it would not be particularly remarkable if one or two of the immigrant families from Outremer also exploited it.

Unlike the simple foot sergeant Johan Sarrasin, Gobert rose higher. Even before he supervised the regional collection of royal revenues, he assisted the *bailli* of Vermandois in an official capacity. He prepared sealed official records and worked in tandem with other *prud'hommes* to oversee the *bailli*'s gracious jurisdiction (the registering of private contracts and agreements) in Laon per se.[73] By ordinance, the *bailli* selected such *prud'hommes* from among locals who were educated and had a reputation for discernment and integrity.[74] Gobert received the administrative (civilian) rank of castellan in this service by 8 January 1287 ("Gobert qu'on dist Sarrazin, chastelain").[75] He continued to be so attested in 1288, 1289, 1290, 1293, 1295[76]—indeed, at least through 1299 ("Gobert dis Sarrazins, chastelains le roi à Loon, garde de par le roy dou seel de la baillie de Vermandois à Loon estauvlit").[77] An excellent, though more spectacular parallel is King Philip IV the Fair's godson of the same name, born a Jew, who became a paramount figure in the administration of the royal forests and in the court circle.[78] Like Gobert, he went

73. Louis Carolus-Barré, "L'ordonnance de Philippe le Hardi et l'organisation de la juridiction gracieuse," *Bibliothèque de l'École des chartes* 96 (1935): 5–48 (26).

74. Carolus-Barré, "L'ordonnance de Philippe le Hardi," 43.

75. Carolus-Barré, "L'ordonnance de Philippe le Hardi," 26.

76. Carolus-Barré, "L'ordonnance de Philippe le Hardi," 26; Auguste Matton, *Inventaire sommaire des Archives départementales antérieures à 1790: Aisne, archives ecclésiastiques—série G et H*, vol. 3 (Laon: A. Cortilliot, 1885), 5 and 16, H17, and G2.

77. "Cartulaire de Saint-Vincent de Laon (Arch. Vatican., Misc. Arm. X. 145): analyse et pièces inédites," ed. René Poupardin, *Mémoires de la Société de l'histoire de Paris et de l'Île de France* 29 (1902): 173–267 (246). Carolus-Barré, "L'ordonnance de Philippe le Hardi," 28; Matton, *Inventaire sommaire des Archives départementales*, 52, H311.

78. Joseph Strayer, *Reign of Philip the Fair* (Princeton, NJ: Princeton University Press, 1980), 59 and elsewhere; Franklin Pegues, *The Lawyers of the Last Capetians* (Princeton, NJ: Princeton University Press, 1962), 124–40.

by either of two names, *Philippe le Convers* or *Philippe de Villepreux.*[79]

Gobert appears to have broadcast his identity as one of those brought, in his case as a young boy, from the land of the Saracens by King Louis IX. He did so by means of his personal seal, which bore the small image of a royal head and on the reverse a bonneted head. Louis Carolus-Barré and Louis Douët d'Arcq before him may have gone too far in their seeming attempt to link this latter element of the seal's iconography to Outremer by offering an alternative reading of the bonnet as a turban.[80] Carolus-Barré's interpretation of the royal head—"Saracen" rather than "Assyrian," Douët d'Arcq's classicizing reading—may nonetheless be correct.[81] The royal head looks *leftward*, representing, again following Carolus-Barré, a *speaking* king.[82] One might conjecture that the king images the assumption of power over *his* Muslims, the words of *his* mouth bringing them to the Christian faith, then *his* instructing/inspiring the personage on the reverse, namely, Gobert, represented by the bonneted head, *turned right* to receive the king's assurances.

Paris, one might hope, with its magnet-like economic attraction and as the location from which the man who brought the settlers to France ruled, might also offer good evidence of the converts and their descendants' other occupations, especially with its rich records on the guilds. At first sight, this seems to be the case, because a number of residents of the capital in the later thirteenth century identify explicitly as immigrants to France from Outremer: a certain Ysabel and her son, Colin; two other men, a

79. Jean Favier, "Les légistes et le gouvernement de Philippe le Bel," *Journal des savants* 2 (1969): 92–108 (96).

80. Carolus-Barré, "L'ordonnance de Philippe le Hardi," 27; *Collection des sceaux*, 3 vols., comp. Louis Douët d'Arcq (Paris: Henri Plon, 1863–1868), vol. 2, 314 no. 5302.

81. Carolus-Barré, "L'ordonnance de Philippe le Hardi," 27.

82. Carolus-Barré, "L'ordonnance de Philippe le Hardi," 27.

Roger and a Robert. Probably many others also came from there, even if the descriptor *d'Outremer* does not appear.[83] The problem, however, is that the tax lists of Paris, from which the evidence mostly comes, date from after the fall and abandonment of the port of Acre to its Muslim conquerors in 1291. Refugees from the devastated city in 1291 included both leading elements and ordinary people who took flight in available ships as best they could, a scene described vividly by the writer known as the Templar of Tyre.[84] Among the ordinary people would have been concubines, menials, seamstresses, and simple laborers in the crusaders' pay—Christians, Jews, perhaps a few pagan slaves and Muslims, the last fearing retribution from their coreligionists for serving Islam's enemies. A promise of conversion was probably the condition imposed in these anguished hours by those organizing the evacuation for permission to board a departing ship. This is probably why many Jews, refusing to convert and hoping against hope, opted to remain behind in Acre. These men and women did suffer imprisonment.[85] Yet their fate was less severe than that of crusaders slain in or just after battle and those Muslims who failed to escape and whom the conquerors perceived as traitors and executed. Sources on both sides of the fighting are in accord that the slaughter was awful.[86] Consequently, the Jews' survival seemed nothing short of miraculous to them. Rabbi Isaac ben Samuel chose to attribute

83. For the evidence: *Compte général du receveur d'Artois*, nos. 369, 2078, 3351, and 3365; *Comptes sur tablettes de cire de la chambre aux deniers*, 879; *Paris sous Philippe-le-Bel, d'après des documents originaux, et notamment d'après un manuscrit contenant le role de la taille imposée sur les habitants de Paris en 1292*, ed. Hercule Géraud (Paris: Crapelet, 1837), 116 and 136. See also Farmer, *Silk Industries of Medieval Paris*, 31.

84. *Crusade and Christendom*, 484; David Nicolle, *Acre 1291: Bloody Sunset of the Crusader States*. Oxford: Osprey, 2005.

85. Kaufmann Kohler and M. Seligsohn, "Isaac Ben Samuel of Acre," online at http://www.jewishencyclopedia.com/articles/8213-isaac-ben-samuel-of -acre.

86. *Crusade and Christendom*, 486, 488, and 490.

his imprisonment rather than execution to his resort to the mystical practice of "reciting the name of God's sword from *Shiʿur Qomah* [The Measure of the (Divine) Body], a practice taught him by two French rabbis."[87]

Upon his release, Rabbi Isaac went to Spain, but many of the original refugees who took ship in 1291 had come to France and may in time have established themselves in the crowded, prosperous capital city.[88] It had a notable silk industry, as Sharon Farmer has demonstrated, one part of which manufactured goods, in particular purses in the "Saracen" style.[89] The style was not simply a style: it implied a particular kind of weaving developed in the Middle East. At its best and most expensive, the cloth did not interweave "linen or cotton with silk."[90] One may speculate that immigrant Middle Eastern seamstresses who had served as lady's maids in Acre knew how to produce the purses in either the expensive all-silk or the cheaper form. If a few of the immigrants from the fall of Acre had the skills, perhaps they found employment and mobility in this occupation. They may also have piqued the curiosity of Louis IX's converts and their descendants living in Paris at the time, no matter either party's craft. The matter must rest here until further research clarifies it, if it can.

Another occupation or profession was a possibility for the boys among Louis IX's converts who arrived in France as adolescents, lads who learned French well but did not forget their colloquial Arabic (or, if once pagans, their *lingua tartarica*, as later records describe such speech[91]). What a remarkable pool of boys

87. Bohak, "God's Right Eye and Its Angel in Jewish and Christian Magic," in *Anges et démons d'orient et d'occident*, ed. Flavia Buzzetta, 63–89 (Paris: Éditions Kimé, 2017), 66; Kohler and Seligsohn, "Isaac Ben Samuel of Acre."

88. Farmer, *Silk Industries of Medieval Paris*, 31.

89. Farmer, *Silk Industries of Medieval Paris*, 27, 59, 77, 131, 293 n. 59, and 301 n. 24.

90. Farmer, *Silk Industries of Medieval Paris*, 77.

91. "Studium grece lingue, arabice et tartarice": in "Supplique de l'Université au pape pour la fondation d'un collège oriental à Paris," ed. Henri Omont, *Bulletin de la Société de l'histoire de Paris et de l'Ile de France* 18 (1891): 164–65 (165).

and, then, young men to educate in Latin at the schools, send on to the University of Paris for further study, and possibly prepare for future preaching missions, furtherance of the dream of conversion, in the homelands of their fathers and mothers. The idea was not new. Jacques de Vitry, the northern Frenchman from the Paris suburb of Vitry-sur-Seine who served as bishop of Acre from 1216 to 1228, told a story relevant here. Jacques was present at the conquest and brief occupation of Damietta in 1219. The crusaders took many Muslim prisoners, combatants and civilians, in the conquest and in other engagements. Of these people he wrote, "We selected 400 of the stronger and better off and kept them" to exchange for Christian prisoners in Muslim hands. However, the crusaders did not need to retain all their captives and sold many into slavery. An exception was made, however, for roughly five hundred young unmarried males "whom he [Jacques] acquired with great effort and at great expense." They were baptized and constituted a thank-offering, the "first fruits to God and the Lamb." However, "others, beyond those whom [he] kept, [he] handed over to certain of [his] friends in order that they might be raised by them, educated in theology and prepared for the priesthood."[92] Surely this story circulated in Acre, the bishop's old see, in the years a generation later, when Louis IX was resident there and commenced his conversion project in earnest.

Closer in time was a project referenced in a papal letter directed to the chancellor of the University of Paris. Though it is

92. *Thesaurus novus anecdotorum*, ed. Edmond Martène, 5 vols, (Paris: Florentinus Delaulne, 1717), vol. 3, col. 304: "De captivis verò Sarracenis, quos in civitate cepimus, quadringentis de melioribus & ditioribus retentis, ut captivos nostros facta commutatione cum ipsis, recuperare possemus alios omnes, eò quod sumtuosum esset nimis tot homines pascere, vendidimus christianis, ut servirent eis in perpetuum, exceptis parvulis, quos ego cum labore magno & expensis feci reservari: quibus baptizatis, plus quam quingenti, ut credo, post baptismum primitiae Deo & Agno transierunt. Hi sunt qui cum mulieribus non sunt coinquinati, &. Alios autem, praeter illos quos retinui, quibusdam amicis meis commisi, ut eos nutrirent, & litteris sacris ad cultum Dei imbuerent destinavi."

undated, the editors of the *Chartularium Universitatis Parisiensis* on good grounds place it not too long before 22 June 1248.[93] The letter mentions ten students of Near Eastern origin who were being educated at the university. They were there to perfect their Arabic and other Eastern languages in preparation for missionary work ("tam in arabica quam in aliis linguis orientalium partium ... alios in ultramarinis partibus erudiant ad salutem").[94] More information on this project and its financing appears in another letter, a mandate that Pope Innocent IV, relying on information from the chancellor, sent on 22 June 1248 to the abbot and monastery of Saint-Peter of Chartres. The pontiff addressed the problem of providing stipends for the "oriental" boys ("super provisione facienda quibusdam pueris orientalibus"). A number of ecclesiastical institutions were contributing to the stipends. The monks of Saint-Peter's claimed that the size of the subsidy required of them was over-burdensome. The pope showed himself willing to adjust their contribution.[95] As a letter of Pope Alexander IV in 1258 reveals, other ecclesiastical institutions also lodged complaints about the onus of supporting such students.[96] One recalls the resistance of local clergy in the Kingdom of Jerusalem to provide for impoverished Muslim and Jewish refugees while they underwent catechizing, although French ecclesiastics were facing far fewer serious problems than were clerics in the war-torn Holy Land. In any case, as fourteenth-century evidence establishes, the idea of pooling the resources of ecclesiastical institutions to support the faculty and students in Near Eastern languages at the University of Paris would not go away.[97]

93. *Chartularium Universitatis Parisiensis*, ed. Heinrich (Henri) Denifle and Emile Chatelain, 4 vols. (Paris: Delalain, 1889–1894), vol. 1, 212 no. 180 note.

94. *Chartularium Universitatis Parisiensis*, vol. 1, 212 no. 180.

95. *Chartularium Universitatis Parisiensis*, vol. 1, 212 no. 181. On all these matters, see also the prefatory comments to the "Supplique de l'Université au pape," 164.

96. *Chartularium Universitatis Parisiensis*, vol. 1, 372 no. 324.

97. "Supplique de l'Université au pape," 164–65.

It was, as we shall see, a costly project. An entry in the royal accounts for 1239, attested by a royal clerk, records "expenditures for Saracens by Brother Simon of the [Order of the] Hospital" ("Pro expensa Saracenorum, per fratrem Simonem Hospitalis, xxxii l. teste decano Turonensi").[98] Presumably Simon or other members of the Hospitaller Order had brought the probably orphaned little boys from the Kingdom of Jerusalem through Acre around this time, with the king's support. The amount expended, according to this record, was 32 l., a very large sum, and it is not likely to have been a one-off payment. That the Saracens referred to here had converted to the Catholic faith and were not prisoners draws on information the editors of the accounts attribute to Ducange: "Saracenorum ad christianam religionem conversorum."[99] Fiscal records also indicate that the crown paid several apparently young men, including Colin, a page named Hugh, and Big Stephen ("Stephanus Mangnus" [sic]), to travel to Acre to take care of the boys ("ad pueros Acon"), which is to say, to prepare them to act according to the proper ways of French lads and probably tutor them in conversational French.[100] Unfortunately, the editors found the phrase perplexing and hypothesized that the travelers went there to do some kind of service for the sons of the great nobleman John of Acre.[101] On the face of it, this translation—"to [John of] Acre's sons" for "ad pueros Acon"—is wholly improbable.

In any case, the point here is that Louis IX was well aware of what was a longstanding impulse at the University of Paris to baptize young boys born in the Holy Land and bring them to Paris for training for subsequent preaching missions in the Near East. He was also aware of the expense and the difficulties of funding it without the aid of the crown. For him, however, the burden of supporting the students would not have been an ex-

98. *Recueil des historiens*, vol. 22, 589.
99. *Recueil des historiens*, vol. 22, 589 n. 11.
100. *Recueil des historiens*, vol. 22, 591 and 612.
101. *Recueil des historiens*, vol. 22, 591 n. 1.

cuse to abandon or downsize the project. This was emphatically the case inasmuch as after he returned to France and got his finances in order again, he began to pour funds into the university in support of the foundation of the college later known as the Sorbonne, established in the early 1250s by his close friend and court preacher, the moralist Robert of Sorbon. Training up preachers was a principal undertaking of the new college.[102] It was an undertaking to which the king was particularly drawn; he himself on more than one occasion literally preached sermons, behavior not necessarily thought appropriate by certain conservative churchmen, but no matter.[103]

One must acknowledge that the surviving evidence does not always suggest scenarios that pleased the architects of the conversion project. Quite the contrary. It hints at a number of problems, among which were some terribly serious ones. The year 1260 brought the petition of the mayors of the king's good towns to *Parlement*, as we have seen, for a confirmation of their jurisdiction over the converts "when they do wrong," literally "go astray" (*quando delinquunt*).[104] One might surmise that the impetus for the mayors' petition was not an abstract concern for jurisdictional precision but real-life incidents of transgressive behavior, possibly only petty and inadvertent, given the immigrants' undoubtedly low level of knowledge of local ordinances in the first few years after their settlement. Yet, no substantial group of people like those in the circumstances described is

102. Jordan, *Men at the Center*, 7–10 and 32–33; and Miller, *Beguines of Medieval Paris*, 87–88 and 94–100.

103. Jordan, "Louis IX: Preaching"; Anne Lester, "Confessor King, Martyr Saint: Praying to Saint Maurice at Senlis," in *Defenders and Critics of Franciscan Life: Essays in Honor of John V. Fleming*, ed. Michael Cusato and Guy Geltner, 195–210 (Leiden: Brill, 2009), 199; Christoph Maier, "*Civilis ac pia regis Francorum deceptio*: Louis IX as Crusade Preacher," in *Dei Gesta per Francos: Études sur les croisades dédiées à Jean Richard*, ed. Michel Balard, Benjamin Kedar, and Jonathan Riley-Smith, 57–63 (Aldershot, UK: Ashgate, 2001), 59–60.

104. *Olim*, vol. 1, 482 no. 17.

likely to have been wholly free of deliberate lawbreakers, including felons, motivated either by wretched treatment and exas-
peration or by temperament and disposition.

Another indicator of problems comes from information available for the Orléanais in 1260, the same year as the High Court
decision just remarked. The crown settled more than twenty-five
convert households in the Orléanais from 1253 to 1255. One of
their heads of household passed away in 1256, according to a
source recently unearthed by Princeton graduate student Andrew Collings.[105] Presumably the children (including orphans, if
there were any) in the now-dissolved household were displaced
from their still relatively new home, new environment, and new
acquaintances and redistributed to other households. Even more
troubling was (and is) the fact that by 1260 the number of convert households in the Orléanais had declined to eighteen. That
is to say, clerks excised six households from the fiscal records and,
by implication, the residents of those households, including orphans, who dispersed in one way or another.

The records tell us what happened to the heads of these families. They had either died (cause unknown) or fled: "sex alii baptisati quorum quidam sunt mortui, et quidam fugerunt."[106] How
did those who died meet their end? Natural causes? As victims
of neighbors' hatred? Suicide, perhaps? All three religions—
Judaism, Christianity, and Islam—developed blistering cri-
tiques and almost absolute prohibitions of self-killing.[107] (A
limited exception among Jewish thinkers was the suicides
of 1096 to avoid forced conversion.[108]) Yet it is no secret that

---

105. Paris, BnF, Collection Moreau, vol. 177, fol. 175.

106. Bruel, "Notes de Vyon d'Hérouval," 614–15. See also Cochard, *La juiverie
d'Orléans*, 60–61.

107. Jennifer Hecht, *Suicide: A History of Suicide and the Philosophies
against It* (New Haven, CT: Yale University Press, 2013), 45–62.

108. Simha Goldin, *The Ways of Jewish Martyrdom*, ed. C. Michael Copeland,
trans. Yigal Levin (Turnhout: Brepols, 2008), 119–22; Chaviva Levin, "Constructing Memories of Martyrdom: Contrasting Portrayals of Martyrdom in the Hebrew Narratives of the First and Second Crusade," in *Remembering the Crusades:*

extreme loneliness, despair, fear, and regret are formidable emotions. They may either disable actions, including resistance and suicide, or enable them; their effect on human behavior is unpredictable. In truth, I do not know how the converts died, but in whatever manner and circumstances these deaths occurred, the problems faced by the immigrants of the Orléanais prompted appeals to their ombudsman, *Maistre* Denis, which is why his name also shows up in the fiscal records at this point.[109]

As for those who fled, it may be that they did so with their families or even as a group with other immigrant families. If the primary cause of flight was mistreatment or extortion by officials or police who had knowledge of where the converts were settled, the information about this may have been shared unintentionally with the victims. ("Robert Sarrasin, who lives in N-ville, paid up. Why don't you, and spare yourself and your family problems?") In this scenario, the convert's seeking out of Robert and anyone else whose whereabouts came to light might make sense. More than likely, I would suggest, those who fled did reach a collective decision. Yet I also think that they would have opted for different routes and not shared the information with their comrades. This would prevent the recognition, capture, and coercion of one from imperiling others seeking escape from *douce France*.

That there is evidence of flight at all in 1260 completely undermines Théophile Cochard's theory that all the converts brought to France had been orphaned infants. How could infants flee after settlement as brief as five years and no longer than seven? Could seven-, eight-, and nine-year-olds flee? The answer is no. A more serious question is about where the Orléanais converts (adults and/or whole families) might *try* to flee if they had come to rue their baptism or to resent harsh treatment at the

---

Myth, Image, and Identity, ed. Nicholas Paul and Suzanne Yeager, 50–68 (Baltimore: Johns Hopkins University Press, 2012), 50–61; David Berger, "Jacob Katz on Jews and Christians in the Middle Ages," in *The Pride of Jacob*, ed. Jay Harris, 41–63 (Cambridge, MA: Harvard University Press, 2002), 49.

109. Bruel, "Notes de Vyon d'Hérouval," 614.

hands of their neighbors or local police. Was there any hope of a return to the East? Possibly there was. The immigrants had money to sustain them if they ran away, thanks ironically to the crown's own generosity. The somatic markers of Middle Eastern "Arabness" or even Cuman-ness were not so obviously othering as the markers (skin color, hair texture) of, say, sub-Saharan negritude. Only in partisan and polemical art and literature were Muslims and pagans slurred as monsters or as "black Outremer dogs" ("cas negres outramaris") and the like.[110] This was a moral judgment, not a physical description, as Lynn Ramey demonstrates,[111] although it may have affected contemporaneous and later European treatment of blacks, whether Muslim or not—a thorny question. Recall that in captivity Louis IX himself had not recognized his Muslim visitor as northern French by sight. Why? Contemporaries acknowledged that French complexions varied from brown to ruddy, from swarthy to white, "E brun e bai e sor e blanc."[112] And since Antiquity there had been an equally wide variety of complexions in Egypt.[113] There was no perceived disconnect between being a Muslim in Egypt and looking like a northern European Christian that leapt to the king's mind, if one can judge by how he responded when his visitor introduced himself and offered gifts. Louis IX was simply astonished that the man spoke his own language, northern French, so well.

The point is that one should not suppose that the immigrant converts looked any more non-French than Louis IX's visitor stood out as non-Egyptian. Moreover, by 1260 the French speech of many of the immigrants, especially the younger ones who had accompanied fleeing parents, must have been passable, though

110. Strickland, *Saracens, Demons, and Jews*, 159–60, 168, 172–73, and 184; Michael Routledge, "Songs," in *The Oxford Illustrated History of the Crusades*, ed. Jonathan Riley-Smith, 91–111 (Oxford: Oxford University Press, 1997), 107.

111. Ramey, *Black Legacies*.

112. Vander Elst, *The Knight, the Cross and the Song*, 100–1.

113. Benjamin Braude, "Black Skin/White Skin in Ancient Greece and the Near East," in *Black Skin in the Middle Ages/Le peau noire au moyen âge*, 3–13 (Florence: Edizioni del Galluzzo, 2014), 4; Heng, *Invention of Race*, 227.

possibly still accented. However, there were so many dialectical idioms and so many regionally based accents in medieval France[114] that other travelers encountering the would-be escapees on the main roads would have had no reason to regard them as other than French natives. This was so even if these same travelers, Frenchmen and Frenchwomen by birth, did not particularly like the sound of their French. It was, after all, common to disparage dialects, most snobbishly in contrast to Parisian court French, a habit that concurs with the so-called superiority complex of thirteenth-century natives of the capital: ("Paris [*Parisius*] is Paradise [*Paradisius*]"; "Paris has no equal ["Paris est sans pair"]).[115] I imagine, in one possible scenario, the fleeing converts pretending to be on pilgrimage to the Holy Land. After having mastered the rudiments of Catholic teachings, they had participated for a few years in the rituals of worship. They could effectively feign being Christians as long as necessary.

A question often asked is whether one can ignore a principal somatic marker of male otherness among the converts from Islam who took flight, one they shared with Jews: namely, circumcision. It is true that this sign differentiated them from Christian men (non-converts) in the Middle Ages. It was a helpful sign when *ribaus*, Christian laborers of low standing, needed to differentiate Muslim battlefield casualties from crusaders' corpses in order to give the latter Christian burials, as John of Joinville noted in a particularly stark passage of his *Life of Saint*

114. Thelma Fenster, "French Language," in *Medieval France: An Encyclopedia*, ed. William Kibler and Grover Zinn, 370–74 (New York: Garland, 1993), 372.

115. R. Anthony Lodge, *French: From Dialect to Standard* (London: Routledge, 1993), 101; Eric MacPhail, "Ecolier Limousin (Limousin Schoolboy)," in *The Rabelais Encyclopedia*, ed. Elizabeth Zegura, 61–62 (Westport, CT: Greenwood Press, 2004); Boris Bove, "Aux origines du complexe de supériorité des Parisiens: les louanges de Paris au moyen âge," *Mémoires de la Fédération des sociétés historiques et archéologique de Paris et de l'Ile-de-France* 55 (2004): 423–43 (423–36); Léopold Delisle, "Paris et Paradis au moyen âge," *Bulletin de la Société de l'histoire de Paris et de l'Ile de France* 8 (1881): 29–31; Paul Meyer, "Paris sans pair," *Bulletin de la Société de l'histoire de Paris et de l'Ile de France* 10 (1883): 26–28.

Louis. The *ribaus* whom Louis IX hired to do just this when he was in Egypt threw bloated Muslim bodies, identified from their circumcisions ("qui estoient retaillés") into the river, while they consigned the Christian corpses to trench burials ("en grans fosses l'un avec l'autre").[116] The ritual was also a favorite topic for Catholic theologians interested in symbology, baptism's displacement of circumcision.[117]

However, the only plausible circumstance in which a convert might have his circumcision noticed, at least in a region like northern France where homosocial bathhouses were rare,[118] was in the company of prostitutes. A convert in flight might have felt desirous of sex, either for pleasure or as a kind of vengeance or payback for his own ill-treatment, something to the effect of "I shall have my way with *their* women before I leave this accursed land." There were Christian prostitutes who serviced travelers, even in the morally hypervigilant realm of Louis IX.[119] Whether a prostitute would notice a circumcision, particularly on an erect member, is doubtful. Let us grant, however, that she did and queried her customer about it. He would have been wise to say, especially if there were rumors swirling of Saracen runaways, that he was a convert to Christianity from Judaism. His dalliance with the prostitute might have typed him as a less than perfect Christian, but still a Christian after all. Only a fool would blurt out that he was one of those rumored apostates in flight to the Dar al-Islam.

116. Jean de Joinville, *Vie de saint Louis*, 316–19, paragraph 290.

117. See, for example, Andrew Jacobs, *Christ Circumcised: A Study in Early Christian History and Difference* (Philadelphia: University of Pennsylvania Press, 2012) and Kathleen Biddick, *The Typological Imaginary: Circumcision, Technology, History* (Philadelphia: University of Pennsylvania Press, 2003), esp. pages 91–104.

118. Homosocial bathhouses were not rare in Christian Spain. Although authorities probably excluded Muslim males, identified by circumcision, from Catholic bathhouses, there would have been no legal basis to forbid converts from Islam (or Judaism) from using the facilities. Social practice, of course, might differ. Constable, *To Live Like a Moor*, 83.

119. Nowacka, "Persecution, Marginalization, or Tolerance," 185–86.

One wonders whether any of the converts who fled succeeded in reaching the Mediterranean ports in France or Provence, if this was their goal, and took ship to Acre. One wonders, too, what the return would have been like when they docked in the harbor and the former Muslims among them subsequently tried to rejoin their erstwhile coreligionists yet avoid Christian suspicions. The "orthodox schools" of Islamic law certainly "acknowledge the possibility of revocation and repentance (*tawbah*)" after apostasy.[120] *Tawbah* usually needed to take place in a timely manner. The quondam converts might have been able to persuade people familiar with Islamic law of their regret at their offense, the sincerity of their desire to return to the fold, and the necessity they labored under to delay their return. Yet, what could these people have expected from Acre's ordinary Muslims who remembered or had heard of them? A few of the Muslims of Acre who refused to convert in 1253 and 1254—let alone to convert for money, as the scenario might have been represented—possibly rose above any residual resentments. Would others of those who remained faithful tolerate the returnees? Suspicion of allegedly repentant apostates was a traditional concern.[121]

Consider a parallel. Theoretically baptism had no sacramental meaning for Jews, but those who chose to convert and underwent the ceremony nonetheless offended the community they spurned. This fact underlies the humiliation endured by repentant apostates at the hands of those who had remained steadfast in the faith. The dilemma reveals itself in a story told about the early thirteenth-century Rhenish rabbi Judah Hasid. He turned away a contrite new Christian who wanted to do penance and return to Judaism, telling him that he had as much chance of atonement as a dead stick the rabbi was whittling had to sprout green leaves. Angered by the rebuke and spurred by it to do even

---

120. Rudolph Peters and Gert De Vries, "Apostasy in Islam," *Die Welt des Islams* 17 (1976): 1–25 (6).

121. Uriel Simonsohn, "Halting between Two Opinions: Conversion and Apostasy in Early Islam," *Medieval Encounters* 19 (2013): 342–70.

worse things than he had done before, the dejected young apostate departed, but the rabbi, in a sense upbraided by the Almighty, soon summoned him back—for the stick had sprouted. This was how the exemplum represented the situation; that is to say, it did so in accordance with the normative principle well known, if this "popular" story can be trusted, among Jews of all social ranks.[122]

In everyday practice, the dilemma played out differently, but the meaning was similar. In theory, for Jews baptism was nothing but getting wet. Yet apostates, even penitent ones, had obviously once affirmed it was more than this. Consequently, their "conversion" was an abomination to faithful Jews. As a further consequence, they were subjected to a ceremonial "unbaptizing." Faithful Jews used water, analogously to the practices of sympathetic magic, to wash the apostates free of the baptismal water. They rubbed sand roughly on the foreheads of the former converts until they bled, an act that "effectively" effaced the sign of the cross.[123] Might the emotions sparked among the Muslim community of Acre have been similar to those of Jews who, at least initially, shamed repentant would-be converts? In the complex calculus that accompanied flight from France, there was no assurance of a proverbial happy ending.

The mayors' petition of 1260, together with the various Orléanais records, with their allusions to criminal behavior, deaths, and flight, provide a glimpse into some of the converts' unhappiness

122. *Ma'aseh Book: Book of Jewish Tales and Legends*, 2 vols., trans. Moses Gaster (Philadelphia: Jewish Publication Society of America, 1934), vol. 2, 381; *Tales in Context: Sefer ha-ma'asim, in Medieval Northern France (Bodleian Library, University of Oxford, Ms. Bodl. Or. 135)*, ed. Rella Kushlevsky, trans. Ruchie Avital and Chaya Naor, commentary by Elisheva Baumgarten (Detroit: Wayne State University Press, 2017), 718–20.

123. Ephraim Shoham-Steiner, "An Almost Tangible Presence: Some Thoughts on Material Purity among Medieval European Jews," in *Discourses of Purity in Transcultural Perspective (300–1600)*, ed. Matthias Bley, Nikolas Jaspert, and Stefan Köck, 54–74 (Leiden: Brill, 2015), 64–66.

and the fault lines in local society. They challenge the evidence
of smooth integration that one might too rapidly infer from, say,
Dreux of Paris's celebrity wedding. The experiences of the converts, in other words, were multiple and ran the gamut from
hellish to tolerable or even satisfying. Their Christian neighbors'
reactions ranged from hostility to indifference or perhaps beyond indifference to amity at times. Why, for example, would the
author of the extraordinary Marian text *De laudibus beate Marie
virgine*, Richard of Saint-Laurent, imagine a special love the
Virgin had for Jews and Saracens?[124] In a tentative way, Rachel
Fulton Brown suggests that this canon, archdeacon, and peni-
tentiary working in and around Rouen was influenced by the
presence of a Saracen family, if their name, *Salehadin* (weak evidence), signals converts in the city.[125] It would be more persuasive to tie the perhaps exemplary presence of Louis IX's converts
in Rouen to Richard's remark that the Virgin "both loved and
loves everything which is of God, Saracens, Jews, and Christians,
albeit in different ways" ("aliter tamen et aliter"). Richard's precise dates are unknown. He was active by 1230, and though some
historians, such as Fulton Brown, conventionally invoke 1250 (a
stand-in for the noncommittal "mid-thirteenth century"), the
Histoire littéraire de la France suggests a date of ca. 1260 and his
tumulary stone is of the late thirteenth century.[126] A churchman
active in the Rouennais at this time could have seen the Virgin's
work in the converts' adaptation to life in Christendom.

However truly bad, mixed, or truly good individual immigrants' lives were in France (and one might expect this to differ
according to age, health, sex, conventional standards of physical
attractiveness, and occupation), a question remains. How did
Louis IX and his advisers assess the success of the project? On

124. Fulton Brown, *Mary and the Art of Prayer*, 348.
125. Fulton Brown, *Mary and the Art of Prayer*, 544 n. 146.
126. *Histoire littéraire de la France*, vol. 19, 23–27; Henri Omont, "Richard
de Saint-Laurent et le Liber de laudibus beatae Mariae," *Bibliothèque de l'École
des chartes* 42 (1884): 503–4.

this point, I incline toward thinking the king was pleased overall, and that he, his advisers, and their successors regarded the
outcome favorably. Why? Let us turn to the evidence for the
Orléanais one more time. It will prove once again to be useful. It
suggests to me, indeed, that *Maistre* Denis, the ombudsman,
managed to reassure the converts whom he oversaw that the
problems they were facing and from which some of them had fled
would soon pass away on their own or could be resolved and that
there were still grounds for optimism.

Perhaps in Denis's favor was the likelihood that some of the
immigrants, even those singed by the caustic of nativist hostility,
actually yearned to belong to the Christian community. This was
not an unknown sentiment among other converts and would-
be converts, both voluntary and even, after a while, involuntary
ones, trying to make the best out of a fraught existence.[127] For,
while the records for 1260 refer to a reduction of heads of household by six, the records for 1262 testify to the establishment of
three new convert households in the Orléanais.[128] The straightforward explanation is that a few of the underage boys brought
from Outremer in 1253–1254 had reached adulthood, married,
and started families—*French* families—by 1262. They then received the pensions to which they were entitled as adult heads of
household for the remainder of their lives. I see no substantial
reason to doubt that in general the converts, or most of them,
came through the trials of their resettlement successfully, weath-
ered the economic crisis engendered by the famine of 1257–1259,
and survived the animosity of some of their neighbors and the
abuse of certain local authorities. They were not unscathed, for
one knows that years later the offspring of a number of them had
fallen into poverty in the Rouennais and were living in part from

127. William Chester Jordan, "Exclusion and the Yearning to Belong: Evidence from the History of Thirteenth-Century France," in *Difference and Identity
in Francia and Medieval France*, ed. Meredith Cohen and Justine Firnhaber-
Baker, 13–24 (Farnham, UK: Ashgate, 2010).

128. Bruel, "Notes de Vyon d'Hérouval," 614.

royal alms. The king's project was therefore probably less of a success for them in the short run than he imagined it was. Still, they endured.

Perhaps, too, the converts from Outremer were frightened into passivity in France by their intimate familiarity with the price of not appearing to assimilate, let alone of openly declaring their desire to apostatize the Christian faith, if this was their inner hope. Everyone knew that contumacious apostasy was punishable by death. This knowledge in the abstract became vividly immediate in the city of Rouen on 18 April 1266.[129] On that day the Franciscan archbishop of Rouen, Eudes Rigaud, known as Louis IX's closest friend, "adjudged and condemned as an apostate and heretic one who had been converted from Judaism to the Catholic faith." The Jew had apostatized before, been persuaded it was wrong to do so, and recommitted himself to Christianity. He had even been rebaptized when he did so. Thereafter, he had again lapsed and refused "to be restored to the Catholic faith, although several times admonished to do so," wrote the archbishop. The Franciscan's views on the legitimacy of rebaptism may seem eccentric, but for adults the sacrament operated only where conversion was voluntary, and thirteenth-century theologians differed as to the threshold of external encouragement/pressure that might constitute illicit force.[130] Though Eudes's particular rationale cannot be recovered from the surviving incomplete version of his commentary on the *Sentences* of Peter Lombard,[131] it was the punishment that the archbishop ordered meted out to the Jewish convert/apostate that would

129. *Regestrum visitationum archiepiscopi rotomagensis/Journal des visites pastorales d'Eude Rigaud, archevêque de Rouen, MCCXLVIII–MCCLXIX*, ed. Théodose Bonnin (Rouen: A. Le Brument, 1852), 541. Translation from *Register of Eudes of Rouen*, trans. Sydney Brown, ed. Jeremiah O'Sullivan (New York: Columbia University Press, 1964), 618.

130. William Chester Jordan, "Archbishop Eudes Rigaud and the Jews of Normandy, 1248–1275," in *Friars and Jews in the Middle Ages and Renaissance*, ed. Steven McMichael and Susan Myers, 39–52 (Leiden: Brill, 2004), 48–49.

131. Jordan, "Archbishop Eudes Rigaud," 49.

have impressed the inhabitants of Rouen, including particularly "des sarrazins convertis a la foi chretienne" residing in the city. As the churchman noted blandly in the record of his visitations, after his judgment the man "was then burned by the *bailli*."[132] The immigrants' latent fears were made real in the sight and smell, even the mere whispered rumor, of the charred body on the open space, the Mare-du-Parc, where such executions were carried out, just across the Seine from the city and in sight of the cathedral.[133] Rouen was not unique. In Paris only two years later, in 1268, a Jewish convert to Christianity who had persisted in the faith for twenty years and had married a Christian woman, apostatized. Moreover, he had two of his sons circumcised, which deepened the authorities' anger with him. When they arrested him and he suffered condemnation in the bishop of Paris's court as a notorious heretic, he swore, rumor had it, that not all the wood in Paris gathered into one spot and set ablaze could destroy him.[134] (Here, he was perhaps drawing on his memory of a trope found in Hebrew lore, brilliantly explicated by Susan Einbinder.[135]) Adding insult to injury, the *prévôt* of Paris and his men, into whose hands the bishop's court relaxed the apostate, conducted him to the pig market ("in plateam ubi porci Parisius venduntur") for execution. There, they committed him, bound, to the flames, which wholly consumed his body ("ligatus totaliter est combustus"). His ashes they scattered on grounds nearby, adjacent obviously to the swine holding pens.[136] The "lesson" was as pointed for converted Muslims in Paris as for their Jewish counterparts.

---

132. *Regestrum visitationum archiepiscopi rotomagensis*, 541. Translation slightly modified from *Register of Eudes of Rouen*, 618.

133. Elma Brenner and Leonie Hicks, "The Jews of Rouen in the Eleventh to the Thirteenth Centuries," in *Society and Culture in Medieval Rouen, 911–1300*, 369–82 (Turnhout: Brepols, 2013), 377.

134. "Notes sur quelques manuscrits du Musée britannique," 189.

135. Einbinder, *Beautiful Death*, 45–69 and 155–79.

136. "Notes sur quelques manuscrits du Musée britannique," 189.

Fears of a different sort affected the converts' neighbors. Memories had to persist among them about the origin of the immigrants and even of the hostility that had caused a few individuals or families to run away. However, it was the newcomers' strange behavior, one would think, the consequence of ignorance, that fed xenophobia in general and could have given a few converts unsavory reputations that morphed into stereotype and passed into lore. An alleged clairvoyant caught up in a supposed antiroyal conspiracy in 1276 was at first reputed to be a wandering monk, a *sarabita*, in the more or less official history written at Saint-Denis ten years later.[137] Two decades after this, the French translator of this history identified the conspirator as a Saracen convert from eastern France who had traveled to Laon, where he reputedly met with his co-conspirators ("plus avant ver Alemaigne estoit un convers qui avoit esté Sarrasin . . . et moult disoit de choses qui sont a venir").[138] Was this an error in translation or did evidence arise in the interim exposing the renegade monk as a convert from Islam? In whatever way the identification originated, was such an allegation more creditable, given the fact that Muslim converts and their descendants really were dwelling in the Laonnois at this time? John of Joinville himself lamented that some native French but deceitful Christians had fatalistic beliefs that mimicked those of Muslims.[139] If he had called such people Saracens, we might compare his choice to that of medieval critics of usury who impugned Christian moneylenders by likening them metaphorically to Jews.[140] However, John called them Bedouins, *Beduyns*, an arresting choice with its evocation of desert paganism. Did he signal thereby that the king he loved so well had nonetheless erred in bringing the converts, only superficially cleansed of their religious beliefs, from the land of Bedouin error to infect sweet France?

137. *Recueil des historiens*, vol. 20, 502.
138. *Recueil des historiens*, vol. 20, 503.
139. Jean de Joinville, *Vie de saint Louis*, 296, paragraph 253.
140. Jordan, *French Monarchy and the Jews*, 44–45.

The resonances of memory varied, of course. Well into the fourteenth century, it was not unusual to find descendants of the original converts referred to or remembering themselves as the children or from the stock of those whom the holy king had brought back from overseas. One need only recall Gobert Sarraceni's seal, which evoked this pedigree. There is also the entry on the wax tablets for the year 1308 that records alms to the sons of the thirteen convert households in the Rouennais "whom Louis had formerly brought from *Outremer*."[141] The letter of remission of 1350 for Raymond Amfossi of Beaucaire represented his lineage as a token of honor simply because of its association with Saint Louis. How else could anyone have known that this man, living in Languedoc, was a descendant of converts originally settled in the north a century before, if not by his own declaration of it in his plea for mercy when he appealed for a pardon? Did he still possess the letter patent of 1253 or 1254 issued to his ancestor in Acre?

Perhaps he was lying in his assertion. To some extent, even if he were, the point would be the same. Raymond Amfossi expected the invocation of Saint Louis to help him overcome his own troubles. True, the authorities' response to his information, assuming they believed him, could have been a flat refusal, precisely because he had disrespected the memory of the saint by committing a felony. Raymond was extremely fortunate, however, and obtained his remission. One might further ask, though, presuming again that his invocation was not a stratagem pulled from a cap, how long his family or any convert lineage preserved this origin story and, perhaps the same thing, gave it a positive spin in the years and decades to come? In fact, I have not found an explicit later reference than his. Nonetheless, the century it survived as part of his own family lore down to Raymond is impressive in itself.

---

141. *Comptes sur tablettes de cire de la chambre aux deniers*, 817 no. 131; Farmer, *Silk Industries of Medieval Paris*, 287 n. 101.

Yet the memory did perhaps persist even longer. A curious indication of this possibility is demonstrated in the arrival in 1427 of a group of self-ascribed Egyptians at the gates of the city of Amiens, one of the microregions settled by mid-thirteenth-century converts.[142] This group was seeking aid from the burghers. The encounter was the first of a series in the century (1445, 1450, and 1480).[143] The initial group, led by a man named Thomas, claimed to be on its way to Flanders. There were sixteen individuals in total. Taken before the city council for the verification of their identity and for general interrogation, the travelers explained that they had come from the far country of Little Egypt. They were, one would now say, Gypsies, or, more politely, Roma. The nineteenth-century editor of the city council minutes used the then-contemporary term in modern France for these people, *Bohémiens*.[144] However, given the fact that the 1427 reference is almost the earliest in France to people whom historians in hindsight name Gypsies/Roma,[145] the city councilors at the time appear to have taken them for immigrants from Islamic Egypt.

Like the leaders of later such groups, Thomas showed his interrogators a papal letter that identified the band as converts to the Christian faith who desired to escape temptation or coercion to relapse.[146] The letter granted the converts indulgences for their perseverance in the faith and asked those who encountered them during their travels to provide alms. The city councilors believed the letter was authentic. Its *stylus* clearly did not differ markedly, if at all, from that of the indisputably genuine papal letters that were readily available for comparison in ecclesiastical

142. "Apparitions des Égyptiens ou Bohémiens à Amiens, dans le XVe siècle," ed. Hyacinthe Dusevel, *La Picardie* 6 (1860): 432–37 (432–35).
143. "Apparitions des Égyptiens," 435–37.
144. "Apparitions des Égyptiens," 437. See also Paul Bataillard, "De l'apparition et de la dispersion des Bohémiens en Europe," *Bibliothèque de l'Ecole des chartes* 5 (1844): 438–75 (438 n. 1).
145. Bataillard, "De l'apparition et de la dispersion des Bohémiens," 449.
146. "Apparitions des Égyptiens," 433–36.

archives in and around Amiens, an episcopal city with many wealthy abbeys.[147] The commune's fiscal accounts reveal an expenditure of 8 l. *parisis* as alms on the converts' behalf, although the council requested they leave the city within three days. (Amiens's aldermen repeated this charitable gesture on the later occasions as well.) At least a few members of this and other convert groups rested at the inn known as *Aux Sarrazins*,[148] a bed-and-breakfast-cum-drinking-establishment once run by a Saracen convert family, perhaps the last vestige of the residential presence of Louis IX's converts in the city. One cannot be certain of this, of course, since the habit of fancifully named commercial inns, with no reference to real owners, was already taking hold and growing ever more widespread.[149] Nonetheless, this late medieval and early modern usage of "Saracen," "Turk," or "Moor" in the names of hostels often conjoined the epithet with the noun "head," alluding to, if one quaint authority is credible, the violence (the bounty on or the taking of heads) in the long struggle between Christians and Muslims.[150] The Amiens city fathers were continuing a tradition, if my suggestion is correct, but at the same time recalling their predecessors' unease with the permanent residents of a century and a half before by limiting the strangers' sojourn on this occasion to seventy-two hours or less.

However much remembering how the story all began helped the converts of the 1250s and their offspring, on the one hand,

147. For a papal letter sent to the cathedral chapter in 1389—that is, not too long before the first appearance of the Egyptians in Amiens—see *Cartulaire du chapitre de la cathédrale d'Amiens*, 2 vols., ed. Edmond Soyez (Amiens: Yvert et Tellier and Auguste Picard, 1906–1912), vol. 2, 110. The cartulary of the Cistercian abbey of Ourscamp shows that major abbeys would have had scores of such letters: *Cartulaire de l'abbaye de Notre-Dame d'Ourscamp*, ed. Achille Peigné-Delacourt (Amiens: Lemer aîné, 1865), 286–313.

148. "Apparitions des Égyptiens," 436.

149. John Hare, "Inns, Innkeepers and the Society of Later Medieval England, 1350–1600," *Journal of Medieval History* 39 (2013): 477–97 (496).

150. Gilbert Monson-Fitzjohn, *Quaint Signs of Olde Inns* (London: Herbert Jenkins, 1926), 126 and 145.

and their neighbors, on the other, to maintain a sense of separateness or awareness of difference in the first century or so after settlement, the ultimate assimilation of most of the newcomers and their descendants was a fact. Marriages, whether of influential figures such as Dreux of Paris or of less wealthy converts, were the key factor in this and in future full integration. Spread out in far-flung settlements as they were, and in individual households surrounded by those of native families, it would have been difficult for most of the converts to be in regular contact with one another, let alone to seek out marriage partners and practice endogamy. Even in Paris, where particular groups of Christian foreigners did not scatter, but clustered together voluntarily in neighborhoods and tried hard to maintain their conceptual distance from natives and other foreigners, the stimulus of affective ties with local Frenchmen and Frenchwomen was capable of decoupling them from their ethnic communities.[151] A fortiori, it was easier for families who lived cheek by jowl with the native French to assimilate. In a word and in all likelihood, most of them in time became thoroughly Christian and thoroughly French. In every culturally consequential way, their descendants still are.

151. Farmer, *Silk Industries of Medieval Paris*, 33–34.

The Last Crusade

IF LOUIS IX PERSUADED HIMSELF that his effort, limited as it was, to convert Muslims (and pagans) and transform them into sincere Christians was successful, as I have argued in the foregoing chapter, what effect did this perception have on the events of 1270? Benjamin Kedar, Jacques Le Goff, Michael Lower, John Tolan, and many others insist—correctly, I think, given the unanimity of the narrative sources—that conversion was a major motivating factor in the king's last crusade. This expedition took him to his death from illness at the siege of Tunis in 1270.[1] I imagine his last circuit of the domain to the many microregions settled with converts whom he had brought back from overseas as a poignant reminder and renewal of this aspect of his crusade mission.

Then there were the hopes focused on the ruler of Tunis. Geoffrey of Beaulieu, who had been on Louis IX's first crusade and accompanied him once more, asserts that the king believed that the bey was willing to convert, which, as we know, Christians would have expected to lead to the mass baptism of his

1. Kedar, *Crusade and Mission*, 165–69; Le Goff, *Saint Louis*, 42, 291, and 558; Lower, "Conversion and Saint Louis's Last Crusade," 220–31; Tolan, *Saracens*, 203. See also Richard, *Saint Louis*, 560 and 566.

subjects.[2] He only needed a little encouragement—or so the story went.[3] Bits and pieces of information seemed to favor this expectation. John Tolan thinks the bey actually did tell an envoy that he might accept baptism.[4] Moreover, by this date the speculation or wishful thinking that the great Saladin himself might have been willing to convert under the right pressures circulated widely in belletristic texts. No longer a man whom Aman Nadhiri might call a "familiar Saracen" (a Christian knight in every meaningful way but steadfast in his Islamic faith),[5] the representation of Saladin in romances moved toward that of a Muslim waiting only for the proper circumstances to convert.[6] The bey of Tunis was no latter-day Saladin, but he, too, might have a Christian heart *avant le sacrement*.

The crusaders also still recalled those Muslims in Valencia who had accepted baptism in imitation of certain of their defeated leaders.[7] Kedar infers from the chronicler Primat's story of Muslim soldiers feigning conversion in order to penetrate the Christian defenses in the siege of Tunis that the local North African population was very much aware of the invaders' overarching proselytizing goal. Otherwise they would not have decided on the ruse with an expectation of success.[8] The scene, which an artist depicted in a fourteenth-century manuscript of Primat's chronicle shows a group of Muslims—their status as "other" denoted by their brightly striped tunics—approaching Raoul Le-

2. Geoffrey of Beaulieu, "Here Begins the Life," 116–19, paragraph 41; Kedar, *Crusade and Mission*, 166.

3. Siberry, *Criticism of Crusading*, 17–18.

4. Tolan, *Saracens*, 203.

5. Nadhiri, *Saracens and Franks*, 84 and 180. See also Heng, *Invention of Race*, 170–71 nn. 58–61.

6. Samuel England, *Medieval Empires and the Culture of Competition: Literary Duels at Islamic and Christian Courts* (Edinburgh: Edinburgh University Press, 2017), 145 and 158.

7. Kedar, *Crusade and Mission*, 168.

8. Kedar, *Crusade and Mission*, 167–68; Primat, "Chronique," 48–49. See also Louis Carolus-Barré, *Le procès de canonisation de saint Louis (1272–1297): essai de reconstitution* (Rome: École française de Rome, 1994), 77–78.

scot, one of Louis IX's subcommanders, in early August 1270. He succumbed during the encounter.[9] Geoffrey of Beaulieu, who was present during the last moments of Louis IX's life, exquisitely reconstructed in Xavier Hélary's study of the last crusade, also insisted on the king's continuing obsession with his enemies' conversion.[10] The king thought the Dominican Order would be instrumental in this work, although in a bit of overzealous criticism Robin Vose expressed doubt that Geoffrey, being himself a Dominican, could be trusted to have recorded Louis's words faithfully.[11] If he did not, he would have been acting out of character, given his contemporaries' assessment of him. For example, in a letter Abbot Jean of Savigny referred to Geoffrey's praiseworthiness, prudence, experience, and virtue to explain why the Cistercian Order, with which the Congregation of Savigny was associated, chose him and two other distinguished men of the same character to serve on a blue-ribbon panel to resolve a dispute within the order.[12] This was only four or five years before the crusade to Tunis.

Unsurprisingly, the Italian chronicler Salimbene, a Franciscan, emphasizes that Louis IX did bring *Friars Minor* along with him to do some of the expected missionary work.[13] One may reasonably ask why, if this is true, the king would neglect to enlist Dominicans as well, circumstances permitting? After all, it was

9. For a description of the MS, see online http://initiale.irht.cnrs.fr/decor/18318. Professor Cecilia Gaposchkin of Dartmouth College brought this illustration to my attention. It is the cover illustration of the present book.

10. Xavier Hélary, *La dernière croisade: saint Louis à Tunis (1270)* (Paris: Perrin, 2016), 9–11.

11. Vose, *Dominicans, Muslims and Jews in the Medieval Crown of Aragon*, 237–38.

12. Edmond Martène, *Histoire de l'abbaye de Marmoutier*, 2 vols., Mémoires de la Société archéologique de Touraine, 24–25 (Tours: Rouillé-Ladevièze, 1874–1875), vol. 2, 240: "des hommes recommendables par leur religion, par leur prudence, par leur expérience, et dont l'âge avancé joint à la vertu étoit digne de tout respect."

13. Salimbene de Adam, *Cronica*, 2 vols., ed. Giuseppi Scalia (Bari: G. Laterza, 1966), vol. 1, 457.

work with which they were intimately familiar, to judge from their own claims about their successes in converting Muslims even before Louis IX came to Outremer for the first time.[14] Finally, and to return to Geoffrey of Beaulieu, the French king on his deathbed also pondered aloud to his confessor how Christianity might most effectively achieve its universal goal, at least that part of it encompassing the conversion of the Muslims. He alluded to the sine qua non of Arabic-speaking preachers in any proselytizing campaign. (Was he thinking of some of his own converted boys, now grown up?) Everything hinged on the success of the siege of Tunis.[15]

In one sense, the siege was a Christian success in that the Muslims negotiated their "surrender," paid an indemnity, and conceded some commercial rights to the king's brother, Charles of Anjou.[16] Yet nothing more came of the king's longstanding dream of converting the bey or any other "infidels" to the Catholic faith. Most crusaders, many suffering illness, returned home rather than continue on to the Holy Land.[17] Those parts of the treaty with the bey dealing with Christianity, despite some sloppy scholarship that Kedar has identified and excoriated, simply reaffirmed traditional guarantees, such as freedom of worship for local North African Christians.[18] The treaty did not permit Latin Christians to proselytize.

Louis IX's son and heir, Philip III, alluded to his late father's desire to extirpate the "errors" of the Saracens in a letter sent from camp to the ecclesiastical co-regent of the kingdom, Abbot Mathieu of Saint-Denis, describing conditions affecting the crusader army.[19] However, at the time he dictated it, the young man

14. "Einleitung" to Wilhelm von Tripolis, *Notitia de Machometo, De statu sarracenorum*, ed. Peter Engels (Würzburg: Echter, 1992), 34.

15. Geoffrey of Beaulieu, "Here Begins the Life," 120–21, paragraph 44, and 121 n. 284; Kedar, *Crusade and Mission*, 166.

16. Richard, *Saint Louis*, 571–72; Hélary, *La dernière croisade*, 184–89.

17. Hélary, *La dernière croisade*, 192–95.

18. Kedar, *Crusade and Mission*, 168–69.

19. Kedar, *Crusade and Mission*, 166.

was himself recovering from the illness he contracted during the siege.[20] He was unable to follow up immediately on his father's impulse and, in any event, never did—which does not mean that the dream of converting North Africa or Muslims and other non-Christians departed the French imagination forever.

There was some pessimism, of course, as John Tolan has shown.[21] Consider Louis IX's friend, the Dominican Humbert of Romans, and his reflections on the possibilities of Muslim conversion. In the 1260s, his treatise on preaching denigrated Islam in conventional ways.[22] Nevertheless, as master general of his order, he simultaneously supported missions.[23] On the eve of Louis IX's final crusade, he was urging his friars to become familiar with the Qur'an, practical advice to would-be missionaries and polemicists in the vanquished lands in which they hoped to carry out their work.[24] Ultimately, however, after the king's death Humbert's "zeal for external missions faded."[25] He even wrote a short version of his defense of crusading that said expressly that there were no good grounds for trying to convert Muslims. They were too dangerous. Resistance was the only answer to their constant aggression: "De conversione vero Sarracenorum nulla loquitur scriptura, nec in aliquo nos iuvat eorum vita, sed potius multos scandalizant infirmos et inter omnia genera infidelium armis nos fortius impugnare non cessant."[26]

More common, however, and much more optimistic, were the views expressed in the *De recuperatione* literature that developed strategies for the reconquest of the Holy Land after the loss of

20. Hélary, *La dernière croisade*, 165.

21. Tolan, *Saracens*, 245–51.

22. Humbertus de Romanis, *Liber de predicatione, sct. Cruci*, ed. Kurt Villads Jensen, 2007: in *Capitulum quartum*, "Quare crux imponitur peregrinantibus in subsidium terre sancte."

23. Humbert of Romans, *Treatise on Preaching*, ii; Vose, *Dominicans, Muslims and Jews*, 21.

24. Ninitte, "Defining the Perception of Muḥammad and Islam," 20.

25. Vose, *Dominicans, Muslims and Jews*, 48–50.

26. Portnykh, "Short Version of Humbert of Romans' Treatise," 83.

Acre in 1291.[27] Often enough these texts represent the potential new military initiatives as working in tandem with conversion efforts. As Renate Blumenfeld-Kosinski and Marianne Saghy have highlighted, the contemporary author Pierre Dubois developed this notion.[28] Is it merely coincidence that this Norman lawyer and French royal publicist, born around 1250, had served as an advocate in Coutances,[29] in whose microregion, the Coutançais, Louis IX had settled a few of the converts? Had he seen or heard of conversion succeeding there? However that may be, for centuries the idea of a French invasion and Muslim conversion in particular simply would not die.[30]

Ironically, as Yann Potin has shown in a provocative essay, in the long aftermath of the crusade of 1270 North African Muslims fashioned their own legend about the invading king, whom they called the *raydafrance*.[31] Its raw materials, embellished by centuries of retelling, were stories that medieval Arabic chroniclers told of the French king's reputed goodness, recognizing it as a kind of sanctity, even though inferior by being Christian in nature.[32] In the later retellings studied by Potin, Louis IX emerges

27. Jacques Paviot, "Comment reconquérir la Terre sainte et vaincre les Sarrasins?," in *Dei Gesta per Francos: Études sur les croisades dédiées à Jean Richard*, ed. Michel Balard, Benjamin Kedar, and Jonathan Riley-Smith, 79–85 (Aldershot, UK: Ashgate, 2001), 85.

28. Renate Blumenfeld-Kosinski, "Pierre Dubois (*ca.* 1250–1320) et Ernest Renan (1823–1892) en communauté de pensée? Quelques reflexions sur la colonisation et l'éducation des femmes." *Académie des inscriptions et belles-lettres: comptes rendus* Nov.–Dec. 2015: 1531–48 (1533–42 and 1546). See also Michael Evans, "Marriage as a Means of Conversion in Pierre Dubois's *De recuperatione*," in *Christianizing Peoples and Converting Individuals*, ed. Guyda Armstrong and Ian Wood, 195–202 (Turnhout: Brepols, 2000) and Marianne Saghy's introduction to Pierre Dubois, *De recuperatione* (forthcoming).

29. Blumenfeld-Kosinski, "Pierre Dubois," 1531.

30. See, e.g., Joseph Peterson, "'Admiration . . . for All That Is Sincerely Religious': Louis Veuillot and Catholic Representations of Islam and Empire in July Monarchy France," *French Historical Studies* 40 (2017): 475–507.

31. Yann Potin, "Saint Louis l'africain: histoire d'une mémoire inversée," *Afrique et histoire* 1 (2003): 23–74 (49 and 54–58).

32. El Merheb, "Louis IX in Medieval Arabic Sources," 294–97.

as a sublimely righteous man, full of virtues and of profound faith, moved to risk his life to save his enemies and bring them to his faith. Before Tunis, however, with the failure of the Muslim defenders to lay down their arms and convert, he came to the realization that God was punishing him, as He had in the king's first crusade. Angels lifted the metaphorical veil that had for so long prevented the pious ruler from seeing where truth really lay—in Islam, not in Christianity. The God-fearing French king had not died. He had slipped out of the Christian camp, according to the legend, converted to Islam, and remained in Tunisia while the dispirited and disease-afflicted crusader army melted away. (To maintain the persuasiveness of the legend, one would need to presume either that in the chaos of camp life, laborers mistook some of the many bones they loaded on the ships going back home for Louis IX's or that the crusaders conspired to hide the king's defection.) In this version of events, the holy *raydaf-rance* became a devout Muslim sage. Wishful thinking, to be sure, but the legend, a parodic fantasy of retribution, does suggest that Muslims retained the memory of precisely what their crusader opponents—especially Louis IX—had been up to. To this extent, they have been more perceptive than many modern students of his reign.

REFERENCES

Primary Sources

MANUSCRIPTS

I have consulted manuscripts in digital and traditional photograph form and originals in the collections of the University of California–Los Angeles Library, the Archives Nationales [AN], the Archives Départementales [AD], and the Bibliothèque nationale de France [BnF]. The titles/descriptions and shelf numbers of the individual manuscripts are provided in the notes.

PUBLISHED

Actes du Parlement de Paris. 2 vols. Ed. Edgar Boutaric. Paris: Henri Plon, 1863–1867.

Anecdotes historiques, légendes et apologues tirés du recueil inédit d'Étienne de Bourbon. Ed. Richard-Albert Lecoy de la Marche. Paris: Renouard, 1877.

"Apparitions des Égyptiens ou Bohémiens à Amiens, dans le XVe siècle." Ed. Hyacinthe Dusevel. *La Picardie* 6 (1860): 433–37.

Atlas historique de Saint-Denis: Des origines au XVIIIe siècle. Comp. Michaël Wyss et al. Paris: Editions de la Maison des Sciences de l'Homme, 1996.

Aucassin et Nicolette, chantefable du deuxième siècle. Trans. Alexandre Bida and Gaston Paris. Paris: Hachette, 1878.

Beaurepaire, Charles de. "De la Vicomté de l'Eau de Rouen." *Recueil des travaux de la Société libre d'agriculture, sciences, arts et belles-lettres de l'Eure*," third series, 3 (1854): 81–600.

Blessed Louis, the Most Glorious of Kings: Texts Relating to the Cult of Saint Louis of France. Ed. M. Cecilia Gaposchkin. Trans. M. Celia Gaposchkin and Phyllis Katz. Notre Dame, IN: University of Notre Dame Press, 2012.

Borgehammar, Stephan. "Heraclius Learns Humility: Two Early Latin Accounts Composed for the Celebration of *Exaltatio Crucis*." *Millennium (Jahrbuch zu Kultur und Geschichte des ersten Jahrtausends n. Chr./ Yearbook on the Culture and History of the First Millennium C.E.)* 6 (2009): 145–201.

Bruel, Alexandre. "Notes de Vyon d'Hérouval sur les baptisés et les convers et sur les enquêteurs royaux au temps de saint Louis et de ses successeurs (1234–1334)." *Bibliothèque de l'École des chartes*, sixth series, 3 (1867): 609–21.

Carolus-Barré, Louis. *Le procès de canonisation de saint Louis (1272–1297): essai de reconstitution.* Rome: École française de Rome, 1994.

Cartulaire de l'abbaye de Notre-Dame d'Ourscamp. Ed. Achille Peigné-Delacourt. Amiens: Lemer aîné, 1865.

Cartulaire de Notre-Dame de Chartres. 3 vols. Ed. Eugène de Lépinois and Lucien Merlet. Chartres: Garnier, 1862–1865.

"Cartulaire de Saint-Vincent de Laon (Arch. Vatican., Misc. Arm. X. 145): analyse et pièces inédites." Ed. René Poupardin. *Mémoires de la Société de l'histoire de Paris et de l'Ile de France* 29 (1902): 173–267.

Cartulaire du chapitre de la cathédrale d'Amiens. 2 vols. Ed. Edmond Soyez. Amiens: Yvert et Tellier and Auguste Picard, 1906–1912.

Chansons de croisade. Ed. Joseph Bédier and Pierre Aubry. Paris: Honoré Champion, 1909.

Chartularium Universitatis Parisiensis. Ed. Heinrich (Henri) Denifle and Emile Chatelain. 4 vols. Paris: Delalain, 1889–1894.

Chronicles of the Crusades, Being Contemporary Narratives of the Crusade of Richard Cœur de Lion, by Richard of Devizes and Geoffrey de Vinsauf; and of the Crusade of St. Louis, by Lord John de Joinville. Comp. Thomas Johnes and J. A. Giles. London: H. G. Bohn, 1848.

Collection de sceaux. 3 vols. Comp. Louis Douët d'Arcq. Paris: Henri Plon, 1863–1868.

Compte général du receveur d'Artois pour 1303–1304. Ed. Bernard Delmaire. Brussels: Académie Royale de Belgique, 1977.

Comptes du Trésor (1296, 1313, 1384, 1477). Ed. Robert Fawtier. Paris: Imprimerie nationale, 1930.

Comptes sur tablettes de cire de Jean Sarrazin, chambellan de Saint Louis. Ed. Elisabeth Lalou. Louvain: Brepols, 2003.

Comptes sur tablettes de cire de la chambre aux deniers de Philippe III le Hardi et de Philippe IV le Bel (1282–1309). Ed. Elisabeth Lalou. Paris: Boccard, 1994.

Crusade and Christendom: Annotated Documents in Translation from Innocent III to the Fall of Acre, 1187–1291. Ed. Jessalynn Bird, Edward Peters, and James Powell. Philadelphia: University of Pennsylvania Press, 2013.

Decrees of the Ecumenical Councils. 2 vols. Ed. Norman Tanner. London: Sheed and Ward, 1990.

Documents sur les relations de la royauté avec les villes en France de 1180 à 1314. Ed. Arthur Giry. Paris: A. Picard, 1885.

Dubois, Pierre. *De recuperatione.* Trans. Marianne Saghy. Forthcoming.

Du Cange, Charles du Fresne, et al. *Glossarium mediae et infimae Latinitatis.* 10 vols. Niort: L. Favre, 1883–1887.

"E breviario historiarum Landulphi de Columna, canonici Carnotensis." In *HF* vol. 23, 192–98.

"E chronico Normanniae." In *HF* vol. 23, 212–22.

"E chronico Sanctae Catharinae de Monte Rotomagi." In *HF* vol. 23, 397–410.

La fille du comte de Ponthieu, conte en prose: versions du XIIIe et du XVe siècle. Ed. Clovis Brunel. Paris: Honoré Champion, 1923.

Geoffrey of Beaulieu. "Here Begins the Life and Saintly Comportment of Louis, Former King of the Franks, of Pious Memory." In *The Sanctity of Louis IX,* 69–128.

Grandes chroniques de France. 10 vols. Ed. Jules Viard. Paris: Honoré Champion, 1920–1953.

Guillaume de Nangis. "Gesta sancti Ludovici." In *HF* vol. 20, 309–465.

Guillaume de Saint-Pathus. *Vie de saint Louis.* Ed. Henri-François Delaborde. Paris: Alphonse Picard et fils, 1899.

Havet, Jules. "Compte du Trésor du Louvre (Toussaint 1296)." *Bibliothèque de l'Ecole des chartes* 45 (1884): 237–99.

HF. See *Recueil des historiens des Gaules et de la France.*

Humbert of Romans. *Treatise on Preaching.* Ed. Walter Conlon. Trans. the Dominican Students of the Province of St. Joseph. Pine Beach, NJ: Newman Press, 1951.

Humbertus de Romanis. *Liber de predicatione sct. Cruci.* Ed. Kurt Villads Jensen. 2007. Online at http://www.jggj.dk/saracenos.htm.

Inventaire d'anciens comptes royaux dressé par Robert Mignon sous le règne de Philippe de Valois. Ed. Charles-Victor Langlois. Paris: Imprimerie nationale, 1899.

Inventaire des titres de Nevers de l'abbé de Marolles. Comp. Georges de Soultrait. Nevers: Paulin Fay, 1873.

Jacobus de Voragine. *The Golden Legend: Readings on the Saints.* Trans. William Granger Ryan. Princeton, NJ: Princeton University Press, 1993 (2012).

Jean de Joinville. *Life of Saint Louis.* In *Chronicles of the Crusades,* trans. Caroline Smith, 145–336. London: Penguin, 2008.

———. *Vie de saint Louis.* Ed. and trans. Jacques Monfrin. Paris: Garnier, 1995.

Layettes du Trésor des chartes. Ed. Alexandre Teulet et al. 5 vols. Paris: H. Plon, 1863–1909.

Leechdoms, Wortcunning, and Starcraft of Early England: Being a Collection of Documents, for the Most Part Never before Printed, Illustrating the History of Science in This Country before the Norman Conquest. 3 vols. Comp. Thomas Cockayne. London: Longman, Green/Longman, Roberts, and Green, 1864–1866.

Leonis X. Pontificis Maximi Regesta. Ed. Joseph Hergenroether. Freiburg im Breisgau: Herder, 1884.

"Liste des sergents du Châtelet de Paris en 1309." Ed. Marius Barroux. *Bulletin de la Société de l'histoire de Paris et de l'Ile de France* 20 (1893): 36–38.

"Le 'Livre' ou 'Cartulaire' de la Nation de Normandie de l'Université de Paris." Ed. Henri Omont. *Société de l'histoire de Normandie: Mélanges* 8 (1917): 8–114.

Ma'aseh Book: Book of Jewish Tales and Legends. 2 vols. Trans. Moses Gaster. Philadelphia: Jewish Publication Society of America, 1934.

Matthew Paris. *Chronica majora.* 7 vols. Ed. Henry Luard. London: Her Majesty's Stationery Office, 1872–1883.

Medieval Sourcebook: Al-Makrisi: Account of the Crusade of St. Louis. Comp. Paul Halsall. Online at https://sourcebooks.fordham.edu/source/makrisi.asp.

Mystère de saint Louis, roi de France. Ed. Francisque Michel. Westminster: Roxburghe Club, 1871.

"Notes sur quelques manuscrits du Musée britannique." Ed. Léopold Delisle. *Mémoires de la Société de l'histoire de Paris et de l'Ile de France* 4 (1877): 183–238.

Oeuvres complètes de Rutebeuf. 2 vols. Ed. Edmond Faral and Julia Bastin. Paris: A. and J. Picard, 1977.

Old French Prose Legend of Saint Julian the Hospitaller. Ed. Carolyn Swan. Tübingen: Niemeyer, 1977.

Olim, ou Registres des arrêts rendus par la Cour du roi. 3 vols. Ed. Arthur Beugnot. Paris: Imprimerie Royale, 1839–1848.

Paris sous Philippe-le-Bel, d'après des documents originaux, et notamment d'après un manuscrit contenant le role de la taille imposée sur les habitants de Paris en 1292. Ed. Hercule Géraud. Paris: Crapelet, 1837.

"Pope Boniface VIII's Bull *Gloria laus* (11 August 1297)." In *The Sanctity of Louis IX*: 160–72.

Portnykh, Valentin. "Short Version of Humbert of Romans' Treatise on the

Preaching of the Cross: An Edition of the Latin Text." *Crusades* 15 (2016): 55–115.

Primat. "Chronique." In *HF* vol. 23, 5–106.

Recueil des historiens des Gaules et de la France. 24 vols. Ed. Martin Bouquet et al. Paris: V. Palmé, 1840–1904.

Regestrum visitationum archiepiscopi rotomagensis/Journal des visites pastorales d'Eude Rigaud, archevêque de Rouen, MCCXLVIII–MCCLXIX. Ed. Théodose Bonnin. Rouen: A. Le Brument, 1852.

Register of Eudes of Rouen. Trans. Sydney Brown. Ed. Jeremiah O'Sullivan. New York: Columbia University Press, 1964.

Registre criminel de Saint-Germain-des-Prés. In *Histoire des justices des anciennes églises et communautés de Paris,* ed. Louis Tanon, 413–54. Paris: L. Larose et Forcel, 1883.

Renaut de Montauban. Ed. Philippe Verelst. Ghent: Romanica Gandensia, 1988.

"Rôles normands et français et autres pièces tirées des archives de Londres par Bréquigny en 1764, 1765 et 1766." Ed. Léon Puiseux. *Mémoires de la Société des antiquaires de Normandie* 23 (1858): 1–307.

Le Roman d'Aquin. Ed. F. Joüon des Longrais. Nantes: Société des Bibliophile Bretons, 1880.

Rutebeuf. *Oeuvres complètes.* Ed. and trans. Michel Zink. Paris: Bordas, 1989–1990.

Sainted Women of the Dark Ages. Ed. and trans. Jo Ann McNamara and John Halborg. Durham, NC: Duke University Press, 1992.

Salimbene de Adam. *Cronica.* 2 vols. Ed. Giuseppi Scalia. Bari: G. Laterza, 1966.

The Sanctity of Louis IX: Early Lives of Saint Louis by Geoffrey of Beaulieu and William of Chartres. Ed. M. Cecilia Gaposchkin and Sean Field. Trans. Larry Field. Ithaca, NY: Cornell University Press, 2014.

Seventh Crusade, 1244–1254: Sources and Documents. Comp. Peter Jackson. Aldershot, UK: Ashgate, 2007.

"Supplique de l'Université au pape pour la fondation d'un collège oriental à Paris." Ed. Henri Omont. *Bulletin de la Société de l'histoire de Paris et de l'Île de France* 18 (1891): 164–65.

Tales in Context: Sefer ha-ma'asim in Medieval Northern France (Bodleian Library, University of Oxford, Ms. Bodl. Or. 135). Ed. Rella Kushlevsky. Trans. Ruchie Avital and Chaya Naor. Commentary by Elisheva Baumgarten. Detroit: Wayne State University Press, 2017.

Thesaurus novus anecdotorum. Ed. Edmond Martène. 5 vols. Paris: Florentinus Delaulne, 1717.

Usāmah Ibn Munqidh. *An Arab-Syrian Gentleman and Warrior in the Period of the Crusades*. New York: Columbia University Press, 1929.

Wilhelm von Tripolis. *Notitia de Machometo, De statu sarracenorum*. Ed. Peter Engels. Würzburg: Echter, 1992.

William of Chartres. "On the Life and Deeds of Louis, King of the Franks of Famous Memory, and on the Miracles That Declare His Sanctity." In *The Sanctity of Louis IX*, 129–59.

William of Saint-Amour. *De periculis novissimorum temporum*. Ed. Guy Geltner. Paris: Peeters, 2008.

William of Saint-Pathus. See Guillaume de Saint-Pathus.

Secondary Sources

Abulafia, Anna Sapir. *Christian-Jewish Relations, 1000–1300: Jews in the Service of Medieval Christendom*. London: Routledge, 2011.

Abulafia, David. *Frederick II: A Medieval Emperor*. New York: Oxford University Press, 1988.

Akbari, Suzanne. "Embodying the Historical Moment: Tombs and Idols in the *Histoire ancienne jusqu'à César*." *Journal of Medieval and Early Modern European History* 44 (2014): 617–43.

Allan, James. "Muhammad ibn al-Zain: Craftsman in Cups, Thrones and Window Grilles?" *Levant* 28 (1996): 199–208.

Ames, Christine. *Medieval Heresies: Christianity, Judaism, and Islam*. New York: Cambridge University Press, 2015.

———. *Righteous Persecution: Inquisition, Dominicans, and Christianity in the Middle Ages*. Philadelphia: University of Pennsylvania Press, 2009.

Andrews, Frances. *The Early Humiliati*. Cambridge, UK: Cambridge University Press, 1999.

———. *The Other Friars: The Carmelite, Augustinian, Sack and Pied Friars*. Woodbridge, UK: Boydell, 2006.

Angold, Michael. *The Fourth Crusade*. Abingdon, UK: Routledge, 2014.

Arnold, John. "Persecution and Power in Medieval Europe: *The Formation of a Persecuting Society*, by R. I. Moore." *American Historical Review* 123 (2018): 165–74.

Baldwin, John. *The Government of Philip Augustus*. Berkeley: University of California Press, 1986.

———. *Masters, Princes and Merchants: The Social Views of Peter the Chanter and His Circle*. 2 vols. Princeton, NJ: Princeton University Press, 1970.

Bataillard, Paul. "De l'apparition et de la dispersion des Bohémiens en Europe." *Bibliothèque de l'Ecole des chartes* 5 (1844): 438–75.

Beaurepaire, Charles. *Archives départementales antérieures à 1790, Seine-Inférieure: archives ecclésiastiques—série G (nos. 8515–8962)*. Rouen: Julien Lecerf, 1900.

Bennett, Ralph. *The Early Dominicans: Studies in Thirteenth-Century Dominican History*. Cambridge, UK: Cambridge University Press, 1937.

Berger, David. "Jacob Katz on Jews and Christians in the Middle Ages." In *The Pride of Jacob*, ed. Jay Harris, 41–63. Cambridge, MA: Harvard University Press, 2002.

Berkey, Jonathan. "Audience and Authority in Medieval Islam: The Case of Popular Preachers." In *Charisma and Religious Authority: Jewish, Christian, and Muslim Preaching, 1200–1500*, ed. Katherine Jansen and Miri Rubin, 105–20. Turnhout: Brepols, 2010.

Bernard, Daniel. *Légendaire du Berry: au coeur de l'imaginaire populaire*. Saint-Cyr-sur-Loire: Alan Sutton, 2005.

Biddick, Kathleen. *The Typological Imaginary: Circumcision, Technology, History*. Philadelphia: University of Pennsylvania Press, 2003.

Biller, Peter. "Goodbye to Waldensianism?" *Past & Present* 192 (2006): 3–33.

Blancard, Louis. *Le bésant d'or sarrazinas, pendant les croisades: étude comparée sur les monnaies d'or, arabes et d'imitation arabe, frappées en Égypte et en Syrie, aux XIIme et XIIIme siècles*. Marseilles: Barlatier-Feissat, 1880.

Blumenfeld-Kosinski, Renate. "Pierre Dubois (*ca.* 1250–1320) et Ernest Renan (1823–1892) en communauté de pensée? Quelques reflexions sur la colonisation et l'éducation des femmes." *Académie des inscriptions et belles-lettres: comptes rendus* Nov.–Dec. 2015: 1531–48.

Bohak, Gideon. "God's Right Eye and Its Angel in Jewish and Christian Magic." In *Anges et démons d'orient et d'occident*, ed. Flavia Buzzetta, 63–89. Paris: Éditions Kimé, 2017.

Bolton, Brenda. "A Show with a Meaning: Innocent III's Approach to the Fourth Lateran Council, 1215." In *Innocent III: Studies on Papal Authority and Pastoral Care*, 53–67. Aldershot, UK: Variorum, 1995.

Bove, Boris. "Aux origines du complexe de supériorité des Parisiens: les louanges de Paris au moyen âge." *Mémoires de la Fédération des sociétés historique et archéologique de Paris et de l'Ile-de-France* 55 (2004): 423–43.

Braude, Benjamin. "Black Skin/White Skin in Ancient Greece and the Near East." In *Black Skin in the Middle Ages/Le peau noire au moyen âge*, 3–13. Florence: Edizioni del Galluzzo, 2014.

Brenner, Elma, and Leonie Hicks. "The Jews of Rouen in the Eleventh to the

Thirteenth Centuries." In *Society and Culture in Medieval Rouen, 911–1300*, 369–82. Turnhout: Brepols, 2013.

Brissaud, Jean. *A History of French Public Law*. Trans. James W. Garner. Boston: Little, Brown, 1915.

Brown, Elizabeth. "A Sixteenth-Century Defense of Saint Louis' Crusades: Étienne le Blanc and the Legacy of Louis IX." In *Cross Cultural Convergences in the Crusader Period: Essays Presented to Aryeh Grabois on His Sixty-Fifth Birthday*, ed. Michael Goodich, Sophia Menache, and Sylvia Schein, 21–48. New York: Peter Lang, 1995.

Brown, Peter. *The Rise of Western Christendom: Triumph and Diversity, A.D. 200–1000*. 2nd edition. Oxford: Blackwell, 2003.

Brown, Reva Berman, and Sean McCartney. "Living in Limbo: The Experience of Jewish Converts in Medieval England." In *Christianizing Peoples and Converting Individuals*, Ed. Guyda Armstrong and Ian Wood, 169–91. Turnhout: Brepols, 2000.

Buc, Philippe. "Crusade and Eschatology: Holy War Fostered and Inhibited." *Mitteilungen des Instituts für Österreichische Geschichtsforschung* 125 (2018): 304–39.

Burns, Robert. *Muslims, Christians, and Jews in the Crusader Kingdom of Valencia*. Cambridge, UK: Cambridge University Press, 1984.

Burr, David. *The Spiritual Franciscans: From Protest to Persecution in the Century after Saint Francis*. University Park: Pennsylvania State University Press, 2001.

Carolus-Barré, Louis. "L'ordonnance de Philippe le Hardi et l'organisation de la juridiction gracieuse." *Bibliothèque de l'École des chartes* 96 (1935): 5–48.

Carré de Busserolle, J.-X. *Dictionnaire géographique, historique et biographique d'Indre-et-Loire et de l'ancienne province de Touraine*. 6 vols. Mémoires de la Société archéologique de Touraine, 27–32. Tours: Rouillé-Ladevièze, 1878–1884.

Cartier, Étienne. "Remarques." *Revue numismatique* 12 (1847): 124–50.

Catlos, Brian. *Muslims of Medieval Latin Christendom c. 1050–1614*. Cambridge, UK: Cambridge University Press, 2014.

Cazelles, Raymond. "La condition du Parisien vers 1300." *Bulletin de la Société de l'histoire de Paris et de l'Île de France* 93 (1966): 49–50.

———. "La réunion au domaine royal de la voirie de Paris (1270–1363)." *Bulletin de la Société de l'histoire de Paris et de l'Île de France* 90 (1963): 45–60.

Charansonnet, Alexis, and Franco Morenzoni. "Prêcher sur les reliques de la

Passion à l'époque de saint Louis." In *La Sainte-Chapelle de Paris*, ed. Christine Hediger, 61–99.

Chazan, Robert. *The Jews of Medieval Western Christendom, 1000–1500*. Cambridge, UK: Cambridge University Press, 2006.

Cheyette, Frederic. "The Royal Safeguard in Medieval France." *Studia Gratiana* 15 (1972): 631–52.

Cochard, Théophile. *La juiverie d'Orléans du VIe au XVe siècle*. Orléans: Georges Michau, 1895.

Cochet, Jean Benoît Désiré. *Répertoire archéologique du département de la Seine-Inférieure*. Paris: Imprimerie nationale, 1871.

———. *La Seine-Inférieure et archéologique*. Paris: Derache, 1864.

Constable, Olivia Remie. *To Live Like a Moor: Christian Perceptions of Muslim Identity in Medieval and Early Modern Spain*. Ed. Robin Vose. Philadelphia: University of Pennsylvania Press, 2018.

Cruz, Joan. *Saints for the Sick*. Charlotte, NC: TAN Books, 2010.

Dancoisne, Louis. *Numismatique béthunoise*. Arras: Alphonse Brissy, 1859.

Davis, Adam. *The Holy Bureaucrat: Eudes Rigaud and Religious Reform in Thirteenth-Century Normandy*. Ithaca, NY: Cornell University Press, 2006.

Dejoux, Marie. *Les enquêtes de saint Louis: gouverner et sauver son âme*. Paris: Presses Universitaires de France, 2014.

Delisle, Léopold. "Paris et Paradis au moyen âge." *Bulletin de la Société de l'histoire de Paris et de l'Ile de France* 8 (1881): 29–31.

Derville, Alain. *Saint-Omer des origines au début du XIVe siècle*. Lille: Presses Universitaires de Lille, 1995.

Devaux, Jules. "Petits problèmes historiques." *Annales de la Société historique et archéologique du Gâtinais* 8 (1890): 95–109.

Di Cesare, Michelina. "Reading the Bible through Glass: The Image of Muhammad in the Sainte-Chapelle." In *The Image of the Prophet between Ideal and Ideology: A Scholarly Investigation*, ed. Christiane Gruber and Avinoam Shalem, 187–200. Berlin: De Gruyter, 2014.

Diehl, Peter. "Overcoming Reluctance to Prosecute Heresy in Thirteenth-Century Italy." In *Christendom and Its Discontents: Exclusion, Persecution, and Rebellion, 1000–1500*, ed. Scott Waugh and Peter Diehl, 47–66. Cambridge, UK: Cambridge University Press, 1996.

"Dissertation sur les dépenses et les recettes ordinaires de saint Louis." *HF* vol. 21, liii–lxxvii.

Duval, Louis. "Domfront aux XIIe et XIIIe siècles." *Bulletin de la Société historique et archéologiquede l'Orne* 8 (1889): 530–77.

Eddé, Anne-Marie. "Saint Louis et la Septième Croisade vus par les auteurs arabes." *Cahiers de recherches médiévales (XIIIe-XVe s.)* 1 (1996): 65–92.

Einbinder, Susan. *Beautiful Death: Jewish Poetry and Martyrdom in Medieval France.* Princeton, NJ: Princeton University Press, 2002.

Ellenblum, Ronnie. *Frankish Rural Settlement in the Latin Kingdom of Jerusalem.* Cambridge, UK: Cambridge University Press, 1998.

Elliott, Jessica. "Jews 'Feigning Devotion': Christian Representations of Converted Jews in French Chronicles before and after the Expulsion of 1306." In *Jews and Christians in Thirteenth-Century France*, ed. Elisheva Baumgarten and Judah Galinsky, 169–82. New York: Palgrave Macmillan, 2015.

El Merheb, Mohamad. "Louis IX in Medieval Arabic Sources: The Saint, the King, and the Sicilian Connection." *Al-Masāq: Journal of the Medieval Mediterranean*, 28 (2016): 282–301. DOI: 10.1080/09503110.2016.1243780.

England, Samuel. *Medieval Empires and the Culture of Competition: Literary Duels at Islamic and Christian Courts.* Edinburgh: Edinburgh University Press, 2017.

Evans, Michael. "Marriage as a Means of Conversion in Pierre Dubois's *De recuperatione Terre Sancte*." In *Christianizing Peoples and Converting Individuals*, ed. Guyda Armstrong and Ian Wood, 195–202. Turnhout: Brepols, 2000.

Fancy, Hussein. *The Mercenary Mediterranean: Sovereignty, Religion, and Violence in the Medieval Crown of Aragon.* Chicago: University of Chicago Press, 2016.

Farmer, Sharon. *The Silk Industries of Medieval Paris: Artisanal Migration, Technological Innovation, and Gendered Experience.* Philadelphia: University of Pennsylvania Press, 2017.

Favier, Jean. "Les légistes et le gouvernement de Philippe le Bel." *Journal des savants* 2 (1969): 92–108.

Fenster, Thelma. "French Language." In *Medieval France: An Encyclopedia*, ed. William Kibler and Grover Zinn, 370–74. New York: Garland, 1993.

Fernández, Damián. *Aristocrats and Statehood in Western Iberia, 300–600 C.E.* Philadelphia: University of Pennsylvania Press, 2017.

Fesler, James. "French Field Administration: The Beginnings." *Comparative Studies in Society and History* 5 (1962–1963): 76–111.

Field, Sean. *Courting Sanctity: Holy Women and the Capetians* (working title). Ithaca, NY: Cornell University Press. In press.

———. *Isabelle of France: Capetian Sanctity and Franciscan Identity in the*

Thirteenth Century. Notre Dame, IN: University of Notre Dame Press, 2006.

Flaubert, Gustave. "La légende de saint Julien l'Hospitalier." In *Trois contes*, new ed., 89–164. Paris: Bibliothèque-Charpentier, 1908.

Folda, Jaroslav. *Crusader Art in the Holy Land, from the Third Crusade to the Fall of Acre, 1187–1291.* Cambridge, UK: Cambridge University Press, 2005.

Forcadet, Pierre-Anne. "Les premiers juges de la Cour du roi au XIIIe siècle." *Revue historique de droit français et étranger* 94 (2016): 189–273.

FranceArchives. https://francearchives.fr/en/.

François, Michel. "Notes sur les lettres de rémission transcrites dans les registres du Trésor des chartes." *Bibliothèque de l'Ecole des chartes* 103 (1942): 317–24.

Friedman, Yvonne. "Women in Captivity and Their Ransom during the Crusader Period." In *Cross Cultural Convergences in the Crusader Period: Essays Presented to Aryeh Grabois on His Sixty-Fifth Birthday*, ed. Michael Goodich, Sophia Menache, and Sylvia Schein, 75–87. New York: Peter Lang, 1995.

Fudeman, Kirsten. *Vernacular Voices: Language and Identity in Medieval French Jewish Communities.* Philadelphia: University of Pennsylvania Press, 2010.

Fulton Brown, Rachel. *Mary and the Art of Prayer: The Hours of the Virgin in Medieval Christian Life and Thought.* New York: Columbia University Press, 2018.

Gaposchkin, M. Cecilia. "Making Capetian the Cross of Christ: A Paper in Honor of Peggy Brown,." Paper presented at "Paradigms and Personae in the Medieval World: A Symposium in Honor of Elizabeth A. R. Brown." Graduate Center, City University of New York, 16 March 2018. Typescript in the possession of the author of this book.

———. *The Making of Saint Louis: Kingship, Sanctity, and Crusade in the Later Middle Ages.* Ithaca, NY: Cornell University Press, 2008.

———. "The Place of the Crusades in the Sanctification of Saint Louis." In *Crusades: Medieval Worlds in Conflict*, ed. Thomas F. Madden, James Naus, and Vincent Ryan, 195–209. Burlington, VT: Ashgate, 2010.

Garcia-Serrano, Francisco. "Friars and Royal Authority in the Thirteenth-Century Castilian Frontier." In *Authority and Spectacle in Medieval and Early Modern Europe: Essays in Honor of Teofilo F. Ruiz*, ed. Yuen-Gen Liang and Jarbel Rodriguez, 104–17. London: Routledge, 2017.

Geneanet. https://pt.geneanet.org/.

Giard, Michel. *Dictionnaire du Cotentin.* [Brest]: Le Télégramme, 2012.

Gillingham, John. *Richard I.* New Haven, CT: Yale University Press, 1999.

Giry, Arthur. *Manuel de diplomatique.* Paris: Hachette, 1894.

Given, James. *Inquisition and Medieval Society: Power, Discipline, and Resistance in Languedoc.* Ithaca, NY: Cornell University Press, 1997.

———. "Social Stress, Social Strain, and the Inquisitors of Medieval Languedoc." In *Christendom and Its Discontents: Exclusion, Persecution, and Rebellion, 1000–1500,* ed. Scott Waugh and Peter Diehl, 67–85. Cambridge, UK: Cambridge University Press, 1996.

Goldin, Simha. *The Ways of Jewish Martyrdom.* Ed. C. Michael Copeland. Trans. Yigal Levin. Turnhout: Brepols, 2008.

Griffith, Reginald. *Sir Perceval of Galles: A Study of the Sources of the Legend.* Chicago: University of Chicago Press, 1911.

Haldon, John. *The Empire That Would Not Die: The Paradox of Eastern Roman Survival, 640–740.* Cambridge, MA: Harvard University Press, 2016.

Hare, John. "Inns, Innkeepers and the Society of Later Medieval England, 1350–1600." *Journal of Medieval History* 39 (2013): 477–97.

Head, Thomas. *Hagiography and the Cult of Saints: The Diocese of Orléans, 800–1200.* Cambridge, UK: Cambridge University Press, 1990.

Hecht, Jennifer. *Suicide: A History of Suicide and the Philosophies against It.* New Haven, CT: Yale University Press, 2013.

Hedeman, Anne. *The Royal Image: Illustrations of Grandes chroniques de France, 1274–1422.* Berkeley: University of California Press, 1991.

Hélary, Xavier. *La dernière croisade: saint Louis à Tunis (1270).* Paris: Perrin, 2016.

———. "Les rois de France et la Terre sainte: De la croisade de Tunis à la chute d'Acre (1270–1291)." *Annuaire-Bulletin de la Société de l'histoire de France* (2005), 21–104.

Heng, Geraldine. *The Invention of Race in the European Middle Ages.* Cambridge, UK: Cambridge University Press, 2018.

Hillenbrand, Carole. *The Crusades: Islamic Perspectives.* Edinburgh: Edinburgh University Press, 1999.

Hindley, Alan, Frederick Langley, and Brian Levy. *Old French–English Dictionary.* Cambridge, UK: Cambridge University Press, 2000.

Histoire littéraire de la France. New ed. 45 vols. Paris: V. Palmé, 1865–.

History of the Crusades. 2nd ed. 6 vols. Ed. Kenneth Setton. Madison, WI: University of Wisconsin Press, 1969–1989.

Holt, Peter. *The Age of the Crusades: The Near East from the Eleventh Century to 1517.* London: Longman, 1986.

Hood, John. *Aquinas and the Jews*. Philadelphia: University of Pennsylvania Press, 1995.

Horowitz, Jeannine. "Popular Preaching in the Thirteenth Century: Rhetoric in the Fight against Heresy." *Medieval Sermon Studies*, 60 (2016): 62–76.

Hoyt, Douglas. "A Chronology of Notable Weather Events," 4 August 2011. Online at http://www.breadandbutterscience.com/climatehistory.pdf.

Illiers, Louis d'. *L'histoire d'Orléans*. New ed. Orléans: Lodé, 1954.

Jackson, Peter. *The Mongols and the West, 1221–1410*. Abingdon, UK: Routledge, 2014.

Jacobs, Andrew. *Christ Circumcised: A Study in Early Christian History and Difference*. Philadelphia: University of Pennsylvania Press, 2012.

Jacoby, David. "Society, Culture, and the Arts in Crusader Acre." In *France and the Holy Land: Frankish Culture at the End of the Crusades*, ed. Daniel Weiss and Lisa Mahoney, 97–137. Baltimore: Johns Hopkins University Press, 2004.

Jordan, Alyce. "Seeing Stories in the Windows of the Sainte-Chapelle: The *Ars Poetriae* and the Politics of Visual Narrative." *Mediaevalia* 23 (2002): 39–60.

———. *Visualizing Kingship in the Windows of the Sainte-Chapelle*. Turnhout: Brepols, 2002.

Jordan, William Chester. "'Amen!' Cinq fois 'Amen!': les chansons de la croisade égyptienne de saint Louis, une source négligée d'opinion royaliste." *Médiévales* 34 (1998): 79–91.

———. "Anti-Corruption Campaigns in Thirteenth-Century Europe." *Journal of Medieval History* 35 (2009): 204–19.

———. "Archbishop Eudes Rigaud and the Jews of Normandy, 1248–1275." In *Friars and Jews in the Middle Ages and Renaissance*, ed. Steven McMichael and Susan Myers, 39–52. Leiden: Brill, 2004.

———. "Communal Administration in France, 1257–1270: Problems Discovered and Solutions Imposed." *Revue belge de philologie et d'histoire* 59 (1981): 292–313.

———. "*Etiam reges*, Even Kings." *Speculum* 90 (2015): 613–34.

———. "Exclusion and the Yearning to Belong: Evidence from the History of Thirteenth-Century France." In *Difference and Identity in Francia and Medieval France*, ed. Meredith Cohen and Justine Firnhaber-Baker, 13–24. Farnham, UK: Ashgate, 2010.

———. *The French Monarchy and the Jews from Philip Augustus to the Last Capetians*. Philadelphia: University of Pennsylvania Press, 1989.

Jordan, William Chester. *From England to France: Felony and Exile in the High Middle Ages.* Princeton, NJ: Princeton University Press, 2015.

―――. *From Servitude to Freedom: Manumission in the Sénonais in the Thirteenth Century.* Philadelphia: University of Pennsylvania Press, 1986.

―――. "The Gleaners." In *Boundaries in the Medieval and Wider World: Essays in Honour of Paul Freedman,* ed. Thomas Barton, Susan McDonough, Sara McDougall, and Matthew Wranovix, 201–20. Turnhout: Brepols, 2017.

―――. *The Great Famine: Northern Europe in the Early Fourteenth Century.* Princeton, NJ: Princeton University Press, 1996.

―――. "Learning about Jews in the Classroom: A Thirteenth-Century Witness, UCLA Library, Rouse MS 17." In *Envisioning Judaism: Studies in Honor of Peter Schäfer on the Occasion of His Seventieth Birthday,* ed. Ra'anan Boustan et al., vol. 2, 1247–60. Tübingen: Mohr Siebeck, 2013.

―――. *Louis IX and the Challenge of the Crusade: A Study in Rulership.* Princeton, NJ: Princeton University Press, 1979.

―――. "Louis IX: Preaching to Franciscan and Dominican Brothers and Nuns." In *Defenders and Critics of Franciscan Life: Essays in Honor of John V. Fleming,* ed. Michael Cusato and Guy Geltner, 219–35. Leiden: Brill, 2009.

―――. "Marian Devotion and the Talmud Trial of 1240." In *Religionsgespräche im Mittelalter,* ed. Bernard Lewis and Friedrich Niewöhner, 61–76. Wiesbaden: Harrassowitz, 1992.

―――. *Men at the Center: Redemptive Governance under Louis IX.* Budapest: Central European University Press, 2012.

―――. "The Psalter of Saint Louis (BN MS Lat. 10525): The Program of the Seventy-Eight Full-Page Illustrations." *ACTA* 7 (1980): 65–91.

―――. "Supplying Aigues-Mortes for the Crusade of 1248: The Problem of Restructuring Trade." In *Order and Innovation in the Middle Ages: Essays in Honor of Joseph R. Strayer,* ed. William Jordan, Bruce McNab, and Teofilo Ruiz, 165–72. Princeton, NJ: Princeton University Press, 1976.

―――. *A Tale of Two Monasteries: Westminster and Saint-Denis in the Thirteenth Century.* Princeton, NJ: Princeton University Press, 2009.

Jotischky, Andrew. *The Carmelites and Antiquity: Mendicants and Their Pasts in the Middle Ages.* Oxford, UK: Oxford University Press, 2002.

Kedar, Benjamin. *Crusade and Mission: European Approaches toward the Muslims.* Princeton, NJ: Princeton University Press, 1984.

―――. "Latins and Oriental Christians in the Frankish Levant, 1099–1291." In *Franks, Muslims and Oriental Christians in the Latin Levant: Stud-*

ies in Frontier Acculturation, 209–22. Aldershot, UK: Ashgate/Variorum, 2006.

———. "Multidirectional Conversion in the Frankish Levant." In *Varieties of Religious Conversion in the Middle Ages*, ed. James Muldoon, 190–99. Gainesville: University Press of Florida, 1997.

———. "Muslim Conversion in Canon Law." In *The Franks in the Levant, 11th to 14th Centuries*, 321–32. Aldershot, UK: Ashgate/Variorum, 1993.

———. "Passenger List of a Crusader Ship, 1250: Towards the History of the Popular Element on the Seventh Crusade." *Studi medievali* 13 (1972): 267–79.

———. "The Subjected Muslims of the Frankish Levant." In *The Franks in the Levant, 11th to 14th Centuries*, 135–74. Aldershot, UK: Ashgate/Variorum, 1993.

Keene, Derek. "Crisis Management in London's Food Supply, 1250–1500." In *Commercial Activity, Markets and Entrepreneurs in the Middle Ages: Essays in Honour of Richard Britnell*, ed. Ben Dodds and Christian Liddy, 45–62. Woodbridge, UK: Boydell, 2011.

Kumler, Aden. *Translating Truth: Ambitious Images and Religious Knowledge in Late Medieval France and England*. New Haven, CT: Yale University Press, 2011.

Labarge, Margaret. "Saint Louis et les juifs." In *Siècle de saint Louis*, ed. Régine Pernoud, 267–74. Paris: Hachette, 1970.

Lambert, Malcolm. *Medieval Heresy: Popular Movements from the Gregorian Reform to the Reformation*. 3rd ed. Oxford: Blackwell, 2002.

Latham, R. E. *Revised Medieval Latin Word-List*. London: Oxford University Press, 1965.

La Tramblais, Louis de. "De la signification et de la convenance des noms de lieux en Berry, et particulièrement dans le département de l'Indre." *Compte rendu des travaux de la Société du Berry* 13 (1866): 330–66.

Le Goff, Jacques. *Saint Francis of Assisi*. Trans. Christine Rhone. London: Routledge, 2004.

———. *Saint Louis*. Paris: Gallimard, 1996.

Legrand, Maxime. "Les ruines romaines et les mosaïques de Souzy-la-Briche." *Annales de la Société historique et archéologique du Gâtinais* 3 (1885): 85–121.

Lekai, Louis. *The Cistercians: Ideals and Reality*. Kent, OH: Kent State University Press, 1977.

Le Nain de Tillemont, Louis-Sébastien. *Vie de saint Louis, roi de France*. 6 vols. Ed. J. de Gaulle. Paris: J. Renouard, 1847–1851.

Lépinois, Eugène de. *Histoire de Chartres*. 2 vols. Chartres: Garnier, 1854–1858.

Lester, Anne. "Confessor King, Martyr Saint: Praying to Saint Maurice at Senlis." In *Defenders and Critics of Franciscan Life: Essays in Honor of John V. Fleming*, ed. Michael Cusato and Guy Geltner, 195–210. Leiden: Brill, 2009.

———. "What Remains: Women, Relics and Remembrance in the Aftermath of the Fourth Crusade." *Journal of Medieval History* 40 (2014): 311–28.

Levin, Chaviva. "Constructing Memories of Martyrdom: Contrasting Portrayals of Martyrdom in the Hebrew Narratives of the First and Second Crusade." In *Remembering the Crusades: Myth, Image, and Identity*, ed. Nicholas Paul and Suzanne Yeager, 50–68. Baltimore: Johns Hopkins University Press, 2012.

Lew-Williams, Beth. *The Chinese Must Go: Violence, Exclusion, and the Making of the Alien in America*. Cambridge, MA: Harvard University Press, 2018.

Lexique de l'Ancien Français. Comp. Frédéric Godefroy. Paris: H. Welter, 1901.

Liénard, Félix. *Dictionnaire topographique du département de la Meuse*. Paris: Imprimerie nationale, 1872.

Lodge, R. Anthony. *French: From Dialect to Standard*. London: Routledge, 1993.

Lower, Michael. "Conversion and Saint Louis's Last Crusade." *Journal of Ecclesiastical History* 58 (2007): 211–31.

MacPhail, Eric. "Ecolier Limousin (Limousin Schoolboy)." In *The Rabelais Encyclopedia*, ed. Elizabeth Zegura, 61–62. Westport, CT: Greenwood Press, 2004.

Maier, Christoph. "*Civilis ac pia regis Francorum deceptio*: Louis IX as Crusade Preacher." In *Dei Gesta per Francos: Études sur les croisades dédiées à Jean Richard*, ed. Michel Balard, Benjamin Kedar, and Jonathan Riley-Smith, 57–63. Aldershot, UK: Ashgate, 2001.

Makariou, Sophie. "Baptistère de Saint Louis." In *Les arts de l'Islam au musée du Louvre*, ed. Sophie Makariou, 282–88. Paris: Hazan and Musée du Louvre, 2012.

———. *Le Baptistère de Saint Louis*. Paris: Somogy, 2012.

Malaviya, Govind. "Review: Sensory Perception in Leprosy-Neurophysiological Correlates." *International Journal of Leprosy and Other Mycobacterial Diseases* 71 (2003): 119–24.

Mallett, Alex. *Popular Muslim Reactions to the Franks in the Levant, 1097–1291*. Farnham, UK: Ashgate, 2014.

Malloy, Alex, Irene Preston, and Arthur Seltman. *Coins of the Crusader States 1098-1291: including the Kingdom of Jerusalem and Its Vassal States of Syria and Palestine, the Lusignan Kingdom of Cyprus (1192-1489), and the Latin Empire of Constantinople and Its Vassal States of Greece and the Archipelago*. 2nd ed. Fairfield, CT: Berman, 2004.

Martène, Edmond. *Histoire de l'abbaye de Marmoutier*. 2 vols. Mémoires de la Société archéologique de Touraine, 24-25. Tours: Rouillé-Ladevièze, 1874-1875.

Mas Latrie, Louis de. *Histoire de l'île de Chypre sous le règne des princes de la maison de Lusignan*. 3 vols. Paris: Imprimerie impériale, 1852-1861.

Massoni, Anne. "Saint-Germain-l'Auxerrois de Paris à la fin du moyen âge." *Bulletin de la Société de l'histoire de Paris et de l'Ile de France* 141 (2014): 17-33.

Matton, Auguste. *Inventaire sommaire des Archives départementales antérieures à 1790: Aisne, archives ecclésiastiques—série G et H*. Vol. 3. Laon: A. Cortilliot, 1885.

Mémoires et notes de M. Auguste Le Prevost pour servirr à l'histoire du département de l'Eure. 3 vols. Ed. Léopold Delisle and Louis Passy. Évreux: Auguste Hérissey, 1862-1869.

Menache, Sophia. "Written and Oral Testimonies in Medieval Chronicles: Matthew Paris and Giovanni Villani." *Medieval Chronicle* 6 (2009): 1-30.

Meschini, Marco. "The 'Four Crusades' of 1204." In *The Fourth Crusade: Event, Aftermath, and Perceptions*, ed. Thomas Madden, 27-42. Aldershot, UK: Ashgate, 2008.

Metcalf, David. *Coinage of the Crusades and the Latin East in the Ashmolean Museum Oxford*. London: Royal Numismatic Society/Society for the Study of the Crusades and the Latin East, 1995.

Meyer, Paul. "Paris sans pair." *Bulletin de la Société de l'histoire de Paris et de l'Ile de France* 10 (1883): 26-28.

Mézeray, François de. *Histoire de France depuis Faramond jusqu'au règne de Louis le Juste*. Vol. 2. 2nd ed. Paris: Denys Thierry et al., 1685.

Michel, Robert. *L'administration royale dans la sénéchaussée de Beaucaire au temps de saint Louis*. Paris: Alphonse Picard et fils, 1910.

Miller, Kathryn. *Guardians of Islam: Religious Authority and Muslim Communities of Late Medieval Spain*. New York: Columbia University Press, 2008.

Miller, Tanya. *The Beguines of Medieval Paris: Gender, Patronage, and Spiritual Authority*. Philadelphia: University of Pennsylvania Press, 2014.

Monson-Fitzjohn, Gilbert. *Quaint Signs of Olde Inns*. London: Herbert Jenkins, 1926.

Mooney, Catherine. *Clare of Assisi and the Thirteenth-Century Church: Religious Women, Rules and Resistance.* Philadelphia: University of Pennsylvania Press, 2016.

Moore, John. *Pope Innocent III (1160/61–1216): To Root Up and to Plant.* Leiden: Brill, 2003.

Moore, Robert. *The Origins of European Dissent.* New York: Blackwell, 1985.

Moréri, Louis. *Le grand dictionnaire historique, ou Le mélange curieux de l'histoire sacrée et profane.* 10 vols. Paris: Les libraires associés, 1759.

Morlet, Marie-Thérèse. *Étude d'anthroponymie picarde: les noms de personne en Haute Picardie aux XIIIe, XIVe, XVe siècles.* Amiens: Musée de Picardie, 1967.

Morton, Nicholas. "The Teutonic Knights in the Holy Land, 1190–1291." Interview online at https://boydellandbrewer.com/medieval-herald -teutonic-knights (accessed 13 December 2017).

Nadhiri, Aman. *Saracens and Franks in 12th–15th Century European and Near Eastern Literature: Perceptions of Self and the Other.* London: Routledge, 2017.

Nicolle, David. *Acre 1291: Bloody Sunset of the Crusader States.* Oxford: Osprey, 2005.

———. *The Fourth Crusade 1202–04: The Betrayal of Byzantium.* Oxford: Osprey, 2011.

Niermeyer, J. F. *Mediae Latinitatis, lexicon minus.* Leiden: E. J. Brill, 1976.

Ninitte, Florence. "Defining the Perception of Muḥammad and Islam in Vincent of Beauvais' *Speculum historiale* and Its French Translation by Jean de Vignay." *Vincent of Beauvais Newsletter* 41 (2017): 15–34.

Les noms de lieux in Eure-et-Loir (microtoponymie). Vol. 4: *Canton de Courville (28 1 12).* Chartres: Société archéologique d'Eure-et-Loir, 1995.

Nowacka, Keiko. "Persecution, Marginalization, or Tolerance: Prostitutes in Thirteenth-Century Parisian Society." In *Difference and Identity in Francia and Medieval France,* ed. Meredith Cohen and Justine Firnhaber-Baker, 175–96. Farnham, UK: Ashgate, 2010.

Omont, Henri. "Richard de Saint-Laurent et le Liber de laudibus beatae Mariae." *Bibliothèque de l'École des chartes* 42 (1884): 503–4.

Park, Danielle E. A. *Papal Protection and the Crusader: Flanders, Champagne, and the Kingdom of France, 1095–1222.* Woodbridge, UK: Boydell, 2018.

Parkes, James. *The Jew in the Medieval Community: A Study of His Political and Economic Situation.* 2nd ed. New York: Hermon Press, 1976.

Pastoureau, Michel. *The Devil's Cloth: A History of Stripes and Striped*

Cloth. Trans. Jody Gladding. New York: Columbia University Press, 2001.

Pattenden, Miles. "The Canonisation of Clare of Assisi and Early Franciscan History." *Journal of Ecclesiastical History* 59 (2008): 208–26.

Paul, Nicholas. *To Follow in Their Footsteps: The Crusades and Family Memory in the High Middle Ages.* Ithaca, NY: Cornell University Press, 2013.

Paviot, Jacques. "Comment reconquérir la Terre sainte et vaincre les Sarrasins?" In *Dei Gesta per Francos: Études sur les croisades dédiées à Jean Richard,* ed. Michel Balard, Benjamin Kedar, and Jonathan Riley-Smith, 79–85. Aldershot, UK: Ashgate, 2001.

Payne, Richard E. *A State of Mixture: Christians, Zoroastrians, and Iranian Political Culture in Late Antiquity.* Oakland: University of California Press, 2015.

Pearce, Raymond, David Lloyd, and David McDonnell. "The Post-Christmas 'French' Storms of 1999." *Weather* 56 (2001): 81–91.

Pegg, Mark. *The Corruption of Angels: The Great Inquisition of 1245–1246.* Princeton, NJ: Princeton University Press, 2001.

———. *A Most Holy War: The Albigensian Crusade and the Battle for Christendom.* New York: Oxford University Press, 2008.

Pegues, Franklin. *The Lawyers of the Last Capetians.* Princeton, NJ: Princeton University Press, 1962.

Peters, Edward. *Inquisition.* Berkeley: University of California Press, 1988.

———. "There and Back Again: Crusaders in Motion, 1096–1291." *Crusades* 5 (2006): 157–71.

Peters, Rudolph, and Gert De Vries. "Apostasy in Islam." *Die Welt des Islams* 17 (1976): 1–25.

Peterson, Joseph. "'Admiration . . . for All That Is Sincerely Religious': Louis Veuillot and Catholic Representations of Islam and Empire in July Monarchy France." *French Historical Studies* 40 (2017): 475–507.

Phillips, Jonathan. *The Fourth Crusade and the Sack of Constantinople.* New York: Viking, 2004.

Phillips, Jonathan, Thomas F. Madden, Marcus Bull, and Andrew Jotischky, eds. *The Cambridge History of the Crusades.* 2 vols. Cambridge, UK: Cambridge University Press, expected 2018.

Pierce, Jerry. *Poverty, Heresy, and the Apocalypse: The Order of the Apostles in Medieval Italy, 1260–1307.* New York: Continuum, 2012.

Potin, Yann. "Saint Louis l'africain: histoire d'une mémoire inversée." *Afrique et histoire* 1 (2003): 23–74.

Powell, James. *Anatomy of a Crusade, 1213–1221.* Philadelphia: University of Pennsylvania Press, 1986.

Ramey, Lynn. *Black Legacies: Race and the European Middle Ages.* Gainesville: University Press of Florida, 2014.

———. *Christian, Saracen and Genre in Medieval French Literature.* New York: Routledge, 2001.

Randolph, Adrian. "The Bastides of Southwest France." *Art Bulletin* 77 (1995): 290–307.

"Regions of France." Online at http://www.regions-of-france.com/regions.

Reimitz, Helmut. *History, Frankish Identity and the Framing of Western Ethnicity, 550–850.* Cambridge, UK: Cambridge University Press, 2015.

Reyerson, Kathryn. "Medieval Hospitality: Innkeepers and the Infrastructure of Trade in Montpellier during the Middle Ages." *Proceedings of the Western Society for French History* 24 (1997): 38–51.

Reynolds, Elizabeth. "The Development of Stained Glass in Gothic Cathedrals." *JCCC Honors Journal* 4 (2012): 1–11.

Rice, David. *Le Baptistère de Saint Louis.* Paris: Éditions du Chêne, 1951.

———. "The Blazons of the 'Baptistère de Saint Louis.'" *Bulletin of the School of Oriental and African Studies* 13 (1950): 367–80.

Richard, Jean. *Histoire des croisades.* Paris: Fayard, 1996.

———. *Saint Louis.* Paris: Fayard, 1983.

"Richard of Chichester (Richard de Wych)." In *Oxford Dictionary of Saints,* ed. David Farmer. 5th ed. Online at http://www.oxfordreference.com/view/10.1093/acref/9780199596607.001.0001/acref-9780199596607.

Riley-Smith, Jonathan. *The Crusades, Christianity, and Islam.* New York: Columbia University Press, 2008.

Riley-Smith, Jonathan, Jonathan Phillips, Alan Murray, Guy Perry, and Nicholas Morton. "A Database of Crusaders to the Holy Land, 1095–1149." Online at https://www.hrionline.ac.uk/crusaders.

Roberg, Burkhard. *Das zweite Konzil von Lyon [1274].* Paderborn: Ferdinand Schöningh, 1990.

Roblin, Michel. *Le terroir de Paris aux époques gallo-romane et franque.* Paris: A. et J. Picard, 1951.

Rollo-Koster, Joëlle. "From Prostitutes to Brides of Christ: The Avignonese *Repenties* in the Late Middle Ages." *Journal of Medieval and Early Modern Studies* 32 (2002): 109–44.

Roserot, Alphonse. *Dictionnaire topographique du département de la Haute-Marne.* Paris: Imprimerie nationale, 1903.

Routledge, Michael. "Songs." In *The Oxford Illustrated History of the Crusades,* ed. Jonathan Riley-Smith, 91–111. Oxford: Oxford University Press, 1997.

Rubenstein, Jay. *Armies of Heaven: The First Crusade and the Quest for Apocalypse*. New York: Basic, 2011.

———. "Lambert of Saint-Omer and the Apocalyptic First Crusade." In *Remembering the Crusades: Myth, Image, and Identity*, ed. Nicholas Paul and Suzanne Yeager, 69–95. Baltimore: Johns Hopkins University Press, 2012.

Runciman, Steven. *A History of the Crusades*. 3 vols. Cambridge, UK: Cambridge University Press, 1951.

Sackville, Lucy. *Heresy and Heretics in the Thirteenth Century: The Textual Representations*. York: York Medieval Press, 2011.

Sadourny, Alain. "Les rentes à Rouen au XIIIe siècle." *Annales de Normandie* 21 (1971): 99–108.

La Sainte-Chapelle de Paris: Royaume de France ou Jérusalem céleste? Ed. Christine Hediger. Turnhout: Brepols, 2001.

Saussey, Charles (Carolus Sausseius). *Annales ecclesiae aurelianensis saeculis et libris sexdecim*. Paris: Hieronymus Drouart, 1615.

Schmieder, Felicitas. "Christians, Jews, Muslims—and Mongols: Fitting a Foreign People into the Western Christian Apocalyptic Scenario." *Medieval Encounters* 12 (2006): 274–95.

Schulenberg, Jane Tibbetts. "Women's Monasteries and Sacred Space: The Promotion of Saints' Cults and Miracles." In *Gender and Christianity in Medieval Europe*, ed. Lisa Bitel and Felice Lifshitz, 68–86. Philadelphia: University of Pennsylvania Press, 2008.

Sède, Sophie de. *La Sainte-Chapelle et la politique de la fin des temps*. Paris: Julliard, 1972.

Severt, Jacques (Jacobus Servertius). *Chronologia historica*. 2nd ed. Lyon: Simon Rigaud, 1628.

Shoham-Steiner, Ephraim. "An Almost Tangible Presence: Some Thoughts on Material Purity among Medieval European Jews." In *Discourses of Purity in Transcultural Perspective (300–1600)*, ed. Matthias Bley, Nikolas Jaspert, and Stefan Köck, 54–74. Leiden: Brill, 2015.

Siberry, Elizabeth. *Criticism of Crusading, 1095–1274*. Oxford: Clarendon Press, 1985.

Sibon, Juliette. *Chasser les juifs pour régner*. Paris: Perrin, 2016.

———. *Les juifs au temps de saint Louis*. Paris: Albin Michel, 2017.

Simonsohn, Uriel. "Halting between Two Opinions: Conversion and Apostasy in Early Islam." *Medieval Encounters* 19 (2013): 342–70.

Sivan, Emmanuel. *L'Islam et la croisade: Idéologie et propaganda dans les réactions musulmanes aux croisades*. Paris: Maisonneuve, 1968.

Spiegel, Gabrielle. *The Chronicle Tradition of Saint-Denis.* Brookline, MA: Classical Folia Editions, 1978.

Stacey, Robert. "The Conversion of Jews to Christianity in Thirteenth-Century England." *Speculum* 67 (1992): 263–83.

Stanton, Charles. *Medieval Maritime Warfare.* Barnsley, UK: Pen and Sword Maritime, 2015.

Strayer, Joseph. *The Administration of Normandy under Saint Louis.* Cambridge, MA: Mediaeval Academy of America, 1932.

———. *The Reign of Philip the Fair.* Princeton, NJ: Princeton University Press, 1980.

Strickland, Debra. *Saracens, Demons, and Jews: Making Monsters in Medieval Art.* Princeton, NJ: Princeton University Press, 2003.

Taylor, Julie. *Muslims in Medieval Italy: The Colony at Lucera.* Oxford: Lexington Books, 2003.

Thompson, Augustine. *Francis of Assisi: A New Biography.* London: Cornell University Press, 2012.

timeanddate.com. Online at https://www.timeanddate.com/.

Tolan, John. "Royal Policy and Conversion of Jews to Christianity in Thirteenth-Century Europe." In *Contesting Inter-Religious Conversion in the Medieval World,* ed. Yaniv Fox and Yosi Yisraeli, 96–111. London: Routledge, 2017.

———. *Saracens: Islam in the Medieval European Imagination.* New York: Columbia University Press, 2002.

Upper Normandy Weather and Climate. Online at http://www.regions-of-france.com/regions/upper_normandy/weather/.

Vander Elst, Stefan. *The Knight, the Cross, and the Song.* Philadelphia: University of Pennsylvania Press, 2017.

Vaughan, Richard. *Matthew Paris.* Cambridge, UK: Cambridge University Press, 1958.

Vicaire, Marie-Humbert. "La naissance de Sainte-Marie de Prouille." In Pierre Mandonnet, *Saint Dominique: l'idée, l'homme et l'oeuvre,* vol. 1, 99–114. Paris: Desclée De Brouwer, 1937.

Vincent, Nicholas. "'Corruent Nobiles!': Prophecy and Parody in Burton Abbey's Flying Circus." In press.

Vitraux de Notre-Dame et de la Sainte-Chapelle de Paris. Comp. Marcel Aubert et al. Paris: Caisse nationale des monuments historiques, 1959.

Vose, Robin. *Dominicans, Muslims and Jews in the Medieval Crown of Aragon.* New York: Cambridge University Press. 2009.

Ward, Rachel. "The 'Baptistère de Saint Louis'—A Mamluk Basin Made for

Export to Europe." In *Islam and the Italian Renaissance*, 113–32. London: Warburg Institute Colloquia, 1999.

Wood, Charles. *The French Apanages and the Capetian Monarchy 1224–1328*. Cambridge, MA: Harvard University Press, 1966.

Worcester, Thomas. "The Classical Sermon." In *Preaching, Sermon and Cultural Change in the Long Eighteenth Century*, ed. Joris van Eijnatten, 133–72. Leiden: Brill, 2009.

INDEX

Jews, Christians, and Muslims from the Ancient to the Modern World

EDITED BY MICHAEL COOK, WILLIAM CHESTER JORDAN, AND PETER SCHÄFER

A NOTE ON THE TYPE

THIS BOOK has been composed in Miller, a Scotch Roman typeface designed by Matthew Carter and first released by Font Bureau in 1997. It resembles Monticello, the typeface developed for The Papers of Thomas Jefferson in the 1940s by C. H. Griffith and P. J. Conkwright and reinterpreted in digital form by Carter in 2003.

Pleasant Jefferson ("P. J.") Conkwright (1905–1986) was Typographer at Princeton University Press from 1939 to 1970. He was an acclaimed book designer and AIGA Medalist.

The ornament used throughout this book was designed by Pierre Simon Fournier (1712–1768) and was a favorite of Conkwright's, used in his design of the *Princeton University Library Chronicle*.

Printed in the USA
CPSIA information can be obtained
at www.ICGtesting.com
JSHW021314220724
66829JS00018B/133

9 780691 210414